School Music Administration
and Supervision

KEITH D. SNYDER

Head of the Music Department
California State College
at Los Angeles

School Music

Administration

and Supervision

SECOND EDITION

Allyn and Bacon, Inc.   Boston, 1965

We wish to thank those who supplied the photographs which appear on the following pages:

Pages 26, 28, 110, 132, 133, 134, 160, 239 (top), 240, 252, 253 (bottom), 254. Courtesy American Music Conference, Chicago, Illinois. Used by permission.

Pages ii and iii. Courtesy William J. Kasza. Used by permission.

Pages 239 (bottom), 253 (top). Courtesy Alma H. Peterson, New Orleans, Louisiana. Used by permission.

Pages 27, 238. Courtesy Paramount Unified School District, Glenn Starr, Music Supervisor. Used by permission.

Library of Congress Catalog Card Number: 65-17188

Printed in the United States of America

First printing . . . May, 1965
Second printing . . . November, 1967

To my wife Evelyn and

our sons Keith and Ben

with love and gratitude

Foreword

No MATTER what the size of a school or school system, the administration of school music has a direct bearing on the success or lack of success of the school music program. To all who are concerned with the teaching of music in the elementary and secondary schools, this text is a welcome addition to the literature of music education. *School Music Administration and Supervision* meets a professional need of long standing.

The author presents the subject in a style that is direct, logical, and convincing. This book deserves the attention of both experienced and inexperienced music educators because the administration of school music is in need of careful and thorough study on both the graduate and undergraduate levels of instruction.

As one reads the text, it becomes apparent how much it offers in the way of practical information for the guidance of the school superintendent, the principal, the curriculum director, and those teaching professional education courses. The author offers guidance in the field of school music that will enable those in general school administration to understand the problems that face the music educator in the performance of his duties.

The music educator who, in addition to his musicianship, develops a competency in the administrative aspects of the profession strengthens his work and his effectiveness. He understands his role as a member of the educational team. He knows what must be done to organize, develop, and maintain a strong instructional program. He works well with superintendent, principals, supervisors, and teachers; consequently, he improves the instructional program in music.

The music educator must be a competent musician, but success in the field demands musicianship plus administrative ability; it demands a working knowledge of good administrative practice. Most of the problems brought by teachers and supervisors of school music to the music education departments of colleges and universities are administrative problems. The music educator seeks help in matters dealing with curriculum development, lines of responsibility, administrative functions, budgets, scheduling, and a host of other problems treated here. This book will serve well in undergraduate methods courses, courses in the supervision and administration of school music, and graduate seminars in music education. Students completing their training with the basic knowledge of school music administration that the author provides will be better equipped for professional leadership and will be in a position to improve the quality of music instruction in our schools.

The author has had a long, varied, and successful experience in school music. In his writing, he has made good use of his experience and study in the field of school music administration. He has also secured valuable assistance from others in the field. The proper use of this book should prove to be extremely valuable to all who seek to improve the teaching of music in our schools.

WILLIAM R. SUR
Chairman, Music Education
Michigan State University

Preface

THE WIDE VARIETY of curriculum offerings and services in public education today has created a need for an impressive number of specialists in each school system. These experts are frequently required to serve as administrative heads of their particular departments. The music educator in even the smallest school is expected to shoulder certain administrative responsibilities, although his professional preparation may have included little or no specific training for these tasks.

The foregoing statement casts no reflections upon the already distraught music educator—rather it points up his unique problem. In preparing himself for his profession, he has, of necessity, been concentrating upon developing his musicianship, in itself a full-time job; for any art form that demands performance skills as well as esthetic insights calls for detailed and meticulous preparation.

A music educator cannot, however, be a musical person alone; he must also be an educator and possess a personal warmth that invites the confidence of people of all ages, both children and adults. He must understand the nature and processes of human growth and development and practice ways of teaching that bring optimum results in changed lives for the people of his community. He must possess a sound educational philosophy and be able to see the relationship between his special subject and the total curriculum of the school.

No four- or even five-year training program can possibly give our professional music educators the training they need in order to acquire all of the above qualities, yet provide them with initial competence for administering the music education program for their schools and communities. This book hopes to help fill the gap by providing a source to which music educators may turn for assistance, as they seek to perform the tasks expected of them.

No attempt has been made to prescribe a single pattern of action in the various areas of administrative concern; rather, the intent has been to point out basic philosophies and concepts upon which procedures best able to meet local problems and purposes can be built or developed.

This book is written for the music educator seeking help in discharging the administrative duties of his office. By its careful study, he may acquire sufficient initial competence for performing those functions required of him. Those who have been active in the field for many years will be able to use it for re-evaluating and redesigning professional activities. Music educators in training may receive from its pages a better understanding of one important phase of their new profession. Principals, superintendents, and others in administrative positions, may gain added insights into the problems confronting the music educator, and as a result, all professional educators may work together more effectively in the great task of training young people for making their full contributions to our democratic society.

The author is deeply indebted to many people for inspiration, guidance, and assistance, in the development of this book. He sincerely appreciates the encouragement and stimulation given his thinking by his close friend and teacher, Dr. James L. Mursell of Teachers College, Columbia University. William J. Kasza, a good friend and former colleague from the Art Department of Los Angeles State College, furnished the creative ideas and preliminary sketches for most of the illustrations and took several of the photographs used in the book. Valued friends and colleagues in the music education profession have helped by their inspiration, advice, and criticism. Students with whom the writer has been privileged to work during more than twenty-five years of teaching in public schools and colleges have made their special contributions. To all those who have aided in any way, the writer proffers an earnest and heartfelt thank-you. To his wife, Evelyn, for her loyalty, devotion, and helpful criticism, he is especially indebted and deeply grateful.

KEITH D. SNYDER

The author is indebted to the following people and organizations for photographs, building plans, budgetary information, and other illustrative material. He greatly appreciates their generosity in supplying these materials.

J. Raymond Brandon, North Little Rock, Arkansas
Wellington A. Brewster, Nanuet, New York
George A. Christopher, Port Washington, New York
Ward Cole, Frostburg, Maryland
Robert Delwarte, Reseda, California
Wiliam C. Hartshorn, Los Angeles, California
Edward J. Hermann, Baton Rouge, Louisiana
Thomas Hill, Fairfax, Virginia
Harry Hinckley, Springdale, Arkansas
Carl Kronberg, Fresno, California
Ruth Lawrence, Fargo, North Dakota
Eddie Lupiani, Baldwin Park, California
Catherine McHugh, Fayetteville, Arkansas
L. E. Opp, Bozeman, Montana
Alma H. Peterson, New Orleans, Louisiana
H. Armstrong Roberts, Philadelphia, Pennsylvania
Glenn Starr, Paramount, California
Donald R. Sullivan, Arlington, Massachusetts
Vito Susca, Pacoima, California
Advertisers Photographing Company, Chicago, Illinois
American Music Conference, Chicago, Illinois
California State College at Los Angeles, California
Music Industry Council, Washington, D.C.

Preface to the Second Edition

W HEN A PERSON is confronted with the second edition of a book, undoubtedly one of his first questions will be, "How does this edition differ from the previous one?" This is a perfectly proper query, and an author should answer it.

Throughout the process of revision I have kept the potential user uppermost in my mind. My purpose has been to assist him in his efforts to attain a working knowledge of the basic concepts of leadership in music education. This has been accomplished in several ways.

First of all, outdated, hard-to-locate bibliographical items have been deleted and more available, more recent ones added.

Each chapter in the revised edition has a list of *Suggested Activities* and suggestions *For Further Reading*. The former are possible projects, the development of which will assist the reader in grasping the conceptual and practical implications of the chapter. The readings offer literature to be explored to further develop insight into the areas under discussion.

The basic organization of the book remains the same as that of the first edition. However, several sections have been either rewritten for greater clarity or reorganized for a more logical presentation of the concept being developed.

The discussions of some areas have been extended and amplified in the light of present-day knowledge and practice. This has been done in areas in which significant changes have occurred during the years since the manuscript for the first edition was prepared.

Diligent efforts have been made to heighten the value of the entire book to the neophyte music educator. The experienced music teacher, as well, will find it a valuable tool for reevaluating and improving his work. It also is hoped that the book will prove helpful to the school superintendent, principal, or supervisor who is seeking to better understand and support the many-sided music program in his school.

KEITH D. SNYDER

Contents

5 — PUBLIC RELATIONS, 111

Leadership in Operational Activities

6 — SCHEDULING, 135

7 — EQUIPMENT, MATERIALS, AND SUPPLIES, 161

8 — BUDGET AND FINANCE, 193

9 — SPACE AND HOUSING, 215

A Summary and Challenge

Appendixes

School Music Administration
and Supervision

CHAPTER 1

Introduction

THE MUSIC EDUCATOR'S JOB is a complex fabric of interwoven duties and responsibilities. Its pattern and design can be understood only after an intensive study of the cloth as a whole and a detailed examination of its various threads. One very important thread running throughout the fabric is that of administrative functions and responsibilities. In addition to the usual duties such as teaching, conducting, guidance, and counseling, there are materials, equipment, and supplies to be purchased and cared for, curriculums to be developed, schedules to be made, and budgets to be built and administered. These and many other responsibilities are a vital part of the music educator's job. In order to be successful and serve his community most effectively, he must develop competence in all of these administrative details. Competence cannot be developed in all areas until an understanding of the job itself has been reached.

The first chapter of this book will be directed toward developing insights into the job as a whole before considering the individual channels of administrative activity that are of concern to the music educator. It has been the writer's observation and experience that the music educator often fails to understand clearly his position within the total framework of educational structure. It is against this backdrop that the music educator's job is seen in its proper perspective. Our first step, therefore, will be to examine carefully the organizational framework within which the music educator works.

The Framework

The public schools of America are firmly established upon the principle that education is a responsibility of the state. In order to carry out this responsibility, the state enacts laws delegating authority for the formation of schools to each community or local school district. These laws make possible the levying of taxes in support of the schools, prescribe what shall be taught, in some instances, and compel all children to attend school up to a certain minimum age. In recent years, the governments of most states have developed some form of financial assistance to the local school districts, adding support to that supplied by the local district. Direct federal aid to local schools has been limited. Certain vocational fields and special fields, such as agriculture and home economics, receive aid through the Smith-Hughes Act and similar acts of Congress. Some federal funds have been allocated for building construction in critical areas, but the chief burden of financing the school and its program rests with the local district and the state.

LOCAL STRUCTURE — The local units or school districts establish and maintain schools in their areas, enact policy, determine the operational pattern, and provide the physical facilities, materials, equipment, staff, and the major portion of the financial support. The full responsibility for operating and controlling the schools rests with these local units.

Although the responsibility for maintaining, operating, and controlling a school rests with the community as a whole, a small body known as the board of education or school committee is set up, elected or appointed, to serve as the agent of the community. Since this representative group is made up of citizens who have had little or no professional training in operating and managing schools, it delegates its authority and responsibility to an educational administrator, usually called the superintendent of schools. Even though the title given this person may vary from community to community, his functions remain quite constant. He is the organizational head and assumes full responsibility for the operation of the school.

Most school systems are of such magnitude and scope that one person cannot attend to all phases of the school's operation. This necessitates the addition of other personnel to share the administrative responsibilities. Separate school units or buildings are administered by principals who are held responsible for their particular units. They are accountable to the superintendent of schools and operate under authority delegated from him. What goes on in each school is the responsibility of the superintendent. Obviously, it is impossible for any one individual to administer all of the varied and complex educational processes delegated to him by the board of education. He, therefore, selects and employs other people with special interests, training, and talents, to assist him in discharging the obligations of his office.

Principals are usually responsible for sizable units of the total school structure and, they, too, are unable to perform personally all of the duties assigned to them. This necessitates delegating some of their responsibilities to other qualified personnel. Directors of special areas such as music, physical education, and guidance, are among those who fall into this category.

Finally, we should not overlook the classroom teacher who often assumes responsibilities other than his regular classroom work.

Figure 1 shows the line of responsibility for educating the youth of our country. It flows directly from the state to the local district, through the board of education to the superintendent, and on to the principals. The activities of each school are the responsibility of the principals, assisted by the directors of special areas, the classroom teachers, and the heads of special services.

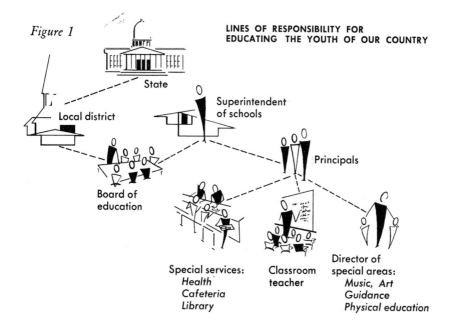

Figure 1

LINES OF RESPONSIBILITY FOR EDUCATING THE YOUTH OF OUR COUNTRY

State

Local district

Superintendent of schools

Board of education

Principals

Special services:
  Health
  Cafeteria
  Library

Classroom teacher

Director of special areas:
  Music, Art
  Guidance
  Physical education

SUPPORTING STRUCTURES — The direct line of responsibility for the operation of schools flows from the state to the local communities as described above. In order to assist the local districts or units, there are two basic supporting structures whose chief functions are to regulate, lead and advise, and, in certain instances, to operate educational units. These supporting structures are the state department of education and the county school department. Figure 2 shows the local structure being supported by the state on the left and the county on the right. These two structures, their officers and functions, require some discussion for an understanding of the over-all framework.

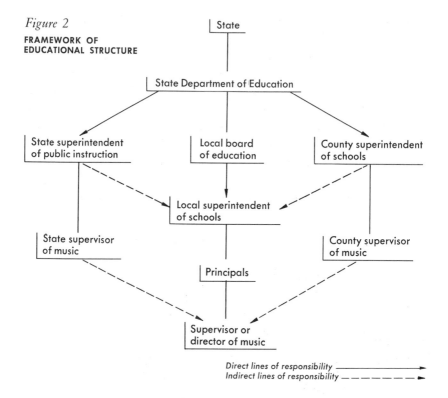

Figure 2

FRAMEWORK OF
EDUCATIONAL STRUCTURE

State

State Department of Education

State superintendent of public instruction

Local board of education

County superintendent of schools

Local superintendent of schools

State supervisor of music

County supervisor of music

Principals

Supervisor or director of music

Direct lines of responsibility —————————➤
Indirect lines of responsibility — — — — — — ➤

STATE DEPARTMENT OF EDUCATION   The actual structure, the offices created by it, and the titles given its officers, vary somewhat from state to state.
In spite of this superficial variance, the purposes and functions retain a high
degree of similarity. The music educator should look to these agencies for the
assistance they can and will give to his local program.

The body of citizenry known as the state must do its business, regulate
and support its affairs, by whatever means its constitution or charter provides.
Every state has created a department of education for the express purpose of
discharging its responsibilities for education within its borders. The chief
official in charge of this department is the superintendent of public instruction.
He assembles a staff of competent people to assist him in doing the work expected of him and his department.

Frequently, one or more of the staff selected by the state superintendent
is directly or indirectly responsible for the music programs of the schools of
the state. This person is usually called the state supervisor of music. Although
the titles given to him may vary from state to state, the functions of his office
remain much the same.

The functions of the state official in charge of music may be summed up in one word—leadership.[1] The local music educator may look to the state music officer for the same type of leadership and activities at the state level that that he himself expects to exercise at the local. For information on the structure within his own state, the local music educator should get in touch with his state department of education and his state music supervisor, if his state has one.

COUNTY DEPARTMENT OF EDUCATION   Each governmental unit in our democratic society has a department or agency responsible for education. The federal government has its Office of Education in the Department of Health Education, and Welfare. The state has its department of education or department of public instruction. The local government has its board of education or school committee. The county government, not previously mentioned or discussed, also has its department or office, with its chief responsibilities centering on leadership and service to the schools of the county.

Some county school offices have direct responsibility for operating the schools of the county in much the same manner as the local board of education. In other counties, the school department serves in an advisory and leadership capacity more nearly approximating that of the state department of education. In either event, it is a part of the governmental structure and a part of the framework within which the local music educator must work.

Frequently, the county office has a music supervisor, consultant, coordinator, or director, and often a staff of assistants, to help him in discharging his responsibilities. Some states operate their schools with no state supervisor of music, relying wholly upon the county office for administrative services. Others have neither state nor county supervisors, but rely entirely upon the local district and its supervisor, director, or coordinator, for leadership in music education. Still others have state and county as well as local supervisors or directors of music education.

All of the various school structures, at their different levels, have exactly the same goal or purpose—providing the youth of our land with the best possible education. Each seeks to work with, and through, the others to arrive at these ends.

DELEGATION OF RESPONSIBILITY AND AUTHORITY — The fact that a school hires a music specialist indicates that the school administration and the board

---

[1] A complete discussion of leadership appears later in this chapter. The presentation there focuses upon the music educator's leadership in his local school and community. The quality and functions of leadership are the same whether exercised locally or at the state level; only the area of influence differs.

of education have realized that their school cannot produce the type of education they seek for their community without his help. They have, therefore,
delegated part of their responsibility to him. The degree of responsibility, the
amount of such responsibility, and the kind of responsibility, so delegated to
the music specialist will depend upon the superintendent and how much he
transfers or retains unto himself.

The good administrator will see to it that the responsibilities he delegates
to the music educator are clearly defined and that each responsibility is accompanied by the necessary kind and amount of authority. Unless such authority
is delegated, there is no power to get the job done. *Authority is the energizing
force that makes possible the fulfilling of responsibilities.* Responsibility without authority is like an automobile with an experienced, licensed operator
present to drive it, but no gas in the tank to make the car perform the functions for which it was made.

The preceding outline briefly describes the framework of responsibility
and authority within which the music educator must do his job. He will be
guided by it, controlled by it, working freely within its boundaries. Only in
this manner, can the music educator do the job expected of him by the community he serves.

NAMING THE JOB — In order to keep our thinking clear while we focus our
attention upon the music specialist and his administrative responsibilities and
functions, it will be necessary to define some terms or titles that will be in
constant use throughout the remainder of the book. There has been, and still is,
much confusion in the terminology applied to the music specialist. For present
purposes, the chief titles currently in use will be defined functionally; that is,
they will be defined in terms of the duties involved in their jobs.

It is unfortunate that many of the terms used in designating the music
educator's job today are held over from the days of authoritarian administration.
Since this is the case, we are faced with the dilemma of giving an authoritarian
title to a democratic process or creating new titles that are not widely accepted
and therefore not readily understood. Throughout this book, the familiar titles
will be used even though by so doing some embarrassment is caused the writer.
It is far better to embarrass the writer than confuse the reader!

DIRECTOR OF MUSIC   The director of music bears the full responsibility
for the total program of music, no matter what the separate number and kinds
of duties may be. He is, in a very real sense, the administrator responsible for

the entire music program. He very often operates upon authority delegated directly from the superintendent of schools and is therefore responsible to him. Throughout the book, this title will be used, because it is the only one that is associated with full and complete responsibility for the music program.

SUPERVISOR OF MUSIC   The title of supervisor designates a person who is primarily responsible for the quality of instruction provided in music. His chief areas of concern are curriculum development, instructional improvement, general planning, and evaluation. He is usually responsible to the principals of the schools to which he is assigned or to the director of music, if the school system employs one.

MUSIC COORDINATOR   This is a new term coming into more general use. His duties are similar to those of the supervisor but, as the title implies, is responsible for the coordination of all the music work in the school and community, as well as assisting in the coordination of music with the other curricular areas of the school. He, like the supervisor, is responsible to the director of music, if the system has one, or to the principals of the buildings he serves.

MUSIC CONSULTANT   The educator bearing this title is primarily a resource person who assists the general classroom teacher in providing more adequate musical experiences for the children involved. The title is coming into use in those school systems developing child-centered curriculums; that is, those breaking away from the traditionally subject-centered curriculums.

MUSIC TEACHER   This person is the specialist in closest contact with children and is responsible for instruction in the area to which he is assigned. He is responsible to the principal of his building and, through the principal, to the director of music, if the school system is so organized.

It must be remembered that there can be no clear-cut separation of these various titles designating the functions of music specialists in the public schools today. Usually, the term in use in any given school is determined by convenience or convention. It is desirable, however, for each school system to determine and define exactly what each music specialist is expected to do and consistently use an appropriate title when referring to his area of responsibility.

It must be clearly understood, also, that in many schools a single person may discharge the functions of two or more of these title areas, in which case the most appropriate and all-inclusive one should be the one used.

For example, Miss Allegretto Subito has been hired by the Board of

Education in Chromatic Cascades as a music specialist; they refer to her as the music teacher. The community is not large, and Miss Subito is the only specialist employed in the area of music. It is understood that her chief work will be that of performing such duties as directing the orchestras and choirs, teaching general music in the junior high school, and visiting the elementary classrooms as frequently as time will allow.

It is obvious that she will be responsible for much of the actual music instruction in Chromatic Cascades. However, since she works with the other teachers in the schools of the district, helping them with music for their assembly programs, or providing illustrative material for their study units, or suggesting music experiences to enrich their daily routine, she is serving as a music consultant.

In the normal course of her duties, Miss Subito will help Mrs. Singlightly, the fourth grade teacher, handle the music in her classroom more successfully. She will also seek to convince Miss Monotone, the second grade teacher, that she can teach her own music by means of instruments, phonograph records, and other means available today. In these instances, our music teacher is acting as a supervisor as well as a consultant.

Sooner or later, the Superintendent of Schools, Dr. Major Minorchord, will ask Miss Subito to prepare a budget in support of the music program for the following year. He, in all likelihood, will ask her to suggest to him what added facilities, equipment, and staff, are needed to provide adequately for the music work in the expected growth of the community. In these instances, she is functioning as a director of music.

This example, whimsically fictitious though it may be, is a true description of the responsibilities placed upon countless music specialists in communities and school districts all over the land. The music specialist *is* an administrator for his school and community.

With the organizational backdrop in mind, we can turn to the music educator's job, single out its components parts, and study them in some detail.

The Music Educator as Administrator

ADMINISTRATION DEFINED — There is a natural tendency for man to organize his work. Even a person working alone plans or organizes the sequence of his endeavor in order to get the job done as efficiently as possible. When two or more persons are working at the same or related tasks, a higher type of planning and organization is necessary. There must be unity of purpose and coordinated activity if the desired results are to be obtained.

When larger groups are assembled to work toward common goals, a unifying force is even more necessary. The organization may be arrived at cooperatively, as a group assembling to clean up the church yard; or it may be imposed by a single source, such as a farmer hiring a group of workers to harvest his crop. Whether the leader emerges from the group or is appointed by a higher authority, a single person is needed to give the signal to start the task, to set the organization into operation. This leader, or director, coordinates and controls all of the efforts of the workers toward the end product or the goals set for the work effort. This person is the administrator of the project.

All types of human endeavor make use of administrative practices. Some are good and some are bad; some are simple, others complex. The purpose is always the same—to get the job done as quickly and effectively as possible.

Administration is the unification of several factors that do not operate separately and independently, but simultaneously and cooperatively. In order to understand the true nature of administration, it is necessary to break the complex down into its several parts, observe the functions of each, and see how each contributes to the welfare of the whole. Jesse B. Sears, a well-known authority in this field, identifies three basic elements in administration—administrative authority, administrative organization, and administrative procedure. These three elements Sears defines more sharply as *power, process,* and *mechanism.*[2]

Power is the energy to get the work done, the authority to establish an organization and to set it into motion. In the public school, this power stems partly from the laws of the land and partly from social pressures that have decreed that public education is desirable. This power is assigned to the board of education in our American school structure. The board delegates the authority or power to the superintendent of schools who, in turn, delegates portions of it to principals, directors, assistant superintendents, teachers, custodians, and clerks.

The *process* is the way in which this power is used for getting the work done. It assembles the personnel, the materials, the facilities, for educating and assigns duties and responsibilities to see that the job is done.

The *mechanisms* are the channels of effort applied to the task toward the achievement of the purposes for which the schools are created.

Administration is partly power, partly process, partly mechanism, and partly work to be done. The power would have no meaning unless

[2] Jesse B. Sears, *The Nature of the Administrative Process*, New York, McGraw-Hill Book Co., 1950, p. 24. Used by permission.

it issued in activity and produced the process. The process would have no meaning if it were not applied to tasks we want performed. The mechanism could mean nothing if the power did not flow through it to the work and if it were not designed to fit the work. Without power, process, and mechanism, one could see the work to be done, perhaps, but could not think of the administrative aspect of the work as a separate task. That is, power, process, mechanism, and work to be done are the terms in which administrative thinking goes on.[3]

The music educator will find that as he fulfills his duties within the school system and community, he will be dealing with these three elements of administration. His power, the energy to get the work done, will come in the form of delegated authority from the superintendent of schools directly or through other administrative offices of the school organization. He will be concerned with the process, the use of this power, in assembling the personnel, the materials, and the various facilities, for accomplishing the educational tasks assigned to the music department. He will see to it that the channels of effort, the mechanisms, are functioning properly and are aimed directly at the goals set for the department and the school. He is, in truth, making use of these administrative principles in all he does.

ADMINISTRATION FUNCTIONS — Now that we have discussed the three basic principles that underlie all administration, we will examine the integral parts of the administrative process. We shall describe in detail a typical school-community music project similar to one that a music educator may be called upon to handle. From this illustration, it will be possible to extract and study the basic functions of the administrative process.

The school system at Key Center is not large, but the community is proud of the music department and the work it has been doing with and for its children. Several years ago, toward the end of the school term, a spring festival was given that served as a crowning climax to the year's activities. The festival has been an annual event ever since.

The school has its stadium and athletic field in a setting that provides a natural amphitheater for events of this sort. There is also a community auditorium large enough, and with ample facilities, for such a program. There are choirs, bands, and orchestras, at the elementary, junior high school, and senior high school levels. There is also a community chorus and a fire department

[3] *Ibid.*, p. 31. Used by permission.

band, both of which are prominent in the musical life of the community. In addition to the special groups at each level of the school, the individual classrooms at all levels have been accustomed to using music as an integral part of their activities. All participate in some way in the annual festival.

The festival chairman, who might be the director of music, forms committees early in the school year to lay plans and set up the organization necessary for carrying them to completion. These committees are made up of school staff members, parents, and pupils. The program committee contacts all of the participating organizations and groups in order to determine the contributions each will make to the festival. The committee also has charge of the printed souvenir program to be distributed the day of the festival. There is a staging committee that plans for the physical facilities necessary for the concert. This committee will see to it that a temporary stage is erected on the athletic field; it will also provide ushers and stage hands to handle the movement of the people in the audience and to move equipment on stage as the various performing groups appear, perform, and leave the stage. The publicity committee will arrange for all advance publicity and advertising; it will see that the press is furnished with passes to the festival. A finance committee will build and execute the festival budget, organize and execute the ticket campaign, and authorize the expenditure of all funds necessary to finance the festival. Undoubtedly, there will be other committees or subcommittees to handle specific details of the festival; certainly, such a community-wide project will necessitate a large organization for laying and carrying out plans for its realization.

The date will be set for the festival, and the timing of the work of each committee and individual geared to reach its culmination in the final concert. Since this concert is to be staged out-of-doors, alternate plans are formed in case the day agreed upon is unfit for such an event. An alternate date may be selected, or the performance may be transferred to the community auditorium. All dates, plans, and schedules, are clearly publicized so that all persons working on the project may know the goals and plans of the others in order to synchronize their efforts with those of the entire group. The chairman of the festival and his steering committee keep in close touch with all preparations, slowing down those moving too fast, speeding up those that are lagging behind, so that the entire activity may be kept in balance.

The day of the festival arrives and everything takes place according to schedule, with only a few minor delays. Fortunately, the weather is good so that the alternate plans do not need to be used. The newspapers send reporters to write reviews of the festival. Those committees whose work was finished at the beginning of the festival itself close out their work and disband. Those who have responsibility for cleaning up after it is over continue to function. All of the money is collected and disbursed; the profit realized is turned over to the treasurer of the school board to be used in a way previously agreed upon.

A few weeks after the festival is over and all the committee work finished, the chairman of the festival calls the chairmen of all the chief committees and all other interested people to a meeting to hear reports from the various committees and to study the educational, musical, and social benefits of the festival. The newspaper reviews are carefully studied to get the opinion of the press about the festival's strengths and weaknesses. The children of the school have been discussing the event in their classes and homerooms; each group has a report written, telling how it has gained from the experience and what it thought could be done another year to make the festival better. As the committee of the whole studies these reports and shares experiences, they begin to lay plans for the festival to be given next year. One important suggestion is that there be a standing festival committee in the community to become the steering committee for the annual festival concert. It is felt that the event has grown so much in size and scope that it is not possible to set up the organization and carry all the plans through to completion within the school year itself. It is thought better to have a permanent standing committee to give the entire project continuity from year to year and to make possible an earlier start the following school year.

The situation just described might well happen in any community in the land. It certainly has happened, with individual variations, of course, in many, many communities already. Obviously, it is the result of a school and community setting a goal for themselves and organizing to bring it about. Its operation contains all of the functions of administration. There is a recognized goal or purpose; there is planning to bring about the realization of the established goals; there is organizing; there is directing; there is evaluating; and there is improving. Now let us turn our attention to these six administrative functions, examine them closely, and see how they operate.

DEFINING PURPOSE   The first stage in the administrative process is that of defining the purpose or desired outcome of any activity for which the music educator is responsible. This function is basic in all operations, from the simplest to the most complex. It is only after establishing goals or desired results that a person in an administrative position can properly lead others through the various sequences of activity that result in intelligent decision and effective action.

The music educator, in his capacity as leader of an organization within an organization, must be sure that the goals his group sets for itself are compatible with the established or evolving purposes and policies of the local school and community. In other words, the goals of the department cannot be in conflict with, or contrary to, the goals of the total school. The suborganization must support and strengthen the larger organization at all times.

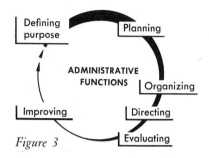

Figure 3

PLANNING   The second stage of the administrative process is that of thinking through problems and procedures before acting upon them; in other words, planning. No organization can operate efficiently and effectively unless it lays thorough and systematic plans. This function of the administrative process charts the course to be followed in the journey toward the goals established in the first stage. It also studies the requirements of the course of action in terms of persons to perform tasks, materials and equipment needed to carry out the tasks, time in which to do them, and the sequence or order in which they are to be performed.

Sears recognizes three types of planning as basic to this stage—positive, negative, and emergency.[4] Positive planning is the setting up of positive patterns of action, setting forth the things that are to be done. The negative aspect of planning is setting up blocks or barriers to prevent undesirable or unwanted things from happening in the course of carrying out a positive plan.

The community, planning for its music festival, will undoubtedly make arrangements with the police for officers to assist in directing traffic flow and automobile parking. Although this planning is positive in nature, its chief purpose is negative. Those responsible for the music festival wish to *prevent* accidents, traffic jams, and unsafe parking conditions. By thus negating traffic hazards, the positive plans, the festival itself, may be more certain of successful completion.

The third type of planning is emergency planning. No matter how carefully an organization or a person thinks through possible pathways to the achievement of a purpose, emergencies will arise. Good administration will have made plans for meeting and solving them. This often involves quick, on-the-spot planning, but the ground work for such planning should be well laid in advance. For example, Key Center planned its music festival to be held

[4] *Ibid.*, pp. 54–58. Used by permission.

out-of-doors. They also made arrangements, however, for holding the performance at a later date or in the community auditorium, in case of bad weather. This latter plan was an emergency plan and every bit as important as the positive and negative ones.

Each of these three types of plans must also be considered in relation to the element of time, so important to all planning. Some plans are to cover a long time span—months, even years; others are for shorter periods—weeks, days, even hours. For example, the music director in a certain school has worked out with his staff a five-year plan for purchasing additional band and orchestral instruments, as well as replacing those presently owned which no longer give good service or are too expensive to maintain. This is a long-range plan, but it will also contain plans for the instruments to be purchased possibly this month, or even right now. Perhaps a band director is confronted with a request, which must be honored, to take his band to a neighboring community to participate in a parade next week. This will require quick planning, but it is of shorter duration than the plans he must make for the same band to participate in the Memorial Day Parade of his own community six months from now. The short-term plans, however, must be as thoroughly worked out and executed as the long-range ones are.

ORGANIZING   Organizing is the the third function of the administrative process. It involves assembling the persons, securing the materials and equipment, checking available facilities or creating new ones, and putting them all into position for carrying out the plans that have been created. It is a time of marshaling forces to activate the plans. This phase of administration is often likely to appear as reorganization, regrouping and realigning the available or procurable forces for better goal achievement.

DIRECTING   The organization, after it is created or assembled, must be set into motion in order to turn out the product for which it was created. The order to begin must be given, and action must be continuous until the goals are reached. This is directing. The administrator in this phase of his work is like the engineer who throws the switch to cause power to activate the machinery for turning out the product. Throughout, the administrator must keep an attentive eye upon the efficient functioning of the organization to be sure it is working properly and is moving in the necessary direction. He must also know when to make emergency repairs and when to turn off the power in order to redirect the energy in a better direction.

This phase is also concerned with the coordination of the entire activity of the organization, making sure that all channels are in proper relationship with the others, that each step complements all others, that the entire operation is in balance, working together as a well-knit, integrated unit, that no one phase runs ahead of another and weakens or postpones the full realization of the purposes set for the entire organization. It may also involve changing the direction of one phase of the organization, if that is necessary. The directing function of the administrative process is like operating a car; the machine must be started, put in gear, steered through traffic, kept on the road, accelerated here, braked there, stopped from time to time for refueling and service, and brought to a stop at the desired destination.

EVALUATING   The fifth function of the administrative process is that of evaluating. The administrator must maintain a questioning or examining attitude at all times, looking for weaknesses and remaining aware of strengths. The product of the properly functioning organization must be studied and tested as it develops and after it is completed, to see if it meets all expected specifications. The process must be evaluated to determine its efficiency and effectiveness. The results of evaluation become the basis for reorganization, for redirecting, for replanning, for redefinition of goals and purposes. This testing, this appraising function, is the basis for, and gives the information necessary for, the next and last function of administration.

IMPROVING   The good administrator will never be satisfied with his organization and its product. He will always be seeking ways and reasons for improving himself, his school, and the product of the school. This drive for improvement will set the entire chain of stages into action again; purposes will be reviewed and altered, plans will be redesigned, organization will be revised, directing will change for the better, and all of these processes will again be tested and ways sought to bring about their improvement.

With a knowledge of the nature of administration and how it works, we can now turn our attention to the core of administrative practice.

Leadership

The ability to instill enthusiasm for a task confronting a group and the ability to inspire united effort toward its fulfillment are the basic elements contained in leadership. This definition is a very concise statement of the nature of leadership. Like all such brief explanations, it oversimplifies a complex and closely coordinated set of attributes and action patterns. It must be remembered that this quality or ability called leadership is not a tangible substance that can be handled or set aside and studied carefully. It is a composite of many factors, and they vary from situation to situation; they do not remain constant. Certain guiding principles can be isolated and discussed, however.

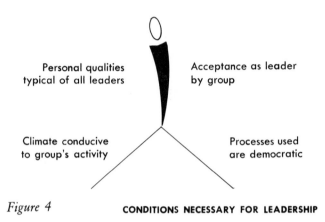

Personal qualities
typical of all leaders

Acceptance as leader
by group

Climate conducive
to group's activity

Processes used
are democratic

Figure 4   **CONDITIONS NECESSARY FOR LEADERSHIP**

NECESSARY CONDITIONS — There are four conditions that must be met before a person can lead others. These conditions are operative whether that leadership is to be developed in music, physical education, home-making, or any other field. The pages that follow will be devoted to a discussion of these four conditions.

PERSONAL QUALITIES   The person in a position of leadership, if he is to be effective, must possess those personal qualities that are typical of all leaders.

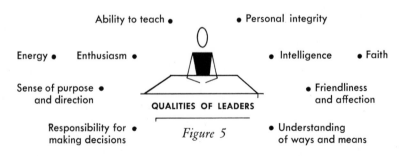

Ability to teach ●   ● Personal integrity

Energy ●   Enthusiasm ●   ● Intelligence   ● Faith

Sense of purpose ●   ● Friendliness
and direction   **QUALITIES OF LEADERS**   and affection

Responsibility for ●   ● Understanding
making decisions   *Figure 5*   of ways and means

Tead has identified ten of these qualities.[5] A slightly paraphrased version will be used for our present purpose. These qualities are presented graphically in Figure 5.

1. *Energy*   A person who expects to lead must possess sufficient physical and nervous energy to meet the demands of the tasks before him. In other words, he cannot "run out of gas" part way through the job. This energy must be of an infectious type, so that it energizes those with whom he works. All who associate with him must feel a lift because of his buoyant energy and spirit. It is also important that the leader be able to control this energy, so that it may be properly directed and focused upon the work to be done.

2. *Purpose and Direction*   The leader must also have a sense of purpose and direction. Before he can hope to lead others upon any course, he must know with certainty where he is going and where he wants his program to go. Without this trait, the leader and those being led will wander aimlessly about, accomplishing little of value. Not only must the leader possess a sense of purpose and direction, but it must be so clear, so positive, that it is easily and clearly communicable to those who are to work toward its fulfillment. After the leader instills his group of workers with his sense of a goal, he must vigorously and enthusiastically sustain it.

3. *Enthusiasm*   A brand of enthusiasm that is felt by all those about him is an indispensable quality for anyone in a leadership position. It must be generated by a heartfelt devotion to the cause, whatever it may be. It is the product of real vigor on the physical side and clearly defined objectives on the mental. Genuine enthusiasm can result only when all forces that sustain and nourish it are in proper balance.

4. *Friendliness and Affection*   No person can lead other people successfully unless he displays genuine friendliness toward, and affection for, all those with whom he works. This affection and friendliness must be real, deep, and sincere. Tead has this to say. "Affection is essential for the leader because it predisposes people toward being influenced," and, "The friendly attitude is the influencing attitude." [6] Becoming acquainted on a sincere, personal basis is the point at which affection and friendliness begin.

[5] Ordway Tead, *The Art of Leadership*, New York, McGraw-Hill Book Co., 1935, Chapter VI. Used by permission.

[6] *Ibid.*, p. 104. Used by permission.

5. *Personal Integrity*   People must be able to trust their leaders. Personal integrity is a personal trait basic to all successful human relations. Certainly, a person in a leadership role cannot even get started, unless he has the complete trust and confidence of those about him. The leader must be sensitive to the standards of taste and morals of his followers; he must not offend them if he is to expect their loyalty.

6. *Understanding Ways and Means*   In every leadership situation, the leader must possess enough understanding of the ways and means, enough understanding of the process by means of which goals are realized, to give wise guidance and direction to the effort as a whole. It is inconceivable that a person ignorant of the field in which he is attempting to lead could convince others of his ability to make decisions that would lead to the objectives established by the group. A person who knows nothing of instrumental music and its problems is not in a favorable position to exercise leadership in this area. Also, a person with no knowledge or feeling for group processes is not likely to succeed in leading people by means of the democratic process.

7. *Responsibility for Decisions*   The leader must be willing to take the responsibility for making decisions and abiding by them. The decision must be made promptly and based upon the best evidence available. A person who postpones and delays decisions will lose the confidence of the group he expects to lead, and will forfeit his leadership. Tead says, "The process of deciding is, psychologically, one of weighing evidence, picturing alternate eventualities and making a choice by which one is willing to stand. Soundness of judgment and courage in facing the outcome are two important conditions." [7]

8. *Intelligence*   The leader must display intelligence in all situations. This means an ability to appraise situations and problems readily; see their significance in the total setting, in the light of present and past experiences; and, from these insights, accurately determine the wisest course of action.

9. *Ability to Teach*   The good leader is also a good teacher. He is able to provide people with the experiences that will increase their understanding of the problems facing them and suitable processes for solution. If the leader is successful in training people to perform better the tasks expected of them, the amount of order-giving can be reduced, and cooperative effort can take its place.

[7] *Ibid.*, p. 122. Used by permission.

10. *Faith* Finally, the leader must have faith. Principally, he must possess faith in people. In addition to this, he must believe that people wish to be led wisely and that they are anxious to follow one who will assist them toward the fulfillment of their aspirations. He must also have faith in his ability to lead and faith in the worthwhileness of the endeavor in which he and his followers are engaged. This faith gives him deep, inner resources without which all other attributes are worthless. A true leader will possess all of these ten personal qualities. They constitute the first condition necessary for effective leadership.

ACCEPTANCE AS LEADER The second condition necessary in any leadership situation is that the leader be accepted in that capacity by the group. A person may be appointed to a position of leadership, but unless the group with whom he is to work receives him in that light, the work to be done will come to a halt. The group must feel that the leader possesses those qualities, has control of those means, that will assist the group in furthering its objectives. He can lead only when a sufficient number of the group believe that he has something of value for them.

CLIMATE CONDUCIVE TO GROUP'S ACTIVITY Leadership is not possible unless the setting, the climate in which people are to work, is conducive to the group's activity. It would be impossible for a leader to lead, and a group to follow, in an atmosphere of distrust and hostility. Only when hostilities are resolved and confidence prevails, can leader and followers work together toward fulfillment of common objectives.

The leader must also realize that he can achieve only to the extent that those he leads are able to achieve and feel their own accomplishments. The mutual feeling that work is being done and goals being reached must prevail at all times.

DEMOCRATIC PROCESSES The fourth and final condition necessary before a person can lead successfully is that the processes by means of which a group works be democratic. Unless this condition is met, leadership does not exist, but is replaced by command. Command is interested in obtaining some action that the commander desires. It is *power over* people. Leadership is interested in how people can be brought to work together for a common end, effectively and happily. It deals in *power with* people. Command is interested only in the result; leadership is equally interested in the process by means of which the result is obtained. When the leader is working with people, he is recognizing the individual worth and contribution each is making to the common effort. This is the very essence of democracy in action.

When the leader possesses those individual qualities typical of the best leaders, when he is accepted by the group he is attempting to lead, when the setting in which he and the group work is conducive to the achievement of goals toward which the group is striving, and when the processes by means of which leadership is exercised is democratic, then and only then can optimum results from leadership be expected.

The music educator is placed in a position favorable for developing himself as a leader and being accepted by his colleagues in such a capacity. He has the special knowledge, skills, and know-how, as far as music is concerned. He is unique in his status as a music specialist; his training and experience have equipped him with the means for helping groups and individuals in clarifying and achieving goals. It was for this purpose that the board of education and the superintendent of schools hired him; it is at the heart of his job—he cannot escape it; he must not attempt to do so, if the work of education through music is to succeed.

It must be clearly understood that the leadership process cannot be outlined in neat, sequential steps. Since it is a process, the nature and detail of that process will vary from situation to situation and from group to group. The leader must see the complete objectives of education and his special area with crystal clarity and be able to show others how these goals may be attained. He must also be able to manipulate the setting so that the goals may be attained. Creative thinking and prudent action are demanded, as well as the ability to apply general principles to specific situations.

AREAS OF LEADERSHIP — The music educator will find himself providing both educational and artistic leadership.

EDUCATIONAL LEADERSHIP   Frequently a person in a school music situation is heard to say: "I haven't the slightest notion about this business of core curriculum, nor do I understand what guidance is all about. Certainly when they get to talking about average daily attendance, I'm completely lost. You see I'm a musician, not an educator, and these other things are no concern of mine." This is tragic. It is just as tragic, however, to hear someone say: "I'm an educator. The quality of music my band or orchestra plays may be less than the best, and perhaps the kids play or sing out of tune, but, you see, I'm not a musician, I'm an educator."

What our schools need are *music educators,* highly trained musicians who are also educators in the broadest sense of the term. They should be working for the educational goals of the community, just as surely as for the musical goals. They should be blending both together for the betterment of each.

The first broad area of educational leadership in which the music educator must engage is the establishment and clarification of goals and purposes. As an educator, he will have a part in the development of school objectives and become familiar with the over-all purposes of the school, as it seeks to serve the needs of the community that supports it. In this work, he will follow the leadership of his superintendent and principals.

While the music educator is following the leadership of his superintendent and principals, he will be leading other members of the school staff in work closely associated with music in education. This is educational leadership at another level. He will be working with classroom teachers, other members of the music staff, parents, laymen, and pupils, in order that music may make its maximum contribution to education as a whole.

The music educator's background of professional training must give him a comprehensive grasp of the underlying philosophies supporting the American concept of education. He must be able to examine critically the issues confronting education today and be able to assist in making decisions that will best serve his community's needs. Also, he must be able to develop capacities for critical thinking within the group for which he is responsible. This is particularly important when a group is considering the goals of music as a special, but contributory, branch of education. It is so easy for persons in music to be carried away by enthusiasm for their art, that they lose sight of the larger goal of education as a whole. Music can be justified in the curriculum of any school only as long as it serves the cause of education as a whole. In truth, no study can be considered valuable unless, by pursuing it, one is enabled to live a richer and more abundant life. It must contribute toward the making of a stronger, happier, better, more cooperative person. To this end, the music educator must exercise his position of leadership.

The second area in which the music educator is called upon to exercise his leadership is that of creating a social climate in which human beings can grow and develop best. This means development of a setting in which the worth and contributions of each individual are respected and treasured; a setting in which each individual *feels* that he is respected and desired as an individual, as a person; a setting where growth is expected to be individual and personal, not stereotyped and uniform; a setting where each individual has dignity and stature; a setting where persons can develop their minds, souls, and bodies, in such a way that they can make their best contributions to society.

The preceding discussion purposely made reference to "human beings." The music educator, as he performs his tasks, is constantly working with people—children, adolescents, adults, men, women, boys, girls—people of all ages and descriptions. No matter what their differences, the social climate around the music educator and the school must be such that each individual can grow and develop to his maximum potential.

The music educator must work to generate enthusiasm for music and the unique contribution it can make to the development of children and adults. His efforts will be directed in many channels, most of which will be discussed later in the book. Curriculum development, community relations, community support and understanding, and human relations, are but a few of the areas in which he will exercise his leadership abilities in developing a social climate in which people can more readily become citizens of whom all can be proud.

ARTISTIC LEADERSHIP   Music, as one of the most powerful and universally esthetic media, impels all music educators to step to the front ranks of those working for esthetically improved curriculums. Many critics of the American educational scene point out that our culture is artistically impoverished and bemoan the lack of cultural refinement in our people. "If the American people do not exhibit the range of well-developed cultural and aesthetic interests that critics of our culture would wish, perhaps part of the cause lies in the culturally poverty-stricken 'minimum essentials' type of elementary and secondary education still too popular in this country." [8]

Leaders in music education will work for a better understanding of the ways in which their art contributes to balancing human personality and making life fuller and richer. They will work toward the development of a truly American art tradition in the schools, in the home, and in the communities. They will work for the development of better facilities for the study and enjoyment of music. They will also work to make all of man's relations with man things of beauty. The school and the community look to the music educator for leadership in this vitally important area of education.

RESPONSIBILITIES — We come now to the point in our discussion where some of the major, broad categories characterizing the music educator's job can be

---

[8] Will French, J. Dan Hull, and B. L. Dodds, *American High School Administration,* rev. ed., New York, Rinehart & Co., Inc., 1957, p. 262. Used by permission.

isolated. Although the separate elements may vary from one school to another, the broad detail is constant. They will only be identified at this point, however; a detailed discussion is reserved for later chapters. The music educator's responsibilities consist of two major types—those in which human relations are at the center and those that are chiefly operational in character.

The entire process of education is human development, and, as a person assumes a leadership role in this process, he must be, or become, an expert in human relations. This applies to the relationships of the music educator with the pupils of the school, the parents, the school staff, the board of education, the community, and the professional organizations. The point is that people work with other people in the school organization so that children may grow and develop all of their capacities to their maximum limits.

Part One of this book will isolate and deal with the areas of leadership in music education in which human relations are found to be the dominant characteristic. Chapter 2 will deal with personal relations; here problems pertaining to staff and personnel, as well as teacher-pupil relationships, will be considered.

The music educator must assume the role of leadership in curriculum development; his particular emphasis will be upon music and its contributions to the curriculum as a whole. This will be discussed in Chapter 3.

The director of music must be a master teacher. He will, therefore, be concerned with the improvement of instruction in music, no matter where the improvement may be needed. This topic is considered in Chapter 4.

School systems, as a whole, are becoming more and more aware of the importance of public relations. Music, because of its very nature, is in the vanguard of subject matter areas concerned with this vital activity. Therefore, Chapter 5 will be devoted to public relations.

Part Two will deal with those responsibilities of the music educator that are chiefly operational in character; that is, they are characterized by their mechanical nature. This does not overlook the fact that the human factor and the necessity for sound human relations are still present and operative; however, these areas are primarily concerned with the operating phase of the school program devoted to music. Such areas as scheduling; equipment, materials, and supplies; budget and finance; and space and housing, will be discussed in Chapters 6 through 9.

Chapter 10 will seek to marshal the thoughts expressed in this book into a guiding philosophy for the music educator to use as he plans for the future.

Summary

Within the framework of responsibility and authority established by the states and delegated to local school districts, the music educator works as a part of a team seeking to put into action the educational program desired by the community. At times, he will perform certain administrative functions within the area assigned to him; at other times, he will work under the leadership of another administrator. He will be putting into practice six administrative functions: defining purpose, planning, organizing, directing, evaluating, and improving. He will be expected to display a degree of educational leadership as well as artistic leadership. His work will consist of working with people, young and old, toward the betterment of society. The material of this chapter is the foundation upon which the remainder of the book is built.

Suggested Activities

1. Draw an organizational chart of the school district with which you are most familiar. Show the lines of responsibility flowing from the state through the local district and on to the music specialist.

2. Draw an organizational chart of a music department with which you are very familiar.

3. Study the structure of schools in your state and county. What provisions are made for a music specialist at the state and/or county level?

4. Using some group with which you are familiar either as a participant or as a close observer, identify the six administrative functions at work.

5. Think of a person whom you regard as an exceptional leader and identify those personal qualities that contribute to his success.

6. In some successful group enterprise with which you are familiar, identify the conditions which make the leader successful.

For Further Reading

American Association of School Administrators, *Staff Relations in School Administration*. Thirty-third Yearbook. Washington, D.C., The Association, 1955. Chapters 1 and 4.

Association for Supervision and Curriculum Development. *Leadership for Improving Instruction.* 1960 Yearbook. Washington, D.C., 1960. Chapters 1 and 2.

James, H. Thomas. "The Nature of Professional Authority." *Phi Delta Kappan.* 40, No. 2:45–48, November, 1959.

Morphet, Edgar L., Johns, Roe L., and Reller, Theodore L. *Educational Administration: Concepts, Practices, and Issues.* Englewood Cliffs, N.J., Prentice-Hall, Inc., 1959. Chapters 1 and 4.

Sears, Jesse B. *The Nature of the Administrative Process.* New York, McGraw-Hill Book Co., 1950. Chapter 1.

PART
ONE

Leadership in

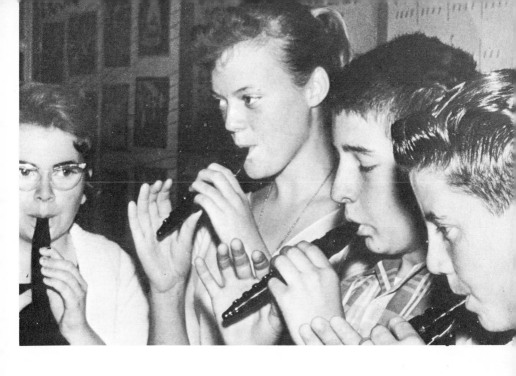

Human Relations

CHAPTER 2

Personal Relationships

WHEN A MUSIC EDUCATOR arises in the morning to prepare himself for the day's activities, he is undoubtedly thinking of the various duties he has to perform before nightfall. His breakfast is interrupted by a telephone call from the mother of one of his choir members, asking if he considers it all right for her daughter, who has a heavy cold, to sing in a trio appearing at the Womens Club that afternoon. After five or ten minutes of conversation, discussing all of the issues in the matter, the mother is satisfied, and the music educator returns to his cold breakfast. As he leaves his house, the boy next door greets him with a request for a ride to the high school. He drives to school and, after parking his car, is swamped by a group of students, chattering about the forthcoming concert to be given at the end of the week. He enters the building, and a pair of irate teachers want to know if it is absolutely essential for two of their pupils to attend his choir rehearsal during the activity period; the students simply *must* make up some work for them.

Our music educator moves through a day that includes classes, conferences, committee meetings, a talk before the Rotary Club luncheon, and a conference on next year's plans with the superintendent of schools. He even finds time to call on the editor of the local newspaper to discuss plans for publicizing the annual spring festival to be held in May.

Throughout the entire day, this music educator is working with, and meeting, people—sometimes formally, sometimes informally. He is talking with parents, students, businessmen, administrators, teachers, and, in all likelihood, the janitor and office secretary. Everything he does brings him into contact with people—young people, older people, musicians, non-musicians, educators, non-educators, business men, professional people, and artisans.

How well he handles these relationships will, in large measure, determine the effectiveness of his work. The music educator who can get along well with people, who can win the respect and confidence of all those with whom he works, will be in a better position for success than one who is antagonistic toward his associates and disliked and distrusted by his fellow workers. This one matter of cordial, effective personal relations is the cornerstone to success in administration.

The ability to work well with people is of paramount importance to those in positions of leadership in public schools. This is as true for the music educator as it is for the principal or superintendent of schools. It is one of the major functions of the leader to stimulate, inspire, and bring about purposeful, cooperative effort on the part of all people actively engaged in the work of the schools.

It is no accident that a person possesses the ability for getting along with, and working well with, people. It has come about as the result of sound planning and development of those behavior patterns that result in proper personal relations. Certain principles, certain guide lines, must be present and operating in all areas of effective human contact. When they are known, observed, and put into practice, better personal relations and more effective leadership will be the result. The next few pages will identify these guide lines and show ways in which they can be developed and put into practice.

Guide Lines

Throughout the following discussion, it must be remembered that, although these guide lines are clear, they are not necessarily distinct one from another. They are not isolated, separate entities. They are interdependent, they operate as a whole, they complement each other. They are but separate threads of a

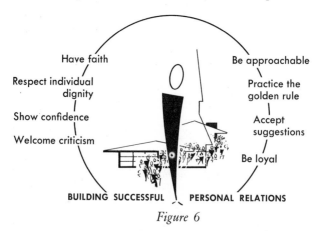

Have faith

Respect individual
dignity

Show confidence

Welcome criticism

Be approachable

Practice the
golden rule

Accept
suggestions

Be loyal

BUILDING SUCCESSFUL   PERSONAL RELATIONS

Figure 6

complete fabric. They are woven together to form the design; they complement and support each other to form the pattern; each one gives beauty and dignity to all the others and, in turn, is dignified and made beautiful by them. It is our purpose to examine each of these guide lines one by one and show their relationship to the whole.

INDIVIDUAL DIGNITY — Human worth, the dignity of the individual, and the value of each person, are foundation stones of our democratic society. Since they are vital to our society as a whole, no organization within our culture can exist and be successful for long without recognizing these truths and patterning policies and actions upon them. This is true just as surely in the school classroom as in the high school glee club; in the music department as in the superintendent's office; in the parent-teachers organization as in the crew of custodians. There can be no exceptions.

There are two aspects of individual dignity that must be identified and discussed separately. The first in uniqueness. It must be recognized that each person is a separate, distinct individual—different from all others. Each person has different abilities from others; each has special experiences in his background that he brings to his work effort. Because of the countless ways in which each individual differs from his colleagues and associates, his contributions to their common endeavor is unique. No one else could do the task in the same manner, nor should anyone be expected to do so. Because each person is unique, he has a right to expect proper recognition of his unique characteristics and a chance to exploit the special abilities with which he is endowed.

Mary Smith and Sally Jones both teach a sixth grade classroom in the same school system. It happens that they share the same birthday, they attended the same schools, enrolled together in college, took the same courses, were members of the same sorority, and began teaching at the same time. In spite of all these similarities in their lives, they are entirely different people and can be expected to teach differently and to make different contributions to the common educational effort. They are different in bodily structure; they have mental, emotional, social, and spiritual differences. They will do things differently, they will react to similar situations in diverse ways, they will lead children and work with adults differently.

The music director must recognize the rightness of this uniqueness, respect it, and capitalize on it, if his work and the work of his department is to succeed. Because each person has a special contribution to make to any organization of which he is a part, the wise administrator will seek out that quality and exploit it to the benefit of the total educational effort.

As each person plans his life and as he works toward the goals he has set, he will find himself in a maze of various and varying positions of responsibility and authority. In any organization of which he becomes a part, some persons will have greater authority than he and others will have less. For example, the music director in a school system of medium size will have greater responsibility and authority for the development of the music curriculum of that school than will the general music teacher in a junior high school of the same system. Similarly, this general music teacher will have more responsibility for the music program of that school than the custodian of the building. Perhaps it would be more accurate to say that each has *different* authority and responsibility, than to say that one has greater authority and responsibility. It is proper to say, and essential to recognize, that each person must be respected for the position he holds in the organization. The rights and privileges of each position must be respected and honored, if good personal relations are to exist. If the music educator desires this respect for his own office, he must be willing to respect the offices of others.

This principle holds true for people outside the school organization as well as for those within it. The pupil deserves respect for his position in society as a learner. The custodian, the secretary, the parent, the science teacher, and all other persons, deserve respect as individuals and as contributing members of society.

COMMUNICATION — Effective administration is a democratic way of living and working. It depends upon free and uninterrupted communication between *all* members of an organization. Individuals and groups must be able to communicate with those possessing higher authority, as well as with those who possess the same or less. All channels of communication must be clearly defined and kept open at all times for discussion of problems and for free exchange of ideas. This principle must function as freely with parents, pupils, and patrons of the school, as with the staff members within the system.

In an organization or society that is functioning properly, it is necessary for all members of the group to have easy access to all lines of communication. Communication is a busy, two-way street. It must be as easy to communicate ideas and experiences *up* the ladder of responsibility and authority as it is to communicate them *down*. There are a few aids to easy communication that might be mentioned.

In the first place, the successful music director must be able to meet people easily and graciously. It must be easy for parents and pupils to come to him for advice and counsel or simply to talk, to visit. There must be no barriers, no restraints, no inhibitions. It must be the business of the music executive to see that all channels of communication are kept open and that new ones are created as the necessities arise.

A few years ago, the writer worked in a school system where the superintendent of schools had an unlisted telephone number. One day when the school offices were closed, the high school band was playing for a parade that had been approved by the administration of the school. During the course of the day, an emergency arose in which it became necessary for the band director to reach the superintendent by telephone. The directory was of no use, Information would not give out the number, and, as a result, valuable minutes were wasted while close friends of the superintendent were called until one was found who knew and would supply the number. The superintendent had closed a line of communication.

Fortunately, in this example, no great harm was done except to the ruffled temper of the band director, but it was known by the community that the superintendent could not be reached by telephone at his home, and many people resented it. The superintendent was known as "difficult to approach," even when in his office at school. This type of restricted communication should be avoided.

It is a good policy for the music administrator to take the initiative in communication with his colleagues and the public that supports the school; this is one way of making certain that lines of communication are open. Seek out individuals and groups and talk over problems and plans with them; this always leads to improved personal relations.

The structure of our democratic society is such that the public is expected and encouraged to make suggestions for the improvement of its organizations. The music educator cannot do lip service to this principle. If he is to operate in a climate of wholesome personal relations, he must willingly and graciously give attentive ear to suggestions for improvement, regardless of their source; they may come from a member of the board of education, a pupil, or the cop on the corner.

Criticism is also expected, even encouraged, in a society dedicated to democratic principles and practices. The music educator must accept all criticism in the spirit offered and act upon it as his judgment permits. A wholesome atmosphere of personal relations will provide a setting in which such criticism can be received with equal graciousness from the janitor or the superintendent of schools.

LOYALTY, CONFIDENCE, FAITH — People are happier and work more efficiently when they see evidence that their leaders are loyal to them and have confidence and faith in them as individuals and as a group. The music educator
who is able to show by his dealings with people that he possesses these traits
and that they are important motivating influences in his life along the pathway
to success.

None of these traits are identifiable by specific actions so much as by a
feeling caught by associates from all the leader says and does. No one in
authority can say to himself, "Now I'm being loyal," or, "Now I'm showing
confidence," or, "Now I'm exhibiting faith." Rather everything that he says
and does shows whether or not he has genuine confidence and faith in, and
loyalty to, all members of his organization, his students, his parents, both as
individuals and as a group.

This condition comes about as a result of the fact that a leader is willing
to work with all people and groups, to share their successes and failures, to
assist with the joint effort, and to help solve personal problems. This willingness, this responsiveness, must permeate all of the administrator's actions. It is
spontaneous, it is wholehearted. It is further apparent in the leader's willingness to defend an individual or a group when either comes under attack.
It is also evident in a desire to support each person's endeavor, no matter how
great or how small.

The music educator must believe and show by his actions that he trusts
people, has faith in their fundamental goodness, confidence in their ability to
make good judgments and decisions, and confidence that, by interaction and
group processes, people will arrive at the best pattern of action for all concerned. He must also be loyal to his community, to his board of education, to
his superintendent and principals, to his colleagues, to the parents and
children of his school, and to all other persons and groups working for the
betterment of the public schools and society.

GOLDEN RULE — This principle, old as it is, is the foundation for all the
previous principles and, in fact, sums them all up. A wholesome atmosphere
of personal relations is bound to result when each person treats all other
people as he himself would like to be treated. The thorough and complete
practice of the Golden Rule will create a school and society in which all
individuals can live in a manner befitting the dignity of human beings.

The gracious music educator will recognize the contributions of others in the progress of the music program. No one likes to be overlooked or neglected. The entire process of education, of which music is a part, is an activity in which many people have made, and are making, contributions. Each person has his share of work and responsibility. Just as a person responsible for failure should be blamed, the person responsible for success should be recognized and commended. A sincere pat on the back will work wonders in developing wholesome personal relations.

The Music Educator's Contacts

As the music educator does his work, he meets and deals with people in many different capacities and situations. The guide lines just presented are basic and will operate in all such surroundings and situations. The remainder of the chapter will be devoted to a discussion of these points of contact, with suggestions for developing and maintaining the best personal relations at all times. There are two major areas to be considered: contacts in the school and contacts in the community.

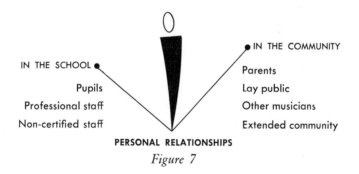

IN THE COMMUNITY

IN THE SCHOOL

Pupils   Parents

Professional staff   Lay public

Non-certified staff   Other musicians

             Extended community

PERSONAL RELATIONSHIPS

Figure 7

SCHOOL CONTACTS — There are three major groups of people in a school system to be considered: the pupils, the professional staff, and the service staff. Each group has several divisions or subgroups. We will discuss them one at a time, beginning with the pupils.

PUPILS Too many music educators lose sight of the fact that the pupils in their schools are human beings with all the rights and privileges allotted to them by our society. They must not be considered less than human because they have not yet reached adult status, but must be accorded the dignity and respect due them as children, adolescents, and young adults. The principles of personal relations, *all of them,* apply to the pupils of our schools as much as they apply to the parents, to the administrators, or to any other category of people.

The music educator's first interest and obligation is to the general student, the one to whom music is not a first interest, but one that contributes to his general cultural development. It is sometimes difficult for a musically trained person to understand that there are perfectly normal people who do not share his unusual interest and enthusiasm for music, but who do have a deep and sincere secondary or lesser interest. If the music educator is to work well with pupils of this type, he must make a strong effort to understand and appreciate their point of view. The music director must help his staff work with and serve this group above all others, for it represents the citizenry who maintain the school and who, therefore, may rightfully expect all of the school's services and facilities to be used for their benefit.

Not only must the music educator serve the interests of the general student, but he must also be alert for those who have latent musical talent which can be developed. There is no greater tragedy than to find individuals who have, through oversight, been unable to develop their special abilities. The music educator must do all in his power to avoid this waste.

The music teacher has an exceptional relationship with music students possessing special talents and interests in music. He should hold himself in readiness at all times to counsel and guide them in their musical development. He should be the person to whom they turn for special advice and guidance in the development of their careers. He should help them chart their program for the future, assist them in establishing realistic goals for themselves, commend them for their achievements, and censure them when these achievements do not match their abilities.

The music educator, in his associations with pupils of all types, must respect them for what they are and what, with proper opportunities, they may become, not belittling or looking down upon their status, but respecting them as growing, dynamic, developing persons. He must conduct himself in such a way that pupils feel free to come to him with suggestions for the improvement of the music program, and he must be able to take student criticisms in a friendly, wholesome manner. He must see to it that pupils have access to all lines of communication, both to him and, through him, to other officers of authority. He must have confidence in his pupils and show it by his actions. Above all else, he must be loyal to each pupil as a person and to them all as a group. There is no more rewarding place to put into practice patterns of treating people as one would like to be treated oneself than with the pupils of the school system in which one works.

PROFESSIONAL STAFF   This group includes all other music specialists in the school system and all classroom teachers; that is, all those who meet pupils in the classroom. It includes the administrative branch, the superintendents, principals, directors of other special areas, curriculum coordinators—in general, those who work with children *through* teachers. It also includes professional service personnel, such as health officers, guidance officers, attendance officers; in other words, those who offer professional service to the pupils of the school system. Each of these groups will be discussed separately.

1. *Music Teacher*   In even the smallest schools, there will be many people who are concerned with, and who make contributions to, the music program. There will be classroom teachers (especially at the elementary level), special music teachers, and possibly supervisors of special areas. To a large extent, the size and structure of the music department will determine the existing relationships. Certainly good personal relations must be operative within the music department of the school, if the best work is to be done. When all members of the staff are working in close mutual cooperation, it may seem unnecessary for one person to serve as a head. However, if the program is to be unified and effective, one person should be charged with the responsibility, and given the necessary authority, for seeing that the work is done.

The music director, the administrative head of the staff, will be expected to exercise all of the qualities of leadership discussed in Chapter 1, and, by practicing the principles of personal relations discussed earlier in this chapter, he can make his leadership effective. He will see to it that all members of his staff have a part in the formation of the policies and plans of the department. He will encourage and reward initiative. He will develop leaders within the group itself. He will permit and encourage each person to make his own unique contribution to the progressing program of the department and the school. The long-term results of their common endeavor will be determined by the manner in which the music director exercises the principles of personal relations.

There will be many types of personalities represented within the music staff. They will have many different beliefs about the status of music in the curriculum of the school. They will have many ways of doing their work. Each must be handled in such a way that the pupils of the school may receive maximum benefit from their musical experiences. The music director most favorably equipped for successful leadership in music education is the one who shows by his actions that he respects each individual's uniqueness and status, is himself willing to receive suggestions and criticisms, has implicit confidence in his associates and in the democratic process, is loyal to his staff individually and collectively, keeps all lines of communication clear, and practices the Golden Rule.

2. *Teaching Personnel*   The music educator must constantly remind himself that he is a part of a team and that his teammates have their own special role to play in the great game of education. Their contributions are just as important as his, and the efforts of all must be closely coordinated and integrated if the goals of education are to be reached. The director of music must of necessity develop close personal and professional relations with the classroom teachers, the subject matter teachers, and the directors of other special areas and services.

Each individual of the professional staff has his own unique contribution to make to the work of the school and his own special way in which to do it. The successful music director will respect the personal and professional individuality of each of his colleagues. Each member is entitled to the dignity of his particular position in the overall school structure. The music educator will respect it. He will also make it possible for his professional associates to make suggestions for the furtherance of the music program and the educational program as a whole. He will welcome friendly, constructive criticism. He will work toward as many face-to-face contacts as possible in the solution of professional and educational problems. His confidence in, and loyalty to, people as individuals and as groups will be freely and unreservedly expressed. His every action will give evidence of the Golden Rule in operation.

Undoubtedly, the administration of the school will be working for an efficient, cooperative, well-balanced staff. The music director must assist in this effort. One of the best ways to secure friendship and cooperation is to be friendly and cooperative oneself; show an interest in other teachers and their problems and interests; make offers of assistance and carry them out when accepted; pay friendly visits to classrooms, offices, and homes; practice the two-way street of good personal relations.

As an illustration of cooperation and mutual assistance between staff members, let us consider a situation likely to occur in a typical high school. The choir meets during school time, as do all of the major musical performing groups. The dramatics class and journalism class also have their regularly scheduled meetings. Just prior to the Christmas holidays, the choir needs extra time for final preparations for their Christmas concert. The dramatics class is rehearsing in the same school auditorium in which the concert is to be held. The journalism class is helping prepare copy for a special issue of the school newspaper. There are several students engaged in two of these activities, and some in all three.

This is obviously a situation that could cause much friction between staff members, unless all of them actively seek to work out a satisfactory plan of mutual assistance. The Christmas concert may be scheduled to take place the Sunday afternoon prior to the closing of school for the holidays; the dramatics class play might be postponed and not given until sometime in January; and, by this schedule, the special issue of the newspaper would not appear until five days after the choir's concert. If the teachers help the students to concentrate their efforts on the activity having the most immediate deadline, and if the teachers themselves are willing and anxious to give ground in favor of the most pressing performance, confident that they will receive similar cooperation when they need it, all three activities can receive the maximum amount of attention from students and teachers.

The music educator must be willing to give the same kind of cooperation and support to his colleagues that he expects from them. Offered honestly, sincerely, and humbly, such cooperation will reap a rich harvest of goodwill that can be gained in no other way. It is good policy; it is good personal relations; it is good education.

3. *Administrative Branch*   The director of music is usually responsible to the superintendent of schools and operates under authority delegated from him. This basic channel of responsibility and communication may be altered, depending upon the nature and degree of the responsibilities the superintendent is willing to delegate. It is always wise for a music educator to obtain a clear definition of his areas of responsibility and the person to whom he is accountable. Much confusion and possible embarrassment may be avoided in this way.

There are certain conditions that make it necessary for the director of music to operate within an area of responsibility authorized by the principals. In such circumstances, the music director must communicate to the superintendent through the principals and, through him, to the board of education.

In many school administrative organizations today, the principal is in complete charge of an entire unit of the school system. The superintendent has made him responsible for *all* that goes on within his unit; the staff, the budget, the buildings and grounds, the curriculum, and the special services. Complete autonomy of the school unit is the goal sought. Under these circumstances, a director or supervisor of music, or of any other special field, must work through the principal. The music educator becomes, in effect, a resource person or consultant, available at all times to the principal and his staff.

Bad feeling may be created between the music specialist, who considers music his entire and direct responsibility, and the principal, who feels that the whole school and all that goes on in it, including the music program, is within his area of control. A clear definition of the areas of responsibility and the practicing of the principles of personal relations can overcome this potential trouble.

The board of education is a policy-forming and legislative body that operates under the authority of the state and acts in the best interest of the community it serves. It serves as an official link between the schools and the community. The music educator is accountable to the board of education through the superintendent of schools, whom the board of education has named as its executive officer and charged with the responsibility for operating its schools. Any communication to the board from the music educator should, ethically, go through the superintendent. Certainly the music director should never go over the head of the superintendent to the board directly, except by invitation of the board, whose authority is higher than that of the superintendent. It is earnestly desired that superintendents adopt the policy of inviting their music specialists to meet formally with the board from time to time in order to discuss policies and problems of special interest to the music program of the schools.

Undoubtedly, there will be many opportunities for the director of music to meet individual members of the board of education socially and informally. On these occasions, the music program and its problems may easily become a topic of conversation. However, this is a poor substitute for a more formal and extensive study of the music educator's problems by the entire board of education.

The administrative staff of today's schools contains many specialists of whom the music director is one. Other areas, such as physical education and art, have their directors, supervisors, or consultants. The wise music educator will make full use of their professional services and seek to develop their confidence and friendship. Such personal relations build the most desirable climate for the wholesome growth and development of the children of the community.

In all of his contacts with the administrative branch of the school system, the music educator, to be most effective, must show respect for the status of each person or administrative group; he must be willing to receive suggestions and criticisms; he must understand the lines of communication and abide by them ethically; he must have confidence in his colleagues, as well as his administrators, and be loyal to them all; in his dealings with them, he must treat them as he would like to be treated if their stations were reversed. The practicing of personal relations is a two-way street; it means some giving and some receiving.

4. *Professional Service Group* The modern school utilizes the services of such professionally trained people as guidance counselors, health personnel, physicians, psychologists, librarians, and audiovisual experts. These people work with, and for, the children of the school, but in the area of general services or special services rather than actual classroom contacts. Their contributions to the school are unique and necessary. They can do much to help or hinder the musical experiences offered the pupils of the school and community they serve. The music director who has a genuine interest in securing the best of everything for the pupils of his school will try to work in close cooperation and understanding with this important group of people.

NON-CERTIFICATED STAFF   Another important group of people working in the interests of education for the children of the community is made up of the stenographers and clerks of the office staffs, the building custodians, the cafeteria workers, the bus drivers, and many others. Each has his special contributions to make and his own services to perform in the total educational effort. All too often, their importance is slighted, but recent trends show steady progress is being made toward full recognition and appreciation of their efforts.

No school organization can hope to operate effectively without the active interest and support of the office workers. Keeping records, handling correspondence, duplicating materials for the professional staff to use, and a host of other operations are of vital concern to the music educator as well as to the school as a whole. Friendly gestures of sincere appreciation for their work go a long way toward creating a wholesome atmosphere of cooperation and goodwill.

The importance of the custodians of any school system cannot be overlooked. Those who keep the buildings clean, warm, ventilated, and in repair; those who keep the grounds neat, well-groomed, and beautiful; those who repair broken furniture and equipment; all are as much specialists in education as any one of the professional staff. Very often, they are sound educators and wield tremendous influence upon the lives of the children with whom they come in contact. The music educator must do all in his power to develop understanding and cooperation between his department and the staff of custodians. The music department with its many concerts, night rehearsals, and special equipment, makes many unusual demands upon these people. The principles of good personal relations applied here can pay huge dividends in the development of better educational benefits for the entire community.

COMMUNITY CONTACTS — The personal contacts a music educator is called upon to make in the community that supports his school are many and varied. The brand of personal relations he develops with *all* the people of his community will, in large measure, determine the nature and value of his music program in the school; certainly, it will determine the degree of public support for it. Since it is not possible to discuss in detail all of the circumstances in which these relations occur, we will identify the chief categories and point out the music educator's responsibilities in each.

PARENTS   Those citizens who have children attending the schools of the community will, in all probability, be the most interested lay group. Certainly, it will be the group from which the music director may expect to draw the greatest amount of community support. It is a truism that the people most actively involved in any activity are its staunchest supporters. Since no cause can prosper without a large and loyal group of sponsors, the wise music educator must seek out ways to involve the parents of his school in the support of the program and to secure their participation in its activities. Such cooperation can be brought about only by diligent effort on the part of the music leader of the school. This effort can be successful only when the best patterns of personal relations are practiced between the music educator and the parents of the community.

None of the eight guide lines for good personal relations delineated earlier in this chapter is more important than communication. It is absolutely essential that the parents of the community find it easy to communicate with the music director, and he with them. All possible lines of communication must be carefully laid and constantly tended to be certain that they are clear and available for the transmission of messages from the school to the parent, and from the parent to the school.

Closely related to this guide line is, of course, the important principle that the music educator must be approachable. He must develop the feeling on the part of the entire community that any person or any group is cordially welcomed to discuss matters of mutual interest in the office, on the street corner, or in the home. This means that the music educator has little time to himself and, oftentimes, little privacy. It is worth noting, however, that the programs of music education that best serve their communities and are most active and influential in the lives of their children are headed by musical leaders who are motivated by this self-sacrificial principle.

People are most interested in, and give their most loyal support to, those programs in which they have a chance to participate. They like to help the music teacher and will eagerly respond to suggestions, if they are permitted to carry them out with no undue interruption. Many music educators have made valuable use of formal parent organizations such as Band Mothers Clubs, Choir Parents, and Orchestra Boosters. Without attempting to belittle or frustrate in any way the valuable contributions such groups can make, we must point out that, if these groups are improperly motivated or handled, disadvantageous results may occur.

Such groups may become so single-purpose minded that the larger aspects of music, or education as a whole for that matter, may be restricted or over-looked. There are communities where a strong Band Boosters group is so active in fund-raising and policy-making in the interests of the school band program that little or no consideration is given to other worthy aspects of the music program. Vocal music receives no support, and interest in it is killed by the lack of funds and attention given to it. The orchestral program becomes nonexistent, and desirable musical experiences for the general student are conspicuous by their absence. A warped version of music education in the public schools such as this is more harmful than helpful, when the greater good for the greater number of children is considered.

A more wholesome type of parent organization would be some sort of Music Council that would be interested in, and focus its attention upon, all phases of music in the school and community. Within this council, groups with special interests in the support and welfare of the band, or choir, or orchestra, or general student could be formed, but the council would coordinate and balance the work toward the best interests of all.

There is also a danger that parent groups might become interested in certain phases of the school program to the exclusion and detriment of other important and worthwhile areas. This frequently happens in athletics and has happened in music. The most wholesome conditions result when all groups are coordinated by some form of all-school organization such as the Parent-Teachers Association. The music educator must never lose sight of the fact that he and his program are but parts of the large mosaic called education.

He must not permit those parents in his community with a special interest in the music program to lose sight of it either.

LAY PUBLIC There is always a group of adults in each community that has no children in the public schools but is nonetheless concerned about the school and its offerings. This group includes people who support the music program wholeheartedly, those who actively oppose it, and those who possess all shades of attitudes in between. The principles of good personal relations must be practiced with all of these people, no matter what their point of view may be regarding music in public education.

The effectiveness of the music director's relationships with this group may well make the difference between a narrow, limited music program and one that is visionary and widespread in its influence upon the lives of all people in the community. This is the group that may determine the balance of power between complete and partial support of the musical activities within the school. A wisely planned and properly executed program of good personal relations with this portion of the music educator's community is bound to further the impact of music upon the school children of the community.

OTHER MUSICIANS It is the music director's business to establish good personal relations with the other persons in the community who make music their profession or strong avocational interest. Unless guarded against, there is a possibility that a lack of understanding and cooperation between the school musician and the community musician will exist. By putting into practice the principles of good relations discussed above, this rift can be bridged or avoided.

It must be clearly established that the music department of the school is working for the common good of all. It has no special ax to grind; its primary purpose is to elevate and improve the musical life of the entire community. To this end, all musicians, both in the school and out, must direct their cooperative efforts.

1. *Private Teachers* Frequently, the music teacher with a private studio in the community feels that the school music department, by giving "free" class lessons in piano, voice, and the orchestral instruments, is trying to run him out of business. Nothing could be further from the truth. Both the school and the community music teacher have an important part to play in the musical life of their community; they can play it with profit to all only if they play in harmony and not off key.

2. *Professional Musicians*   The music director must see to it that the work of the school organizations does not make inroads into the domain of the professional performing musician. He can be guided by the *Code of Ethics* adopted jointly in 1947, and renewed annually since then, by the Music Educators National Conference and the Musicians Union. This code clearly establishes the area of activity for the schools and for the professional musician. As long as its definitions are followed, good relations can be developed and successfully practiced by all concerned.

3. *Church Musicians*   Too often, the school musician and the directors of the local church choirs work at cross purposes; sometimes suspicion and jealousy are evident. The closest cooperation between these groups is vital to the healthy musical life of the community. It would be helpful for all to have a clear understanding of each other's areas of service. The music director might well take the lead in the development of such accord. The church choirs should be seen as one of the culminating activities of the school's vocal program, with both the school musician and the church musician working toward this objective.

4. *Music Hobbyists*   All communities have some people who do not make music their full-time profession but use it as a strong avocational interest or part-time profession. This group is often overlooked in the music director's relationships with people in the community. This is the group that is so avid in pursuit of musical satisfactions and whose lives are so enriched by it that they are willing and anxious to share it with the young people of the community. Properly cultivated, this group can become a fertile resource for enriching the school's musical offerings, as well as a strong group for the support of the music program of the school. Carelessness in personal dealings with this group and its members could cause great damage to the music program of the schools in any community.

5. *Music Service Personnel*   No music department could work at peak efficiency, in fact could not even exist for very long, without the goodwill and active support of those people who serve the music profession. The music publishers, the music sellers, the piano tuners, the instrument repair men, and all others who provide the school music field with goods and services are deserving of the best personal treatment the music director and his associates can give them. This mutual dependence upon the goodwill and support of each other is aptly personified in the close working arrangements

and mutual cooperation between the Music Educators National Conference, with its cooperating groups, and the Music Industry Council, with its affiliates. This same cooperation and respect for one another must be carried to the local scene and operate in each community, large and small.

In all of his contacts with people in the community of which his school is a part, the music director has a fertile field in which to plant the seeds of warm, effective personal relations and nurture them into full, flowering, cordial, cooperative endeavor. It must be remembered that the final objective of this program of personal relations is the improvement of musical experiences and satisfactions for the children of the community. The music director and his associates must be motivated by no other purpose. When the guide lines identified and discussed earlier in this chapter are followed and become an integral part of all human relationships in the school and community, the children of the community are bound to benefit.

EXTENDED COMMUNITY Even while keeping his mind and attention centered upon the children of the community, the wide-awake, resourceful music educator recognizes that the field in which he must develop the best personal relations extends beyond the limits of his school district. In this modern age of quick communication and rapid transportation, we all live in a community that is as large as the world itself. It is true that the most frequent and numerous personal contacts are made in the local community, but they in turn reach out with diminishing frequency and intensity through the county, region, state, nation, and even into the international community of nations.

Personal contacts with other music educators, other schools, other parents, other children, must be sought and carefully cultivated. The easiest approach is through the professional organizations with which the music educator affiliates himself. The names and areas of influence for these various organizations will differ, depending upon the locality in which the music educator is working, but they will, in all likelihood, be coordinated by the Music Educators National Conference and its state affiliates. Active participating membership in these organizations will reap untold benefits for the children of all communities.

Patterns of Action

Knowing the guidelines of effective personal relations and recognizing where personal contacts are likely to be made are only a part of the process of human conduct that will lead to a better musical environment and more wholesome musical experiences for the children of our schools. What a person *does* is far more important than what he *knows* about human relations. In this section, we will discuss ways of behaving that will be effective in developing the type of personal relations that will bring us closer to our desired goals. We cannot discuss concrete, step-by-step plans for action, but rather ways of meeting people that will be helpful in fostering the most satisfactory personal relations.

The motivation to behavior that leads to effective personal relations is interest in other people. This interest must completely dominate one's action. It means locating one's interest outside of himself and placing it in the people around him, the ones he meets and those with whom he works.

In a very real sense the effective leader must develop attitudes and interests that are outside himself rather than those which are self-centered. This type of extroversion is attractive to other people and causes them to follow such leaders willingly and eagerly.

There are many manifestations of extroversion. These are the action patterns the leader should seek to adopt. For our present discussion we will mention seven which are basic. The first is really the key to all of the others.

SHOW INTEREST IN PEOPLE — A music educator who does not have a deep, sincere, and abiding interest in people—all sorts of people—is doomed to failure. An interest in people must be the driving force behind all of his efforts. It is at the root of everything he undertakes, it shows in everything he does, it is apparent to all people with whom he comes in contact. It is the first requisite for successful personal relations in action.

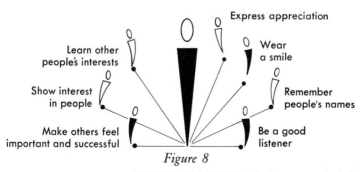

Figure 8

PATTERNS OF ACTION for effective personal relations

This interest in other people will find action in many ways. It will show up in concern for the personal welfare of each individual with whom the music educator deals. He will be willing to identify himself with their hopes and aspirations, to glory in their successes, and to sympathize with their failures. He will show by his every action that he finds pleasure in the company of his colleagues, his students, the parents of his community, and all other people whom he encounters.

LEARN OTHER PEOPLE'S INTERESTS — Discover the interests of those with whom you must deal and make it your business to know enough about these subjects to enable you to converse intelligently about them. Not only will this serve to broaden your own perspective, but it will develop more cordial relationships with your associates and better enable you to plan and carry out the program of music education needed in your community. The investment of a little time and energy spent in familiarizing yourself with the activities and interests of your associates will yield incalculable benefits in improved relationships.

You will be amazed how fascinating the interests of other people are when you take time to study them and give these people an opportunity to teach you about them. This applies in all areas of personal contact: the classroom, the business office, and the convention lobby.

REMEMBER PEOPLE'S NAMES — An individual's name is his most prized possession. It flatters him and makes him feel important to have his name remembered and to be spoken to by means of it. The pupil in the classroom, the parent in the home, the passer-by on the street, the businessman in his store, all respond favorably to the person who has taken enough interest in them to learn their names. This device will work as positively for the music educator seeking a favorable musical environment for his pupils as it does for the politician seeking votes.

BE A GOOD LISTENER — Everyone likes an attentive audience when he gives voice to his problems, plans, hopes, and aspirations. Each person welcomes a chance to express his ideas on a pet subject. The music director who can develop the knack of being a good listener will find a more receptive audience for a recital of his own problems and plans. A person who talks all the time, never permitting the other person to express his point of view, will find it difficult, if not impossible, to secure the support he needs for his own program.

MAKE OTHERS FEEL IMPORTANT AND SUCCESSFUL — Nothing succeeds like success. This is an old saying, but still true. When a person is made to feel important and successful in a task, he radiates enthusiasm and good-will. He is agreeable, cooperative, and anxious to please others. The wise administrator helps make it possible for all members of his organization to recognize their importance to the common endeavor and to feel success in their contributions to it.

This principle is as operative in the classroom as in the staff meeting. A student who is made to feel successful and important will contribute more to the music program and, at the same time, take away more from it. The parent who is made to feel important to the welfare of the music department will contribute more to it and be active in the promotion of those activities that yield more and better musical experiences for the youth of his community.

The successful music executive will handle all situations in such a way that every member of his organization will sense his share of success in any venture and will feel his own importance to the organization. Rather than seeking to focus the spotlight upon himself, he will focus it upon others. He will hasten to give credit where credit is due and be direct and sincere in his praise for work well done, whether it is done by student, parent, lay worker, or a businessman.

WEAR A SMILE — A cheerful countenance is attractive to other people. A smile attracts; a frown repels. The smile must not be forced and stilted, but one that is warm and friendly, one that is the result of genuine inner peace and contentment, one that is the result of a happy personality.

EXPRESS APPRECIATION — Make it a habit to personally thank other people for whatever they have done for you, the leader, personally or for the organization and its work. This appreciation must be sincerely expressed and as easily voiced to a student as to a fellow worker.

The preceding part of this chapter indicates that the practicing of democratic human relationships is imperative. The highest ideals of democracy must permeate all personal relationships and be exercised in all contacts the music educator has with people. The succeeding chapters will be aimed at showing how the music educator can make his personal relationships effective, so that the entire cause of education through music may benefit.

All of the theory discussed in this chapter is meaningless unless the music educator can apply it to his everyday experience in working with the curriculum, his teaching staff, and the public.

New Personnel

The previous portion of this chapter has dealt with the points of contact the music director has with his colleagues, pupils, and community. There is another area of personal concern that contributes to this setting. The next few pages will be devoted to the problem of selecting personnel for the music department and making new teachers feel at home in the school and community.

SELECTING PERSONNEL — The amount of participation expected of the music director in recruiting and selecting teachers for his staff will depend upon the amount of responsibility delegated to him for his task by the superintendent of schools. Often the superintendent will retain full rights to the selection of all personnel. If this is the case, a music educator can do nothing more than work with the teachers assigned him and seek to obtain the best results from their efforts; at the same time, he can try to lead them toward self-improvement on the job. Good administrative practice indicates, however, that if the director of music is made responsible for carrying out the school's program in music, he should assist in selecting the personnel for doing the job. This principle applies particularly to the music staff, but, to a degree, it should apply also to the selection of teachers for elementary schools where music instruction is carried on in the classroom by the room teacher.

Before beginning his search for a new staff member, the music director must clearly establish the nature of the job and the type of person necessary to fill it. An analysis of position and teacher should be conducted cooperatively with the present members of his staff, the principals, the superintendent, and the community. When the nature and purpose of the work to be done is clearly established, the qualities of personality, background, and training necessary in the person to do it can be studied. Without a doubt, details concerning both the job and the needed individual will vary from community to community and from school to school. Keeping this last point in mind, we turn our attention to the basic criteria for selecting a new staff member.

CRITERIA — Although it is not possible to describe in detail the type of person required for a staff member, certain broad areas are constant and definable. It will be necessary to discuss them in some sort of sequence, but by so doing no one quality is to be considered of greater importance than another; actually, it is the composite person and personality who is sought. The following factors are the ones that loom large in the thinking of a person charged with the responsibility for selecting personnel.

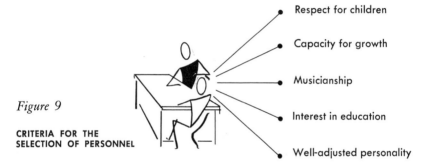

Figure 9

CRITERIA FOR THE SELECTION OF PERSONNEL

- Respect for children
- Capacity for growth
- Musicianship
- Interest in education
- Well-adjusted personality

RESPECT FOR CHILDREN No teacher can be expected to achieve success and make his best contribution to the school and its music program, unless he has a deep and abiding interest in, and respect for, children. The word respect has been chosen with considerable care. It is used because it means to be considered worthy of esteem, to be regarded or treated with honor, to be valued. All people who expect to work with children and influence their lives for good must be convinced of the tremendous worth of each child with whom he comes in contact, including, without discrimination, children of all kinds, races, creeds, and cultures. This quality cannot be superficial; it must be deeply rooted and sincere.

MUSICIANSHIP The music staff member must possess all of the attributes of a first class musical personality: he must have a lively interest in music in all of its phases; he must be anxious to perform it, to hear it, and share it with others; he must have a highly cultivated taste for the finest in music; he must possess the necessary skills for performing, creating, and teaching; his knowledge about music and things musical must be diverse and secure; his musical insights must be deep. In short, he must be a thorough musician in every sense of the term.

Although it is desirable to obtain the services of a performing musician, this skill is by no means an indispensable requirement. There is no doubt that the ability to perform artistically is a valuable asset for the music educator, but there are people who possess other skills that compensate for a lack of it.

A sensitivity for, and an understanding of, group playing and singing is important because so much of the music teacher's time is spent with performing groups, both large and small. The ability to conduct and to play the piano are the most important performance skills to be sought in a music educator.

It must be remembered that the amount of training in music and musical performance does not, of itself, determine the degree of musical sensitivity possessed by a teacher. Musical insight, awareness, and initiative, are products of growth in an environment that fosters such development. College credits are not necessarily proof that a person is musical.

INTEREST IN EDUCATION   If the public schools are to achieve the goals our society expects of them, all persons associated with them must understand the nature and purposes of education in a democratic society. The worker in music must be convinced of the contributions that music can make. He must be as interested in the total development of a child's personality as he is in his musical development. He must have a philosophy of education that is clearly developed and sincere. He must also be able and willing to take his share of responsibility for the work of the school as a whole, including such tasks as homeroom guidance, lunch room supervision, and general committee work. The importance of this quality cannot be too greatly stressed.

WELL-ADJUSTED PERSONALITY   A person who works as intimately with people as does the music educator must be a well-adjusted person. He must have his own physical, mental, emotional, and social behavior so well under control that he can help other people to develop control. His own adjustment to the pressures of everyday living must be such that others will profit by their association with him. He must meet people easily and be at home with the banker, the lawyer, the bricklayer, the housewife, the politician, and children of all types. It is an inescapable fact that the business of education is human relations in practice, and unless a person is able to meet and work with people easily, confidently, and with pleasure, he cannot be successful.

CAPACITY FOR GROWTH   The teacher most sought after is the one who recognizes that his growth is not complete and is willing and anxious to do those things that will contribute to, and promote, further growth.

The person who exhibits a genuine love for children, who is a sensitive musician, who is a sound educator, who possesses a well-adjusted personality, and who shows a capacity and willingness for growth, is to be desired as a music staff member. The final test of these qualities is found in the way that a person behaves in his working with people.

PROCEDURES — No pat procedures or rules of thumb can be given for ways of securing the best teachers for the music department. The alert music director will constantly be seeking good people to fill openings as they occur in his department. He will make it his business to keep in contact with those teachers who show by their work at festivals, clinics, and other activities, that they possess the qualities he seeks for his department. He will establish good relations with those teacher training institutions turning out the type of beginning teacher he wants for his system. He will become acquainted with the best students and observe them in their student teaching duties. He will also watch at work those teachers recommended by his professional friends. The securing of competent staff members will always be a vital concern of the successful music director.

ORIENTATION — When any new person comes into an established organization, there inevitably follows a period of orientation, a time of familiarization with policies and procedures, a time of becoming acquainted with people in school and community, a time of establishing oneself as an integral part of the organization. Everything a music director can do to shorten this period will result in increased efficiency for the entire organization and will be reflected in its product—the education of children.

Work shops conducted prior to the opening of the school year are becoming a common practice in many schools today. Such an activity serves many functions, and one of them is that it provides an orientation process for new teachers. It affords the new staff member an opportunity for becoming acquainted with the other members of the staff, to know them as persons and to know how and where they work. It furnishes him with an opportunity for becoming familiar with the physical plant and the educational equipment with which he will be working. He is able to see other staff members at work upon common problems and to become a part of the process himself. It gives him a chance to get his feet on the ground before he faces his first group of children.

A printed or mimeographed handbook of school and department policy and practice is another valuable means of furnishing a new teacher with the information necessary for a quick and thorough orientation in his job. Its advantage is that it is presented in definite, tangible form. Experience has shown that policies and practices can be interpreted and applied more uniformly when they are written out.

Where superintendents of schools or their assistants have an orientation program for all new members of the system as a whole, the music director will work closely with it and its development. In addition, he must be concerned with the particular orientation necessary for the new music teacher on his staff. The newcomer needs to meet and become acquainted with other members of the staff and to learn their areas of responsibility in relationship to his own. He needs to have opportunities for observing older staff members at work so that he may profit by their greater experience. He should have someone in the department to whom he can go for advice and counsel. It may be the director of music or someone designated by him to be the "big brother" or "big sister" to the new colleague. These are but a few of the ways a new staff member can be quickly and effectively oriented into his new job.

Summary

The way in which a music educator, or any other educator for that matter, gets along with people will in large measure determine the influence he is able to exert upon their lives. One major product of education should always be improved behavior and improved social relationships. This chapter has suggested four principles for guiding the educator in his dealings with people: respecting the dignity of the individual; maintaining open lines of communication; displaying loyalty, confidence, and faith in people; and applying the Golden Rule to all personal relationships.

The music educator meets, and works with, many types of individuals in a great variety of settings. He meets, and works with, his fellow musicians in the school system and in the community. His colleagues are administrators, teachers, custodians, and clerks. His clientele is made up of parents, pupils, and all persons in the community that supports the school. The wholesomeness of all of these personal relationships is governed by the way the music educator lives and works among his fellowmen.

It is not enough for a music educator to know the principles of good personal relations and to recognize all of the points of contact with people, both in and out of the school system; he must also display behavior patterns that will develop the most wholesome environment for fostering relationships that lead to effective cultural improvement for the school and community. Seven patterns of action have been discussed: displaying interest outside of oneself, smiling, speaking to people by name, listening to other people rather than always talking oneself, discussing the other person's interests, making it possible for other people to feel important and successful, and showing appreciation.

A director of music charged with the responsibility of selecting personnel for his staff needs a set of criteria for guiding his thinking. This chapter suggests that a teacher who possesses a genuine respect for children, who is a sensitive musician, a sound educator, has a well-adjusted personality, and shows a capacity for growth, is likely to provide the most beneficial influence upon the lives of the children with whom he comes in contact.

The guiding principles for satisfying personal relations, the points at which human contacts are made, the patterns of personal action, and the criteria for selecting staff members—these points have been the chief focus of this chapter.

Suggested Activities

1. Think of some person whom you regard as an exceptional leader. Analyze your relationship with this person and identify those Guide Lines discussed on pages 30 to 35 that are evident.

2. Do the same with the Patterns of Action discussed on pages 46 to 50.

3. Examine yourself and see how many Guide Lines you consistently follow.

4. Do the same with the Patterns of Action.

5. Think of the several music teachers you have known. How do they measure up to the criteria discussed on pages 51 to 53?

6. Study yourself and determine your strengths and weaknesses in terms of the criteria for personnel discussed on pages 51 to 53.

7. Ask a good friend to identify your strengths and weaknesses in terms of these criteria.

For Further Reading

Flora, Frank E. "Successful Administrative Relationships Make Successful Music Programs." *Music Educators Journal,* 47, No. 5:66–67, April-May, 1961.

Gehrkens, Karl Wilson. "An Old Man's Opinion." *Music Educators Journal,* 46, No. 6:48, June-July, 1960.

Glenn, Neal E. "Human Relations and the Music Supervisor." *Education,* 74, No. 1:27, September, 1953.

Kennelly, E. F. "Human Relations in Personnel Administration for Education." *Education,* 75, No. 4:214–217, December, 1954.

CHAPTER 3

Curriculum

THROUGH THE YEARS, the term curriculum has meant many things. Even today, it has no uniform meaning and must be defined anew by each person who uses it. For our purposes, it will be defined as those experiences provided by the schools for its pupils and in which the pupils participate. The fact that this definition is a broad concept of curriculum cannot be denied. This is not a weakness; rather, the very broadness and all-inclusiveness of such a definition give it strength. When we recognize that a child is a living, growing organism, learning from all of his experiences, both in and out of school, then we realize the need for a broad definition that will take into account the totality of the child's experience within the school.

Educators can no longer abide by a definition that limits curriculum to "courses of study." By course of study, we mean a type of curriculum that attempts to divide all of life's experiences into tight, unrelated segments and to explore each independently of the other. A systematic sequence of problems is laid out in the hope that solving each in turn will lead to a mastery of the subject or area in question. This course of study definition is unacceptable because it excludes too much. Of course, children learn valuable life concepts in many courses of study, but they also learn by means of experiences that lie *outside* the confines of limiting courses of study. The most serious shortcoming of this concept of curriculum is that, in practice, it denies the fundamental idea that persons are different and learn in different ways and by different means.

Not only is this course of study definition of curriculum rejected by today's educators, but they also find unacceptable a definition that includes all of the experiences by which a child learns, both within and outside the school's jurisdiction. It is easy to accept the fact that children learn by their experiences outside the range of the school's influence. In truth, they learn a very considerable amount from these experiences. We cannot, however, permit the school to assume responsibility for learning experiences over which it can exercise no control. We return, therefore, to our original definition that the curriculum of a school consists of the actual experiences of children for which the school is responsible and over which it exercises control.

The Music Curriculum

The music educator will need to paraphrase this definition of curriculum in the following manner: "The music curriculum consists of all the actual musical experiences that children accept under the guidance of the school." Notice the word "accept." No true learning takes place unless there is a desire for such learning on the part of the child. He must possess a willingness to learn. He controls the learning process; he always has, for that matter. No positive musical learning can take place unless the learner accepts the experiences offered. If he rejects them, a negative learning or an absence of learning results. Therefore, the basic objective in curriculum planning and teaching is to bring the child to the point where he will accept the learning experiences offered by the school.

The broadness of our definition does not exclude the necessity for a plan; in fact, it makes it all the more necessary. When the curriculum was narrowly conceived and offered to the child on a "take-it-or-else" basis, its very narrowness made it relatively easy to select experiences, place them in a sequence, and attempt to inveigle the child to move through them systematically. It was like preparing a meal, putting it on a plate before the youngster, and saying, "Here it is, eat it or starve." All too often, children starved musically rather than try to swallow the unpalatable stuff dished up for them.

The curriculum as defined in this chapter is somewhat like a cafeteria where the child holds his empty plate and is permitted to make his selections from the foods attractively displayed before him. We have helped him by placing all of the meat at one place on the counter, the vegetables at another, the salads at another, and the dessert at another. We have also encouraged him to select a well-balanced diet, to understand how to select it, and to know why it is important. We have tried to help him understand that some things go together better than others. The menu and food layout in a cafeteria take planning—the same type of planning necessary for developing a curriculum in music in the broad terms of our definition.

By our definition, the music curriculum is a richly varied group of experiences. It will include the songs sung at opening exercises in the morning, the songs sung on busses going on field trips, the songs sung at football rallies and games. It will include the jam sessions before and after band rehearsal, the concerts, the assembly programs, and all other public appearances. It will include the music from the sound track of a social studies film, the school dances, the singing games at parties. It will also include the songs, dances, singing games, the quiet listening, and the songs made up by groups of children under the guidance of a wise, resourceful teacher in our elementary schools. In short, it will include *all* of the musical experiences of the child under the auspices of the school.

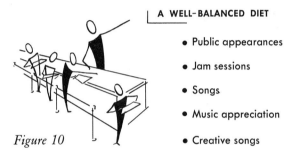

A WELL-BALANCED DIET

- Public appearances
- Jam sessions
- Songs
- Music appreciation
- Creative songs

Figure 10

These broad aspects of curriculum must be constantly in the foreground of the music educator's thinking as he leads others in enriching and expanding the musical experiences his school will offer the children of his community.

Shaping Forces

The curriculum has never been a neat plan devised by professional educators and put into operation in the schools. Although it is true that the leadership of teachers and educators has had its influence through the years, its force has not been as great as might be supposed. The curriculum of any school is the resulting balance between all of the forces that have a part in shaping its nature and content. Chamberlain and Kindred[1] identify six such forces, which we will use as the framework for our present discussion.

[1] Leo M. Chamberlain and Leslie W. Kindred, *The Teacher and School Organization,* 2nd ed., Englewood Cliffs, N.J., Prentice-Hall, Inc., 1949, pp. 325–35. Used by permission.

CUSTOM AND CONVENTION — Some curriculums are based on a "what-was-good-enough-for-their-fathers-is-good-enough-for-the-children" attitude. People are reluctant to alter the pattern of their schools, even though they welcome gladly new ideas, new practices, and new products, in other parts of their culture. The old subject-centered curriculum still persists in spite of the fact that there is considerable evidence to show that it does not prepare one for college or life any better than, if as well as, the newer types of curriculums. Habits and traditions of the past are extremely difficult to break in education, and this one factor alone has been responsible, to a very great degree, for the slow rate of curriculum change.

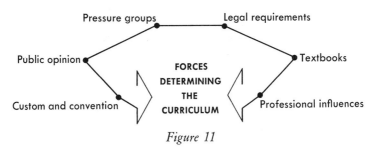

Figure 11

TEXTBOOKS — The subject-centered curriculum placed great stress upon the textbook used in a particular area. For the most part, a single book was depended upon for all information. In this situation, the publishers controlled, to a large extent, the content of any curriculum, since schools and curriculum planners are largely dependent upon the textbook publishers for their source material. Happily, a great wealth of rich and varied material is now available. Publishers, for the most part, with their editors and research personnel, have been more visionary than most schools and communities as far as curriculum development is concerned. What the publishers issue is no longer a limiting factor upon the school curriculum, but rather a tremendous reservoir of stimulating, attractive resource material.

LEGAL REQUIREMENTS — On frequent occasions, the states have exercised their prerogative to prescribe what shall be taught in the schools over which they have jurisdiction. Many experiences are present in the curriculum of today's schools because a state law says they must be there; frequently, the state prescribes the area, the content, and the amount of time each day or week spent upon them. Very often there is so much placed in the curriculum by mandate that it is extremely difficult to offer the useful, varied program that educators desire.

Although one will not quarrel with the principle that states have this right, use of this right does lead to undesirable restrictions at times. When too great a proportion of curriculum content is dictated, other desirable experiences are frequently excluded. Music educators often suffer in this situation. In many states, large blocks of curricular time are devoted to the social sciences, physical education, and language arts, as required by law. These subjects, with other local or academic requirements, often fill the school day so completely that music experiences are denied many students who desire them and would benefit by them. Students are thus denied contact with the auditory arts that would aid in giving breadth to their education and food to their aesthetic souls.

PRESSURE GROUPS — It is unfortunate that the structure of society is such that groups are able to force their special interests upon the general public. It is particularly vicious when such groups, serving minority interests, can force curriculum content to be bent in a direction that benefits them, or, because of prejudice, can force the schools to exclude experiences that would be beneficial to society as a whole.

Pressure groups do not always exert an unwholesome influence. It is true that, on occasion, bands of interested parents have been able to force a desirable change to come about faster than it might have come without such pressure.

The inclusion of music in the curriculum of many schools is a good case in point. Many communities owe their fine music program today to the devoted interest of groups of parents who have banded together and brought pressure to bear upon reluctant or narrow-minded boards of education in such a way that time, space, and public funds, were made available for music instruction and equipment.

PUBLIC OPINION — What the general public believes schools should or should not offer, to a certain extent, controls the nature and content of the curriculum. Certainly, schools cannot move forward any faster than the public that supports them will permit. Some of the attacks upon educational institutions, so prevalent today, have come about because the schools have tried to move ahead faster than the public would allow. The force of public opinion, with its effect upon schools, is good and sufficient reason for the development of a sound public relations program, and such a program will be discussed in Chapter 5.

PROFESSIONAL INFLUENCE — If this force is placed at the end of the list, it does not necessarily mean that it is the weakest of the six influences. It is certain, however, that the professional educator cannot wield his influence with any degree of strength, unless the other five are favorable or at least the balance between them has created a permissive setting in which the professional educator can operate. In the final analysis, the public controls the school and the school curriculum. The professional educator is able to move forward only as far, and as fast, as he is able to educate the public to lead the way.

The place music holds in the curriculums of the schools of America is the result of these forces at work. Some communities give music little or no prominence, possibly because they have not broken sufficiently with the past and thus still consider music a fad and a frill. Other places give music an important place in the curriculum because certain pressure groups have insisted that it be there. Some states require by law certain minimum offerings in music; others stipulate none. Some textbooks in music offer a rich and varied group of musical experiences; others limit all musical activity to singing. Each community establishes its own music curriculum in accordance with the interplay of the six forces just discussed.

Curriculum Change

Just as there are various forces that shape the nature and content of the curriculum, there are also forces that necessitate its change. These forces must also be singled out and understood before the music educator can exercise his leadership toward the development of improved schools.

DYNAMIC CULTURE — A culture that is dynamic must change. The American culture is living, moving, and dynamic. From its beginnings, it has continually sought a better life for all of its members. It has not been content with a *status quo,* but has purposely reached out for new ideas, new forms of technology, new social patterns, always seeking a way of living and working that more nearly reaches the highest pinnacles of happiness and comfort available to mankind. If this were not so, the culture would be static and, to all useful purposes, dead or at least dying. In such a society, it is not possible to go back to the good old days or even to retain them. The very nature of life moves onward, and it is the nature of man to try to make the future better than the past.

As a society changes, its institutions must change—its government, its churches, its homes, its business, its industry. These changes must also inevitably affect the schools; the schools must change as new meanings and new emphases are given to life. A changing society such as ours calls for curriculum change in all educational institutions in order to keep pace at least; more than that, it must foresee and help chart the future in order to prepare for it.

CHILDREN'S NEEDS — The older concept of education gave little concern to the interests and needs of the child in the present. Education was thought to be a preparation for the future. His training was controlled by adults who gave him the experiences they thought he needed. As a result, the child was unable to see the purposes for the requirements made of him. His natural interests were often stifled; certainly they were given little or no consideration. Education was thought to be preparation for life.

The present trend is to consider the pupil's basic drives and develop a curriculum that satisfies them. Educators now know that true learning does not take place unless the learner wants and accepts the experiences offered. Education is, therefore, not preparation for life but life itself. It has been recognized that the best way to prepare for life tomorrow is to live it today.

LEARNING PROCESS CLARIFIED — The older concept of learning thought the mind needed exercise and training, like a muscle. The discipline of doing difficult things, though dull, uninteresting, and useless, was thought to be helpful in training the mind. The entire emphasis was upon learning facts and skills, not upon insight and understanding.

Today, learning is known to involve the entire person—his social, mental, emotional, and physical being. Interest must be keen in the content or subject matter of learning, as well as in the activities that promote it. Also, the results of learning—new skills, new attitudes, new knowledge, new insights—must be clearly recognizable to the learner. He must be aware of all these while he learns.

It is also known that education is a process of growth and development.

The child is a growing, evolving, developing organism, and he must be placed in the most favorable environment if this growth is to be uninhibited. Individuals grow in different ways, at different rates, and at different times. These newer concepts of the learning process demand a fundamental change in the curriculum of the school.

GROWTH AND DEVELOPMENT — Psychologists and educational workers have corrected a good deal of faulty thinking about how an individual reaches maturity. The process of reaching maturity is influenced by the entire environment in which the growth takes place. It is therefore important that the surroundings and activities into which a growing child is placed are favorable to developing all of his resources to their limits.

The older curriculum, with emphasis upon learning facts, was not good for this concept of growth; rather than fostering desirable growth, initiative, and independence, it served as a stifling influence. The more permissive atmosphere of the newer curriculum, centered on the interests and needs of the child, is a setting in which normal, healthy growth can take place; it necessitates a change from the practices existing in many schools and communities today.

Curriculum Development

Who makes the curriculum? The simplest, most direct answer to this question is contained in one word—everybody. The entire focus of education is upon people; education is considered to be an entirely human process for human ends.

Schools were first organized because people wanted certain things for their children. They decided what the work of the schools should be and the way in which it was to be done. As time went by and more and more professionally trained educators were employed by the schools, these educators began to decide what was desirable for the curriculum. The people of the community lost direct control but, even so, retained indirect control and have retained it to the present day. When the schools did not offer what the public thought they should, pressures were applied until the curriculum was in line with community thinking. In our society and system of public education, this will always be so.

The schools in our culture are a cooperative effort with professional educators, pupils, parents, and public, all playing a part. No curriculum can be successful in achieving the goals our civilization has placed upon public education, unless all people are involved in the process of developing such plans, executing them, and evaluating them. All educators and all interested lay people must consider curriculum development their major responsibility, if our schools are to provide the citizens of our society with the kinds of educational experiences they need to assume their proper roles in our culture.

The music curriculum is made by the children as they sing, work, and play together in the elementary classroom. It is made by the room teacher as he uses music to enhance his daily routine. Assembly singing is part of it; singing in the homeroom, singing in French class, singing for square dancing and party games—these are all part of it. It includes the music of pep rallies, school dances, and musical shows. It includes visits to the local churches and radio stations, trips to the local record shops, trips to the contests and festivals. The music curriculum includes *all* of the musical experiences that are a part of the school, and it is made by *all* those people who had a share in bringing these experiences to the children.

The process of curriculum development cannot be outlined in neat steps; it differs from school to school and from community to community. This is as it should be—schools, communities, and people differ, their needs will differ, and approaches to common problems will assume different characteristics. Nevertheless, behind all curriculum development programs is found a framework that is quite constant. In this pattern of actions will be found the six stages of the administrative process developed in Chapter 1. Although the entire problem must be treated as a whole, it will be helpful to our thinking to break it down into its component parts and see how each one operates and contributes to the entire process. The essential characteristics remain the same, whether considering the total curriculum of the school or the music curriculum in particular. In order to guide our thinking more effectively, we shall consider the process from the point of view of the music curriculum.

GROUNDWORK — No activity can be started without some person who believes that his efforts and the enlisted effort of others should be engaged in it. Curriculum development cannot begin until some person is convinced that work in this direction should be begun and is successful in winning others to the same point of view. This starting impulse must spread to include all of the forces and people who will eventually contribute to the process of curriculum building. Although it will undoubtedly take some time before everyone actively connected with the school is convinced that such study is necessary, the step of laying the groundwork is essential if the project is to be effective.

The generating force may come from any one of a variety of places. It may start with the administrators, the superintendent, the principals, the supervisors, or the directors. It may start with the teaching staff at the elementary or secondary level, or with grade groups, or subject area groups, or guidance activities. It may begin with parents who are dissatisfied with the existing curriculum or with a group of children saying, "What do we have to take this stuff for!" No matter where it starts, it must begin somewhere and be permitted and encouraged to grow, until it absorbs all persons who will have a part in its development. This is essential before the other stages can begin to operate.

The process of developing enthusiasm for curriculum study throughout the entire school and community can be handled in many ways. Within the staff, workshops and clinics may be conducted; staff meetings may be devoted to it; conferences may be held with individuals and groups; and committees may begin work on related problems in order to focus the activity. In the community, lay committees may be asked to study specific problems alone or with staff help; study groups may be organized, demonstrations presented, and speakers sent to clubs and social groups. As more and more people become active in the process of studying the school and its program, curriculum study will become the vital concern of an ever expanding group.

DEFINING PURPOSE — After the groundwork is laid, it is necessary to define or develop a philosophy of education from which a philosophy of music education will be a logical outgrowth. This will undoubtedly take some study and time, but it is absolutely vital to the success of the later stages of the process. It must be understood that the basic philosophy may change as the process goes on; without a doubt it will be refined, but it is not possible to start without a belief, a definition of what is valuable, of what is true and right. It will become the creed of all those working on curriculum development— "This I believe."

Let us pause a moment to consider the sources from which this philosophy or purpose will develop, the forces that will bring it about. The first of these influences is the thinking and experiences of all who are concerned with the project. The more people involved in the process, the broader, more inclusive will be the thinking devoted to the development of the philosophy. The advice of people from all segments of the school organization and the community must be actively sought and heeded. A curriculum developed only upon the thinking and experiences of music teachers will be biased and not functional in terms of the school and community needs.

A good cross-section of the music specialists within the local school system, the administration, the parents, civic leaders, and the students themselves, must be organized to bring their best thinking and experience to bear on this definition of purpose. This may be done by such means as workshops, study groups, discussion groups, and committees. The work of any one group must be readily available to other groups working on similar problems, and the thinking of all coordinated into a common statement of purpose.

The second influence that assists in shaping the working philosophy of a school seeking to improve its curriculum derives from other groups who have developed curriculums for their own communities. Some person or group of persons must set about studying the curriculums of other schools and communities. It is important to study not only the published plans but the actual experiences provided for the children in the classrooms. In other words, the curriculum in action should be studied very carefully. It is a true statement that very often there is a wide divergence between what a school *plans* to do and what it actually *does*.

The third source of information for the development of a working philosophy is the careful study of the so-called experts or authorities in the field being studied. These are people who, because of their unusual endowments of intellect, training, and experience, have been able to see beyond the present and show the direction the future must take for the betterment of all mankind. These persons must have a voice in the planning of any curriculum that hopes to meet the needs of the children of our schools. All too often, the thinking of these people has been cast aside as "theoretical" or "impractical" when, in reality, such criticisms of them are the result of narrow, closed attitudes and ideas.

PLANNING — The planning phase of the curriculum development process begins with a study of the community, its needs, its problems, its resources, its people. The community must be studied from a music point of view. This by no means excludes the study of the community as a whole, but the particular emphasis is upon the musical needs, problems, and resources. It is necessary to develop a clear understanding of the nature of musical growth.

As the process, the purpose, and the resources become clearer, goals will be established. Whereas the philosophy established was a belief or a creed, the goals are objectives or mileposts, to be passed in the process of growing into a musical person. They must be clearly seen and clearly defined. Education without goals is like taking a trip without a plan.

If a person has some reason for going from New York City to Lincoln, Nebraska, let us say, he has many routes and many modes of travel open to him. He may fly or go by train, bus or car; he may go by horse and buggy or walk; he may lie down on the ground and hope that someone will pick him up and carry him there. His reasons for making the trip will help him make his decision; there may be an emergency in his family or business, so that speed is of vital importance. In this case, he will probably fly, even though in other circumstances he might be fearful of the dangers of flying or feel himself unable to afford the cost of a plane ticket. He may plan the trip in order to visit his parents and wish to take his family with him, in which case he might go by automobile. Other factors will influence the route he takes in his car. For instance, he may be in no hurry because his vacation period is of sufficient length to make a leisurely trip possible, or he may have former schoolmates, fraternity brothers, or friends he wishes to visit enroute. He may set up a schedule and tell those whom he will visit the day and time they may expect him, thereby setting goals for himself. All of these factors will determine the details of his trip. He has set goals for himself and a mode of travel and, to a certain extent, a time schedule to follow.

Returning to the music curriculum, let us consider its nature and content. After the musical goals for a community have been established and understood, insights into the environment and conditions that validate these goals must be considered. This study of the community, its musical needs, resources, and facilities may, and in many cases undoubtedly will, bring about completely new insights into what the music curriculum must be. It is safe to predict that it will point up vividly the fallacy of the fragmentation of the music curriculum into unrelated, special areas. This fragmentation has long been one of the objects of justifiable criticism of music curriculums.

An extensive, far-reaching curriculum study will build a strong case for a broad, all-inclusive, dynamic program of general music. It will begin in the kindergarten; continue through the elementary school; on into junior high school, at least; and, in all likelihood, through the high school and college. It will be the main current, the main stream, of musical activity and experience of the new music curriculum.

In this broadest, most dynamic sense, general music is the foundation upon which special, selective activities and experiences can be built. Nothing that has been said heretofore should be construed as meaning that the bands, orchestras, choirs, and ensembles, should be discarded or minimized in favor of a general music program; rather, the intention is that the music program should be broadened to include experiences that will permit *all* children to find activities that will permit their maximum musical growth, even though their abilities may deny them admission to the band, the orchestra, or the choir.

In this setting, general music stands upon its own merits, makes its own contribution toward well-rounded, musical growth and is all-inclusive and all-pervading. It is not a watered-down, weakened series of musical experiences, but a strong, progressive force like a river. As a mighty river has many tributaries, each serving its own region in its own way, so will the music curriculum have many contributing influences and activities. The mainstream is known as general music,[2] with the choir, the orchestra, the music appreciation class, the school assembly, and all similar activities at all levels, serving as tributaries flowing into this mighty river. No single activity is considered independent or a separate entity, but rather a part of the larger system, making its own contribution toward the development of musical persons.

A music curriculum thus conceived and executed is all-consuming, because it leaves no one out; all-powerful because it has life, drive, purpose, and is not static; continuous because musical experiences are planned at all chronological levels and for all levels of ability. All its activities and experi-

Special theory
Listening
History activities

Special instrumental
activities

THE GENERAL MUSIC PROGRAM

Special choral
activities

Figure 12   The musical personality

[2] This is not a new idea. The literature on music in the curriculum has made frequent reference to this concept, especially in the last decade or two. Mursell stated it well in his *Education for Musical Growth* (Ginn & Co., Boston, 1948) as well as in other of his works. Both the First and Second Source Books of the Music Educators National Conference have strong statements supporting this point of view. The Fifty-seventh Yearbook (1958) of the National Society for the Study of Education, Part I, makes equally lucid and convincing arguments. Although the profession has known and done lip service to this concept for many years, it is regrettable that more music curriculums have not been established with general music firmly established as the core.

ences, whether general or special, lead to a common, final goal—that of developing a musical person.

GOALS   The first step in establishing educational goals is to develop a clear concept of what the final product is to be. This is not unique to curriculum building but is consistent with all sound planning, whether it be building a house, taking a trip, or manufacturing an automobile. Only when the end product is clearly defined, can effective day-by-day plans be laid for reaching these goals.

One of the major faults of the older concept of curriculum is that only final or distant goals were considered. In this point of view, the present or near future is ignored. School experiences are planned as preparation for adulthood and no consideration given to the needs of childhood. More modern understanding of curriculum calls for just as clear a delineation of distant goals but provides day-by-day experiences in keeping with childhood needs, at the same time progressing systematically to the final goal. To say that long term goals are more important than short term goals is fallacious. However, it is important that long term goals be established *first*.

These short-term goals will undoubtedly change from day to day and week to week. The planned experiences must be flexible enough to include such changes without losing sight of the long-term goals. Adherence to a goal without consideration for day-to-day exigencies is a limited approach that should be avoided.

STEPS TOWARD GOALS   Next, it is necessary to study and provide for the activities and experiences that will lead toward goals. Here we can continue a little further the analogy between education and a trip. Lincoln, Nebraska, is the goal; visiting parents, relatives, and friends, is the purpose; but the way to go, the route, has not been decided upon. Niagara Falls, as well as Chicago and the Great Lakes, is a sight that might be seen on the way. On the other hand, perhaps sightseeing is not desired, and the most direct route is more attractive. Possibly a route going through Washington, D.C., has points in its favor. In any event, some decisions must be made, and those decisions are based on what the traveler expects to get out of the trip while it is in progress.

So it is with a music curriculum. Goals have been set, but the way to travel must be decided upon, the experiences provided that will lead to the established goals. These experiences are located in four major areas; performing, listening, creating, and engaging in rhythmic activity. Although they are discussed separately, it should be remembered at all times that they are interrelated and mutually dependent one upon the other for full fruition. It is difficult, if not impossible, to imagine any musical experience that does not contain certain elements of each of the four major areas of musical experience —performance, listening, rhythmic activity, and creation.

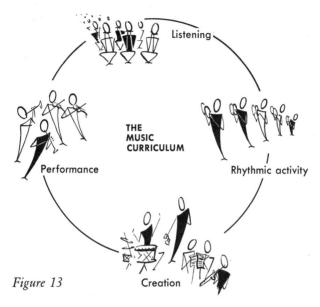

Figure 13

1. *Performance* Music is a performance art. It must be recreated in order to live. It can be enjoyed only by the process of being put into sound, and this process must be repeated each and every time the music is to be experienced. Musical feeling, or musicianship, has a chance for development in the process of performing music.

For the purpose of fostering musical growth and musicianship, the *medium* of musical performance is not as important as the process itself. In other words, it does not matter whether one plays the harmonica, violin, or sings; the important thing is that the person has actually participated in music-making. The musical benefits gained from performance are the same whether a person sings a song or plays upon an instrument; whether he sings or plays a solo or has a part in a large ensemble; whether he plays upon an oboe or recorder, violin or guitar, piano or accordion. This statement is made upon the assumption that the music performed in each case has comparable intrinsic value or worth.

The complete, well-balanced music curriculum will contain opportunities for all sorts of music performance experiences. Singing will become a part of normal classroom activity in the elementary classroom and often in the junior and senior high schools. All schools, both elementary and secondary, will have their general choruses, special choirs, select ensembles, and assembly sings. Instruments will be played in the elementary and secondary classrooms, there will be orchestras and bands at all chronological levels as well as ability levels, there will be small ensembles of all sorts and descriptions. The standard orchestra instruments will be available and taught, but the guitar, the ukelele, the accordion, and all others, will be used as well. All possible types of experiences must be available in order that all students may be reached.

2. *Listening*   Music is the art of sound. It must be heard to complete the artistic act. In this day and age, it is almost impossible to avoid hearing music, with the juke box, the radio, and television, in as widespread use as they are. Certainly, most people experience music by means of the aural activity, rather than through performance or creation.

Although it has become customary to designate aural experiences as listening activities, much more than passive listening is involved. All such activities must contain two chief emphases: the development of tonal perception and the development of tonal imagery. The former deals with the development of an awareness of tonal content and form as stimulated externally; the latter, with an awareness of tonal elements as stimulated inwardly. Each must be developed to some degree before the individual can fully enjoy and participate in any musical activity.

Listening activities, for the most part, are used to identify those experiences that place primary emphasis upon aural participation. This requires generalized ear training. The appreciation lessons, assembly concerts, and inter-grade sings, fall into this category.

Specialized ear training activities are usually associated with specific and detailed listening in connection with performance and creative activities. Pitch discrimination, interval and tonality awareness, and similar concepts, are identified with this class.

Curriculums for the schools of today and tomorrow must provide a generous amount of such experiences for their pupils so that the pupils may derive more benefit from all the music to which they are subjected day after day, whether by choice or not. Listening to music under the guidance of the schools is an experience that leads to the development of musicianship.

3. *Rhythmic Activity*   The rhythmic element in music is one of the most beautiful and most expressive of all the elements that make up the tonal art.

All too frequently, this beauty and expressiveness is lost, ignored, or buried under a faulty concept or approach to teaching and learning rhythm. Although it is not within the province of this book to give an exhaustive discussion of this important phase of the music curriculum, it would be wise for us to consider some of the fundamental characteristics of rhythm, how it is experienced, and the implications this information has for curriculum builders.

It is impossible to develop a simple definition of rhythm. However, we must examine all of its elements one by one and attempt to understand them before we can properly plan to include rhythm in a music curriculum.

First of all, rhythm is a strong organizing influence in music. It is the stuff that holds the complex structure of music together, the adhesive that prevents the various components from flying apart. Various sounds devoid of rhythm will not create music.

Music, properly conceived, is sound patterns moving through time, and it is rhythm that gives organization to the element of time. It gives movement its plan, its design, its force. So we might say that rhythm is measured movement. It is regular, steady, persistent flow. It is like a river or stream, always moving, now slowly and calmly, now a rushing torrent, now skipping and splashing gaily, but always moving on. It is never completely still. Movement in music is the same, and rhythm is the force that brings it about.

How frequently one hears the statement, "I can play all the notes, but I can't get the time." The maker of this remark does not mean "time" at all. Rhythm is the proper term. Time has to do with the minutes and seconds passing by. Rhythm has to do with the division of time into groups or beats or pulsations with varying amounts of stress and release; also, it involves the prolonging of sounds throughout multiple beats or shortening them into fractional pulses.

As music moves through time, the element of rhythm weaves itself around this framework of beats or pulses, much as a vine entwines itself about its trellis. A strong conception of beat is important to give rhythm its feeling of exactness and authority. This should not imply the beat is strict, even, unvarying. The beat is *relatively* strict, even, and unvarying. Nothing kills musical beat as quickly as a strict, mechanical, unvarying beat. The trick is to give beat the feeling of exactness without making it unvarying and mechanical. It is doubtful that the desired freedom can come about without first developing the ability to divide time units into strict beats or pulsations. Flexibility can be acquired after exactness, but the reverse is difficult, if not impossible, to achieve.

These beats or pulsations that we have been discussing have a tendency to group themselves into repetitive patterns of twos and threes. These are identified by accented beats, followed by unaccented ones. In musical terms, this phenomenon is meter. A march has a different meter from a waltz. A lullaby differs metrically from a polka. Such comparisons are obvious. To properly understand rhythm, one must keep in mind that each musical composition has its own metrical design.

Pulsations in music recur at varying rates of speed. Sometimes they are close together, sometimes they are far apart. To identify this attribute of rhythm, it is customary to use the Italian word for time, which is *tempo*.

Three properties of beats or pulsations in music have been discussed. They are regular, they are metrically grouped, and they recur at varying speeds or *tempi*.

Another extremely important concept of rhythm is that its basis in human response and understanding is almost completely physical. Rhythmic skill and understanding involves the muscle structure of the body. Unless rhythm can be felt and reproduced physically, it cannot be useful in music at all. This is really the key to the entire process of teaching rhythm, whether to children or adults. One must be able to move rhythmically before one can perform musically.

What are the implications of all of this for those who must develop music curriculums? First and foremost, teaching rhythm must be approached through bodily movement. Not just any movement, but movement that has the same beauty, grace, flow, and drive, that music has because of its rhythmic structure. The movement should come from within the person; it should not be externally imposed.

To begin with, the movements must be made of large motions using the larger muscles of the limbs and body. From this beginning, skills will gradually be developed using the smaller muscles and members of the body. It is best to start with the child's own natural rhythm, adapting the music to it until he has sensed the exhilaration that comes from bodies and music becoming one in rhythmic motion. After this has been achieved, the learner can gradually be brought to adjust his natural rhythm to that of the music and, by so doing, add variety and flexibility to his movement.

It may seem strange that we have progressed thus far in our discussion without mentioning the symbols of rhythm—the notation. This is entirely proper. Only after pupils become skilled in responding to musical rhythms, should they be expected to cope with the symbols. All too often the beauty, the sweep, the flow, the grace, of musical rhythm is lost to the student because he has been expected to read the notes before he has had a chance to feel the music.

The heading of this area of musical experience is "rhythmic activity." Here lies the crux of the entire matter. Rhythm can be taught only by activity —doing something with the body—not thinking, not reasoning, but moving.

4. *Creation* This is an often neglected and misunderstood area of activity. When a person is truly musical and has developed a feeling for the expressive content of music, why should he not be creative? Certainly the term creative means using musical substance in new ways; it also means using insights in new relationships. In fact, the development of musical insights is itself a creative act. Deciding upon the proper interpretation for a song is creative; improvising a second part to a familiar melody is creative; experimenting with various instrumental combinations is creative. The very essence of all music teaching worthy of the name is creative.

In addition to the establishment of goals and the provision of experiences that will lead to them, the planning stage of the curriculum process should give some consideration to developing ways and means for determining how effective the planned experiences have been in reaching the goals. On an automobile trip, when a goal of 500 miles daily is set and 300 miles actually driven, the goal is missed by 200 miles. Perhaps the objective was too high, perhaps the traffic was unusually heavy, perhaps there were two flat tires and the gas ran out during the day. There may be several contributing factors that need to be known in order to plan more realistically for the next day's journey.

It is not as easy to measure distance traveled in pursuit of an objective of education as it was with our trip by car, but some method of evaluation must be devised in order to determine the efficiency of our planning and the effectiveness of the curriculum. This will be discussed at a later point in the chapter.

ORGANIZING — The next stage in the process of curriculum development is that of organizing. In order to place the developed plans into operation, the necessary resources to make it effective must be assembled and placed into meaningful relationship; in other words, they must be organized. The resources represented by people must be discovered and arrangements made for using them at the proper time and place. These people may represent the staff, the community, the student body, or combinations of all three. In other words, all people who can and will contribute something must be located and arrangements made to include them. All required physical equipment must be procured and placed in readiness for use at the proper time. Instruments, pianos, record players, records, sound film projectors, films, song books, and all such materials and equipment, must be on hand for use when needed. There must be rich resources of song material and instrumental material and other material, the need for which must be anticipated in the plans laid by the groups at work on the project. If trips into the community can provide meaningful experiences toward the realization of the objectives of the curriculum, necessary arrangements should be made. This part of the process is gathering together all of the materials, equipment, supplies, people, and activities needed to make the curriculum a rich and rewarding group of experiences.

DIRECTING — The directional phase of the curriculum process is brought into play when the new plans, or portions of them, are set into operation. It is wise to test out portions of the new curriculum on an experimental basis. This offers a more secure basis for wider, more detailed planning. While the trial program, as well as the program as a whole, is in operation, there will be a need for coordinating the various phases, keeping the entire process in functional relationship with all of its parts.

Using our trip analogy once more, our car must be steered through traffic while we continually watch for the highway signs, the traffic lights, stopping now and then for a rest or to refuel, perhaps to restudy our route map to be sure we are traveling in the right direction. Once our plans are made, they cannot be left to run by themselves; they must be directed.

EVALUATING — As mentioned in the planning section earlier in this chapter, methods for evaluation will have been developed. We are anxious to know the degree of effectiveness of the curriculum, whether or not we are heading toward the established goals and how far we have progressed in that direction. Progress must be evaluated in terms of the near goals as well as those more remote. The chief criterion for evaluation is growth—pupil growth, staff growth, and community growth. The information gained from this stage of the process will be the basis for the next stage—improvement.

IMPROVING — The outcomes of evaluation will set off the entire process once more. Processes will be set up to effect improvement in all aspects of the curriculum and its development. In fact, the desire to improve the school's curriculum started the entire chain of events in the first place.

It is extremely important to remember that, properly conceived, the curriculum must at all times be dynamic, it must be under continuous study for possible improvement. It can never properly become fixed and unchanging; to permit such a thing to happen would deny the entire concept of curriculum built up in this chapter. A curriculum is a continuous, growing, evolving process that involves all the people of the school and community.

In conclusion, it must be remembered that the curriculum, no matter what the subject area under consideration, cannot be imposed, designed or directed, from outside the school or community. It must always be conceived in terms of actual children, who come from actual homes and neighborhoods, who work in actual classrooms under the supervision of actual teachers carrying out the plans developed by the local school. This is the only way to achieve the necessary participation of all people concerned with the curriculum. This is essential if children are to be provided those learning experiences necessary for wholesome, well-rounded growth and development.

Practical Issues

Throughout the previous discussion, an ideal way of thinking about the curriculum and its development was proposed. We must be realistic, however, and realize that as yet all schools are not ready to develop such a curriculum. Until they are, a person working in a situation that is not yet ready for this curriculum should keep it in view as a goal and constantly work to lead his school and community toward it. Many of its processes and values can be realized in even the most traditional systems.

If a music educator *must* develop a course of study, he should not build it by himself, letting it consist of a series of day-by-day "lesson plans"; rather, he should establish very broad goals and create many pathways for reaching them. By all means, he should develop it cooperatively, making use of the thinking of teachers, pupils, and lay people from the community. Its recorded content should be a listing of rich resources available for the development of the desired experiences. By such means, he can approximate the best curriculum development and, at the same time, work toward the time when the curriculum will, in truth, be all of the experiences provided the children under the auspices of the school.

The forward looking music educator will, in all situations, encourage initiative on the part of all teachers—those who are actively teaching music and those who are not. He will welcome the results of independent thinking and group thinking about curriculum on the part of the students, parents,

teachers, and administrators. He will welcome suggestions and eagerly encourage new movements within the framework of the existing curriculum, in
the hope that they will lead the way to its extension into a better, broader
pattern of action. By such methods, the music educator may well be the "little
leaven" that "leaventh the whole lump" and start the entire school and community in the direction of more modern curriculum practices.

Summary

The music curriculum has been defined as all of the musical experiences that
children accept under the guidance of the school. This broad definition gives
the music educator a very wide latitude in which to work. He must recognize
the fact that children learn music and learn about music by all of their contacts
with it, both in the classroom and outside of it. It is incumbent upon the music
educator to do all in his power to make the musical environment of his school
one that will foster desirable growth.

It is recognized that no one person can determine the content and nature
of the music curriculum. Tradition, available textbooks, legal requirements,
pressure groups, public opinion, and professional influences, are the forces
that cause the curriculum to assume the form and experiences it does.

Properly conceived, the curriculum is constantly changing. This is essential, since our culture is continuously changing because of its dynamic nature.
A curriculum that reflects the culture, as a curriculum should, must change
as the society that supports it changes. The changing culture also causes
children's interests and needs to be modified which, in turn, necessitate curriculum changes. The changing educational scene has brought newer understandings of the learning process and a better understanding of human growth
and development. These influences have also been felt in the school's curriculum.

The concept of curriculum developed in this chapter demands recognition
of the fact that all persons connected with the school—parents, pupils, teachers, supervisors, administrators, custodians, and clerks—are actively engaged
in the development of the musical experiences that constitute the music curriculum. As the curriculum is developed, the six administrative functions
known as defining purpose, planning, organizing, directing, evaluating, and
improving, are brought into play. The area of curriculum development is of
most vital concern to the music director. It is the only true reason for his being
a member of the school staff. All of his activity must be directed toward the

improvement of the musical experiences offered the children of his school. This is curriculum.

Suggested Activities

1. Carefully study the music curriculum of a school with which you are familiar. Try to determine whether it was developed by wide participation or by a single person and published as an executive order. Does it provide for all four of the types of experiences discussed on pages 71 to 75?

2. If you know of a school undergoing a major curriculum revision, try to determine the force or forces that initiated the change and what forces are giving it its shape and direction.

3. By direct observation, examine the music curriculum of several near-by schools. To what degree does each put into practice the philosophy that a general music program should be provided at each grade level throughout the system and be the "core" of the entire curriculum? Is the general music offering really general or does it tend to be limited to listening, singing, or some other single experience?

4. Prepare meticulous and detailed plans for a curriculum study in a school district you know. Provide for exercising the administrative functions discussed in this chapter between pages 66 and 77.

For Further Reading

Franseth, J. "Improving the Curriculum and Teaching Through Action Research." *School Life*, 42, No. 4:8–10, December, 1959.

Fraser, Dorothy McClure, and Pullen, Thomas G., Jr. "What to Teach? Curriculum Planning." *National Education Association Journal*, 51, No. 7:34–36, October, 1962.

Hartsell, O. M. "Quality in Elementary School Music." *National Education Association Journal*, 49, No. 3:27–29, March, 1960.

Heffernan, Helen. "Education Through Music," *Education*, 74, No. 1:11–16, September, 1953.

Knuth, William E. "General Music for the General High School Student." *California Journal of Secondary Education*, 30, No. 4:223–226, April, 1955.

Leonhard, Charles. "Place of Music in Our Elementary and Secondary Schools." *National Education Association Journal*, 52, No. 4:40–42, April, 1963.

Music Educators National Conference. *Music Curriculum in Secondary Schools*. Washington, D.C., The Conference, 1959. Pages 7–16.

National Society for the Study of Education. *Basic Concepts in Music Education*. Fifty-seventh Yearbook, Part I. Chicago, The Society, 1958. Chapters 9 and 10.

Pitts, Lilla Belle. "Purposes and Goals of Music Education in 1958," *Music Educators Journal*, 44, 5:19, April-May, 1958.

CHAPTER 4

Improving Instruction

Anyone with administrative responsibilities cannot lose sight of the fundamental principle that administration has no reason for existence except to make the product of the schools better. All administrative activity should lead in this direction. Just as the curriculum and its development are important in working toward this end, so is the improvement of instruction. The music director is actively interested in the development of better teaching, so that the product of this teaching—musical learning—will be improved.

From the outset of this discussion, it is well to remind ourselves that there is no difference between the concerns of the director of music and the supervisor of music, as far as improvement of instruction is concerned. Both will find activity in this area an integral part of their work. The only difference between their offices is in the greater degree of administrative responsibility delegated to the director. The improvement of instruction falls within the domain of both; they must each be vitally concerned with the quality of the learning process in their special area—music.

Another point needs to be made clear before we go any further; that is the relationship of the music specialist to the principals of the schools in which music is being taught. Proper administrative practice makes the principal responsible for the improvement of instruction within his unit. "Principals themselves are seldom qualified as special supervisors, but they are most effective in improving instruction when they bear full responsibility and have access to the counsel and professional guidance of the special supervisors. There is developed between the supervisor and principal a common interest and a spirit of cooperation which serve to improve instruction of the local school and unify the work of the entire school system in the special field of the supervisor." [1] It must therefore be clearly understood that the music specialist is working through the principals and at their pleasure.

[1] Will French, J. Dan Hull, and B. L. Dodds, *American High School Administration,* rev. ed., New York, Rinehart & Co., 1957, p. 112. Used by permission.

This chapter will deal with improving instruction from a functional point of view, concentrating upon curriculum development as an avenue for teacher growth and other means for promoting in-service training and improvement.

Teacher Education

The central person in the development and determination of curriculum is the teacher. When one accepts the fact that a school's curriculum is the experiences provided the children under the guidance of the school, rather than subject matter separated into properly graded segments for their assimilation, such a point of view becomes even more clearly evident. The preceding chapter on curriculum was developed with this principle in mind.

The entire process of curriculum development is to improve the learning situation by organizing the school-controlled experiences so that maximum change in the lives of the pupils will result. This process also brings about improved instruction, because, through teacher participation in the development of curriculum, a better understanding of its vital issues and contributing factors will be brought about. A development of these ideas will be the purpose of this section of the book.

Figure 14

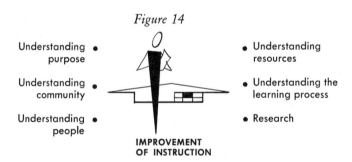

Understanding purpose

Understanding community

Understanding people

Understanding resources

Understanding the learning process

Research

IMPROVEMENT OF INSTRUCTION

UNDERSTANDING PURPOSE — The first step to be taken in the development of curriculum, as already discussed, is the definition of purpose. The end result, the purpose itself, is important but no more so than the process by which it is reached. It is imperative that all who are responsible for bringing defined purposes to fruition understand them thoroughly. Only then can the ultimate goals and objectives of music education be reached. The process by which this understanding is developed is of paramount importance.

Purposes defined by authoritarian means and passed down the line to those who must put them into operation do not beget understanding. Purposes that are not understood and made a vital part of a teacher's pattern of action have no value; they are useless. Democratically, cooperatively defined goals bring all who have participated in their development to a common understanding of the central objectives of education, as well as a special field—in this case, music. Only when the entire staff understands the purposes of its activity, the goals toward which they are striving, can they develop teaching procedures that will result in maximum effectiveness.

No person can take part in an activity without some sort of purpose to motivate him. Teachers would not teach school if they did not have some reason for doing so. Doctors would not be doctors unless they found in their profession the realization of some personal goals. Pupils would not attend school unless they found there the satisfaction of some personal ambition; their purpose may be avoidance of parental displeasure or avoidance of the penalties of the compulsory attendance law.

The quality of the purpose of any endeavor will govern the efficiency and effectiveness of the work directed to those ends. Shortsighted, selfish goals will produce shortsighted, selfish teaching; inspired purposes will produce inspired teaching.

As teachers gain in their understanding and acceptance of the purposes of education in our culture—more specifically, the purposes of music education—their behavior in the teaching-learning situations will improve. This, therefore, is the first step in improving instruction—establishing a goal or series of goals and understanding the reasons for their establishment. This focuses and directs teachers' work as nothing else will.

UNDERSTANDING COMMUNITY — The schools of America are social institutions developed in settings for social purposes. They are meant to serve the needs of the society that created them. Each school has been established to serve not only the national and state needs but the local community as well. Unless it does so, the community withdraws its support, and the work of the school is crippled or nullified. It is imperative, therefore, that each teacher understand the community he serves.

Understanding the community means knowing its entire fabric, its social, political, economic structure, and the forces that make it a living, moving, social organism. As teachers and parents work together in the development of a curriculum for their community and its school, this understanding develops.

Understanding the community also means understanding the resources it contains for education. For the music educator, special concern is exercised for the musical resources of the community and the contributions they can make to the program of education through music.

UNDERSTANDING PEOPLE — The entire business of education is completely absorbed in people. The community is people, the school is people, and the purposes of the school are to effect a change in the behavior of people. The cooperatively developed curriculum will lead to a better understanding of mankind and the forces that modify individual and group behavior. Teachers must know and really understand people of all ages and in all situations as living, striving organisms. The more complete this understanding, the better teachers will be able to cope with all educational problems.

The process of curriculum development brings teachers to a better understanding of the motivations, the drives that cause people to behave as they do. What activities result in satisfactions, the resolution of needs? How do people grow, as children, as adults, as parents? Teachers will teach better when answers to these questions are clearly understood and can become a part of their equipment for accomplishing their tasks.

UNDERSTANDING RESOURCES — The cooperatively developed curriculum has brought the teacher into contact with all the resources at the disposal of the school for carrying out its tasks. He becomes a better teacher because he knows the tremendous reservoir of materials, people, and experiences, both within and outside the community, that he can draw upon in doing his work. He becomes a better teacher because he is able to see beyond a single, or a few, textbooks to the vast amount of printed material available to him. As he understands that resources are more than printed matter, that they include people, activities, experiences, ideas, and thoughts, as well, so the instructional process of which he is a part will become better. Just as children develop by a process of growth, the teacher in his job improves as he grows in his understanding of the school's resources.

The process of curriculum development also enables the teacher to realize the resources he has within himself, to understand them better, to know his own abilities to think, to develop insights, to develop new relationships, to grow in understanding. All of this fortifies the teacher with a sense of personal power that breeds confidence in himself and his ability to do the things that society and the school expect of him.

UNDERSTANDING THE LEARNING PROCESS — No study of the curriculum can possibly proceed properly without consideration being given to the learning process in the light of today's understandings. In fact, a restudy of the learning process may initiate the curriculum study in the first place.

Professional educators, psychologists, and research workers, are constantly adding new information to our store of knowledge about the nature of learning and the processes by which it comes about. These new insights often dictate curriculum change. Many educational experiences are completely outmoded, in the light of present knowledge about learning and how it takes place.

We are concerned in this chapter with the improvement of instruction. Improvement begins with complete understanding of the learning process and the providing of experiences by means of which it can take place.

RESEARCH — There has been a tendency on the part of the rank and file of music educators to be suspicious of research as a useful force in curriculum development and as an avenue of teacher growth. There are several reasons for this state of affairs. In the first place, there has been, and to certain extent still is, a persistent feeling that, because of music's subjective nature, it does not lend itself to scientific investigation. This feeling undoubtedly stems, at least in part, from lack of understanding of the scientific process and the results it can obtain. It is quite easy to appreciate how such a feeling can come about. The typical music educator has not been able to include in his program of training the types of experiences that lead to an understanding and appreciation of the processes of scientific investigation and the contribution such study can make to his chief area of interest; namely, music.

Relatively few music educators have participated in research projects. This lack of personal involvement is another reason for their not understanding research and profiting by the insights that can be gained thereby. It is still axiomatic that insights and appreciations are the result of personal involvement or experience. Later on in this chapter, suggestions will be made which, if followed, will make it possible for the music educator seeking to improve himself and his school to become involved in research and, by means of these experiences, develop the necessary insights for complete use of the scientific process in solving his professional problems. In order to do this, the music educator must get over his fear of possible failure and his "I can't do research because I don't know how" attitude.

All too many music educators simply do not know that there is a sizable body of research in music and music education which, if studied, can be helpful to him as he goes about his tasks. Training institutions in recent years are providing curriculums that are helping eliminate that lack of information. The Music Educators National Conference, its affiliated units, and other professional organizations, are doing their part also. It is the responsibility of the music administrator to assist in this process, as far as his local school staff is concerned.

Altogether too many curriculum decisions have been, and still are being, made by what has been called the "by guess and by golly" line of reasoning. We "guess" that something is right and proper, so "by golly" that's the way it's going to be! It is rather remarkable and certainly puzzling that the American people are perfectly willing, even anxious, to defer judgments and decisions in medicine, business, transportation, communication, and practically all other avenues of their culture, until studies can be made, evidence obtained, and conclusions drawn. Yet in education as a whole, and certainly in music education, they are willing to resort to the "by guess and by golly" method of making judgments.

Greater confidence can be placed in judgments that have been based upon research findings. This evidence may come from two sources: studies made outside the music educator's own school system or studies made within his local system. The body of research in music education is not as great as it is in other disciplines. However, it is growing all the time, and each year brings a noticeable gain in communicating the results of this research to the profession. The music educator must not overlook the fact, also, that much helpful information for his own special field can be obtained from research done in allied or similar fields.

There is one inherent weakness for the music educator attempting to solve his local problems through research done outside his own school system. There has been no personal involvement or participation on the part of his staff, the parents of his community, or himself. This fact tends to lead to lack of understanding of the results and some suspicion of their applicability to the immediate problems at hand. This can be offset by doing on-the-job research for the express purpose of seeking answers to problems and gathering evidence for making valid, prudent decisions. Such research is frequently called action research, done for the express purpose of bringing about change in curriculum, teaching procedure, or any other aspect of the schools that needs improvement.

TYPES OF RESEARCH CONTRASTED   For purposes of differentiation and clear understanding, research done outside of the school, studying its curriculum and seeking to improve it, will be called pure research. That research done within the local school system seeking to improve its work will be referred to as action or "on-the-job" research. It is our purpose now to compare and contrast the two and see what each has to offer the music educator seeking to lead his staff and his community toward improved practice.

Pure research centers chiefly in the graduate schools of the colleges and universities of the land. It deals with problems that are considered to be of value or concern to the profession as a whole. By definition, action research, on the other hand, is done locally for the express purpose of seeking answers to local problems leading to local change. It may very well have implications for other schools and other localities, but this is not its primary purpose.

Pure research is usually done by an individual, often a person seeking an advanced degree. Action research is most frequently group initiated and group executed. One of the great strengths of this type of information seeking lies in the fact that many people are involved in all of its aspects. They tend to place more confidence in the results because they have had a hand in developing them. For the same reason, they are more willing to help effect the change that this type of research suggests.

Pure research often deals with laboratory situations or problems remote from the classroom and rehearsal halls. Action research is centered in the places where children learn and have those experiences wholesome for total growth.

Conclusions are usually in the abstract in pure research, but they usually result in change in schools where action research prevails.

A WAY TO PROCEED   No amount of information about research or knowledge about the different types will be very valuable to the music educator in a leadership position unless he knows how to conduct the research his school system needs. It is the purpose of this section to give a framework for developing research when needed by a group of curriculum workers in music.

The first step is to build up a strong desire on the part of all his associates to do research. This also involves a willingness on the part of all to put the results of such research into action. This is done primarily by persuasive argument. It is also helpful to let the group know about other schools, other groups, that have solved their problems by this means. This may very well be the most difficult step of the process. Nearly all teachers feel more secure when they teach as they were taught for many years. With this feeling of security comes a bias that causes them to feel that the way they know best, in which they feel the most secure, is the right or only way to proceed. A willingness to seek evidence is important, but it is also imperative that a willingness to be persuaded by the evidence be present.

After the willingness to seek answers and the willingness to be persuaded by evidence has been established, the next step to be taken is that of assembling the group that will actually conduct the research. The people for this group will come from the teachers of music themselves, interested lay groups, other interested and qualified persons within the school system, and a consultant from outside the school system, if this is possible.

Choosing the work group and assembling them to begin their tasks is only part of the problem. The music administrator must also be absolutely certain that all of the conditions for effective group research are in operation. Some of these conditions reside in the music administrator himself, and others in the administrative structure of the school system in which he is working. First of all, there must be an entirely free atmosphere for effective give-and-take discussion. All persons must be free to express their thoughts without fear of reprimand or reprisal. The music administrator himself must be able to "take it" when discussion goes contrary to his own thinking.

Every encouragement must be given for truly creative thinking. Ideas, although visionary and far from established practice, must be carefully examined for merit and accepted, modified, or rejected, according to their value to the problem and its solution. The climate of the group must be such that all ideas may be freely presented and frankly discussed. A willingness must be developed to try out new ideas in order to determine their merit; in other words, a willingness to experiment must be fostered.

The group must be given freedom to alter existing practices when the need for such change becomes apparent. They must evaluate practices and procedures often and quickly, promptly discarding the useless and retaining the useful. They must be constantly on the alert to improve their own group work as they seek to find solutions to the problem before them.

The music administrator must see to it that sufficient time is available to all persons making up the experimenting group, so that their work may be carried out without a sense of excessive burden. It is necessary, also, that all required resources be available for the group as it does its work. It is the responsibility of the music administrator to see that all of these conditions are met before the group can be expected to perform properly its assigned tasks.

After the group has been assembled, its first task will be that of defining clearly and concisely the problem for which a solution is being sought. The first tendency is to define in broad, vague generalities. This type of definition is not suitable for research. It must be sharpened until a single or, at the most, two or three closely related problems come into sharp focus. At this stage, it should be written down and all participants agreed that the written statement is clear.

The next task is the establishment of the hypotheses upon which the research will be conducted. An hypothesis is an assumption or guess that, if something is done a certain way, it will yield certain results. An hypothesis, or two or three of them, is necessary before evidence can be gathered; it points the direction of the entire research. The hypothesis is closely related to the definition of the problem. In fact, it is the definition stated in terms of action.

The next step in the process is that of setting up the test procedures. This is closely related to planning and organizing, two of the administrative functions discussed in Chapter 1. A plan for gathering evidence must be made and the resources assembled for getting the job done. With it all, there must be plans for constantly evaluating the procedures and a willingness to revise and improve as the research proceeds. Suitable plans must be made for keeping records and studying the data when they are assembled. Then, and only then, is the plan set into motion for gathering the evidence.

When the evidence has been gathered and carefully studied, it then becomes the basis upon which generalizations or conclusions are made. The music administrator and his co-workers must be very careful that all generalizations are made upon the evidence gathered. Often they must be willing to draw conclusions that are contrary to their beliefs and present practice, when the evidence so demands.

The research process would be incomplete if it were to stop here. Changes in curriculum, method, technique, or practices, must be initiated and supported, based upon the conclusions drawn from the study. Experience has shown that it is easier to effect change when many people have been participating in the research that has dictated this change. They are more easily convinced and more willing to put into practice the changes, when they have been a part of the process dictating the change.

SECURING ASSISTANCE   In spite of a strong desire to use research techniques in solving problems in a school system, there may well be some leaders in music education who are still timid about initiating a research project unassisted. Nowadays many school districts employ directors of research. These people are hired for the purpose of giving advice, aid, and assistance to the educator who wishes to apply research techniques to the solution of a prob!em. Quite frequently county and state school departments have research people on their staffs who may be consulted by teachers employed in school districts too small to hire a research specialist themselves.

Lacking a research specialist in his own district and having no county or state resource to draw upon, the interested music administrator has another source of help. Nearly all colleges and universities that have graduate programs have people who could be hired as consultants to assist in beginning a research project and carrying it to its conclusion.

With all of the help available in local, county, and state school offices, as well as in nearby graduate schools, there is no longer any valid reason for failing to employ research techniques in the solution of educational problems.

A Teacher of Teachers

The drive or urge to improve oneself is basic in human nature. It may have been killed or deadened by unfavorable circumstances or frustrations earlier in life, but the basis for growth and development of a person's powers is centered in this urge, nevertheless. Behind all purposeful work is the desire to advance to something better—a more wholesome way of living, greater prestige, increased economic security. It is upon this basic urge that the director of teachers builds his work.

It is the responsibility of those in positions of educational leadership to provide teachers with situations, incentives, and the know-how, for helping them do their jobs better. All of the principles of developing good teaching-learning situations apply here as much as in the classroom or home. In a very real sense, the director of music is the "teacher" providing experiences whereby his "pupils," the members of his staff, may learn and grow in their profession. The same factors that enter into the learning experiences of the classroom in order to make them good enter into the relationships between the director of music and those who teach music. The director must be adept at manipulating the learning environment in such a way that his teachers may have their greatest possible growth.

INCENTIVES FOR GROWTH — In order to bring about the professional growth of a teacher or a group of teachers, certain incentives must be established. The desire for improved status and professional acceptance and self-pride are inherent in the situation itself, but there are other elements that can and must be created by the director as he works with his group.

GROWTH NECESSITIES

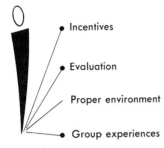

Figure 15

MORALE A group that has clear, positive goals, a sense of knowing where it is going and how it is going to get there, a group that is accomplishing and achieving results, that has a feeling of solidarity, a feeling of pulling together, a oneness, will have the type of morale that provides incentives for each member of the group to grow, to improve in his work. There will be, or can be created, a desire on the part of each individual teacher to want to become better at his task in order to contribute with greater effectiveness to the welfare and work of the group. It is also true that the group will want to become better in order to strengthen each individual within it. The state of mind of a group of teachers is a powerful factor in providing desirable incentives for growth.

A survey made some years ago[2] sought to determine the factors that lead to satisfaction in teaching. More than 1500 teachers in 200 systems located in 43 different states reported that being permitted to assume a considerable degree of professional responsibility, having a voice in policy-making, and working under competent leadership, were important conditions for creating and maintaining high morale. These observations clearly show that a democratic pattern of administration is necessary for teachers to derive the greatest satisfactions from their professional work.

Good working conditions, community acceptance, the correction of grievances, and fairly determined and reasonably adequate salaries, were also named as factors leading to satisfaction in teaching. Although these conditions did not stand as high on the list as those mentioned in the preceding paragraphs, their effect upon the development of favorable or unfavorable morale cannot be overlooked.

There are many things a music director can do in order to foster and develop morale favorable to teacher growth. It is natural for all people to desire appreciation and recognition and commendation for the contributions they have made to the welfare of the group. It is wise to single out those who have made unusual contributions to the work of the school and to recognize their efforts by a friendly thank-you, or by a letter commendation, or by a public statement of appreciation. In a dynamic, active, functioning

[2] Francis S. Chase, "Factors for Satisfaction in Teaching," *Phi Delta Kappan,* 33:127–32, November, 1951. Used by permission.

group with everyone contributing in some way, all should come in for their share of appreciation and commendation and be able to sense the sincerity of the director when he expresses it.

The director who respects his fellow workers as persons and professional colleagues and shows by his actions that this is so, has taken an important step in developing desirable morale. The principles of personal relations developed in Chapter 2 have no better place to be put into operation than in the relationships between the director of music and his staff. Their full employment will assist mightily in the development of growth incentives.

As an individual achieves professional status in the eyes of his community, co-workers, and pupils, his individual morale and the morale of the group tend to rise. The more the director can do to help teachers, especially those in their first years of professional activity, to achieve recognition in the eyes of their fellow men, the more wholesome will be the atmosphere for raising the level of the group as a whole.

RELEASING TALENTS   Each individual has something unique to offer his job and his society. The same holds true for groups. Before these special talents of individuals and groups can develop fully, they must be placed in an environment that encourages their full exploitation. They must be free to experiment, to try out new ideas, to seek better ways of doing their jobs, to initiate new practices, and to feel that their efforts are encouraged and appreciated.

The director of music must make use of these extraordinary contributions for the common good of all; by so doing, he will be building toward the betterment of his staff, his school, and his community. He will bring this about by developing situations and activities that make it possible for each teacher to use his special talents and to develop new ones. This is one way in which he can assist in the creation of incentives for teacher growth.

FINANCIAL REWARDS   Although the salaries teachers are paid are not basic to the development of good morale, nor the size of the paycheck itself an incentive for growth, nevertheless there are factors associated with the financial rewards of music teaching that have a bearing upon our problem. Chase[3] found that when teachers believe their salaries have been determined by a fair process and find them to be reasonably adequate, they tend to disregard them as sources of satisfaction. On the other hand, when resentment arises from salaries believed to be unjust and inadequate, this can be a major contributor to dissatisfaction and, as a result, a deterrent to teacher growth.

[3] *Ibid.*, p. 131. Used by permission.

The trend in present day salary schedules is to recognize training, experience, and competence, in determining the amount of pay teachers receive for their work. As schedules pay more attention to competence, and schools begin to pay more for the services of superior teachers, salaries can become an incentive for teacher growth.

Music teachers often feel that their salaries should be determined by a schedule which differs from that of the regular classroom teacher. This feeling is brought about by the higher cost for the training a music teacher must receive and the amount of work required outside the classroom and after school hours. When one considers that the music teacher usually begins his professional training early in childhood with private music lessons and must continue this sort of training through his college program by paying special fees in addition to the regular tuition, it can be clearly recognized that he has invested far more in his training than the average classroom teacher. Also, when one considers the amount of time and energy spent in out-of-school rehearsals, concerts, and parades, his job is likely to be more demanding than that of the classroom teacher who has no special activities to direct. When these factors are recognized in arriving at a salary for his services, the music teacher is more likely to be happy with his salary provisions.

It is the nature of people in our society to seek compensation for their services at a rate commensurate with their sense of their own worth. In this way, they gain status in the eyes of their community and their professional associates. The morale of the music teacher varies as his salary assists him in reaching the status he desires or as it thwarts his drive toward it.

The music director, as he works to provide his teachers with the salaries they deserve, must remember that the amount of money paid is not as important as the fairness with which the sum is agreed upon and its adequacy in meeting the financial demands of their position in the community.

CREATING ENVIRONMENT FOR GROWTH — It is axiomatic that, if growth is to take place along desirable lines, the environment must be wholesome or one that will contribute to such growth. Certainly, if teachers are to grow, an environment must be provided that makes growth possible.

Such an environment depends upon approaching all problems democratically. It is the only process that permits individuals to assist in making policy and making decisions. It alone permits opportunities for experimentation and the exercising of individual judgments. It is the only pattern that provides opportunities for group processes to work. It is the only process that permits and encourages teacher growth.

It is entirely possible for a teacher, or a group of teachers, to respect and admire an administrator who uses authoritarian methods and to be willing to follow each order or directive and to do all assigned tasks in such a way that they satisfy him and give him pleasure. In such a setting, the morale of the group could be high—but growth thwarted.

The suggestions given in the chapter on personal relations (Chapter 2) have a direct bearing on this problem. The music director seeking maximum growth for his staff will diligently seek to put into practice all conditions that will stimulate and foster healthy growth.

A little later in this chapter (page 99), certain conditions necessary for democratic group action will be presented. These also have a direct bearing upon the establishment of a sympathetic environment for teacher growth.

GROUP EXPERIENCES — Just as the skillful classroom teacher manipulates the situation so that each pupil is provided with the experiences necessary for his best personal growth, so the director controls the environment in such a way that the teachers for whom he is responsible may develop their competence. The next section of this chapter will be devoted to a more complete discussion of ways in which this may be done; however, it is wise to see, at this point, the importance of this problem.

If teachers are to become more skilled in their working with children, their experiences must be of such a nature that growth in these skills can and will take place. All growth in skills comes as a result of increased understandings and insights that, in turn, result from opportunities to experiment, to try out, to do the things that make good teaching possible. The successful music director will see to it that such experiences are provided members of his staff.

EVALUATION — Evaluation, or appraisal, is also a process that properly used and understood, results in teacher growth. The ability to size up progress and chart new directions is an important factor in teaching; it is also important for the director of music to estimate teacher progress and suggest new directions for future activity. The ability to see errors and weaknesses and set up steps for their improvement is vital to the growth process.

There are three commonly accepted types of teacher appraisal or evaluation: the teacher rating scale, personal estimate or subjective judgment, and evaluation of pupil progress. These will be discussed in turn.

The teacher rating scale, of which there are many forms, is an objective measure and quite impersonal. In using it exclusively, it is impossible to bring into focus some of the important factors in teacher growth and effectiveness. Many of the qualities of good teaching, such as the relationships between teacher and pupil, are too personal and subjective to be measured by an objective scale. In modern education, this type of teacher evaluation is falling into disuse.

It is somewhat difficult to develop clearly stated and understood criteria of judgement, when using personal estimate and subjective judgement as an evaluation technique. When teachers and supervisors have mutual confidence and respect in and for each other, this system can operate advantageously. Quite obviously, this situation is to be desired and striven for, but with the full realization that it cannot come about at once.

Measuring the effectiveness of a teacher by the progress pupils show under his guidance also has the disadvantage of being rather subjective and indirect; it has great value, however, in measuring teacher effectiveness in terms of the product. It also overlooks the rather important fact that pupils grow best when the teacher provides them with enough materials and experiences for their needs and then gets out of the way. Just how much of a person's growth is the result of the teacher's effectiveness and how much comes as the result of his own initiative is hard to say.

The teacher of teachers will develop his own techniques for evaluating teacher progress and lead those with whom he works to set up standards and methods for measuring their own growth. The methods used will, in all probability, be a combination, or a composite, of all three principle types, with stronger emphasis upon subjective judgements and measurement of pupil progress.

Direct Methods for Improvement

Everything an administrator does should be steps toward the improvement of instruction. Certainly everything discussed in this book has such an end in view. Although many aspects of the music director's work aim at this purpose indirectly, some of his activity must be focused upon the problem directly. The consideration of the direct actions has been the central purpose of this chapter. The following pages will be devoted to some of the methods the music administrator can use in his frontal attack upon the problem. The specific one, or ones, he will use will depend upon the needs of the individual and the group and the situations out of which they grow. The discussion will proceed from two points of view; those activities using individual contacts will be discussed first, and those using group action will be considered second.

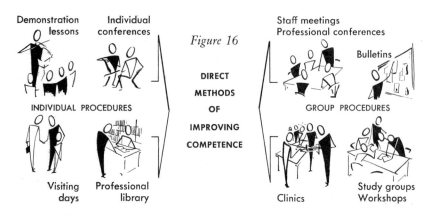

Figure 16

DIRECT

METHODS

OF

IMPROVING

COMPETENCE

INDIVIDUAL PROCEDURES — Much may be accomplished through the enthusiasm and knowledge of the administrator himself. Here is an opportunity for him to put to use his sense of personal relationships in a matter that often requires tact and understanding.

DEMONSTRATION LESSONS   The music administrator is expected to be a superior teacher; this he must be in order to fulfill the duties of the position he occupies. Many times, he can help a member of his staff improve by teaching a class while the person seeking help observes. This activity is usually referred to as the demonstration lesson. The teacher of teachers must enter upon this relationship with an air of helpful humility, and the teacher being helped must desire the assistance. A free, cordial relationship is of paramount importance; forced relationship can lead only to failure.

The person giving the demonstration lesson must be well prepared and have the entire plan so well organized that the lesson taught will be a superior product, but, at the same time, the conditions that led to this excellence must be clearly evident to the observer. It is also important that the conditions that lead to excellence be within the grasp of the observer. It is useless and frustrating to show a person how he can do a job well, when the person does not possess the abilities or equipment with which to do an equally fine job. Setting a goal so high that it cannot be attained is a frustrating experience for a learner; this is equally true of a teacher who wishes to improve. He must be able to see clearly and easily what it is that he needs to incorporate into his own teaching to make it better, but he must be made to feel confident of being able to attain it.

CONFERENCES An individual conference should always follow the demonstration lesson. It offers the supervisor and teacher an opportunity for talking over the demonstration, pointing up high lights, values, and techniques. The conference can be most useful when it follows the demonstration and even more effective when held in privacy. It should never be held in the same room with a group of children. Not only is there danger that the presence of a group will divide the attention of both participants in the conference so that maximum benefits cannot result, but there is also danger that the teacher may lose status with his class, if it is clearly evident to the class that their teacher is seeking help.

The individual conference can also follow a visit of the specialist to a classroom, where he has been called for consultation. To visit a teacher's classroom unannounced and leave without discussing the work going on therein is nothing more or less than bad manners. When a teacher is genuinely seeking help and has asked for a specialist to visit and observe him at work, he deserves the courtesy of an opportunity to talk his problems over at length with that specialist. The conference should, therefore, be scheduled at a time and place that make an unhurried, free, frank, and cordial discussion of the visit possible between teacher and specialist.

Regardless of the reasons for the conference, the music director must be certain that a friendly, confident relationship is established between both persons so that the conversation can be most helpful.

VISITING DAYS In the writer's opinion, this is one of the best devices for improving instruction. When entered into with a genuine spirit of seeking improvement in one's own work, observing another teacher at work in a different school with a different group of children can furnish a teacher seeking help with a wealth of ideas for his self-improvement.

There are two types of learning possible in such an activity. There is a positive type of learning that results from the teacher having opportunities for seeing better ways of attacking and handling problems similar to his own and a negative type that shows him mistakes made by the other teacher. It is frequently possible that seeing another person make a poor attack upon a problem points up one's own similar weaknesses or faulty techniques. In either case, the observant teacher, the teacher seeking greater competency, can profit by the opportunity for visiting another school and seeing other teachers at work.

The administration of all schools and the administrators in special fields should work toward the policy of permitting all staff members a

certain number of days off during the school year for the express purpose
of observing other teachers at work in other school systems. The teacher
should not sacrifice his pay in order to participate in such activity. Properly
conceived, this is a type of in-service training.

PROFESSIONAL LIBRARY   If teachers are to reach the status of other professional workers, they must adopt the best practices followed by other professional people. One of these is certainly the practice of reading and studying
professional literature in order to keep abreast of the developments, current
thinking, and practice, in education.

Each teacher should be encouraged and helped to set aside a certain
portion of each day for professional reading. People guiding the learning of
others should certainly be able to guide their own. It is not always practical
nor is it always wise to take a course at some teacher training institution; also,
it may not be convenient. Very often a person can be helped better by being
encouraged to lay out his own plan of study and growth and given assistance
in following it. It is clearly established that a person working on a felt need
will grow faster than a person working on an unfelt need or a person taking a
course in order to "get three points and place himself in position for the
next increment."

Such a program of professional reading will make mandatory the avail-
ability of a wide range of literature. The director of music can help by using
part of his annual budget to build up a professional library for the exclusive
use of teachers seeking help.

This library should be set up in a central place within the school system
so that teachers may draw from it easily. When it is combined with similar
libraries developed by directors of other special branches, the superintendent
of schools, and the principals, it can become a professional library of high
caliber and a powerful influence for teacher growth. The possession of a
large number of books will not necessarily promote teacher growth unless the
director of music conducts his program of in-service training in such a way
that his staff avails itself of the resources contained in the library.

Every educator should also set aside a part of his own personal budget for
use in building his personal professional library. Appendix A, page 255, contains a list of titles that should, in the opinion of the writer, be a part of every
music educator's library. It is by no means a complete list, but it is considered
to be a minimum start in the right direction.

It is extremely important for teachers to spend part of their professional
reading upon material outside the area of their special interests; music teachers
should study reading, mathematics, history, and English; elementary school

teachers should read about the junior high and senior high schools; classroom teachers should read about guidance and administration; administrators should read about classroom teaching and special fields. All teachers will become better teachers as they broaden the scope of their thinking and experience. The teacher of teachers should help them do just that.

GROUP PROCEDURES — As valuable as individual techniques are, there are also outstanding values to be obtained from group attacks on the problem of improving instruction. It is a well-established principle that group thinking is more powerful than the sum total of all the independent, individual thinking involved in a problem.

It is not intended that the present discussion be an exhaustive treatise upon group processes. Its only purpose is to state and discuss briefly certain principles and conditions that are fundamental to effective group work. This presentation will be organized into three major areas: the group itself, its "feeling" or "tone"; goals; and ways of working together, or procedures. Here, as in so many other areas of educational endeavor, it is impossible to draw sharp lines of distinction between each principal and condition. All are vital parts of the whole and evident in some degree—now greater, now lesser —in any and all group situations.

GROUP FEELING   The way each individual feels about his identification with the group is extremely important. The most prized possession is the self; but, in a group, the individual does not shed his individuality; rather, he adds to it a feeling of "we-ness." He must be eager to be known as a member of the group, anxious to work in the group's *best* interests, and concerned in aiding in the solution of its problems. He must feel an important part of the group, its cause, and its work.

The atmosphere of the group must give each member a sense of freedom and, at the same time, a feeling of being bolstered up and supported by the group. Members of a group cannot work successfully together when they fear loss of status if their expressed views are contrary to that of the group or a status leader (individual in a place of higher authority) within the organization. All fear of censure, real or imagined, must be removed from the members of the group.

There must be free and easy discussion among all members of a group. The exchange of ideas must be free and uninhibited. This type of interaction fosters creative thinking that is one of the vital powers of the group. There must be a willingness to discuss all sides of a problem and weigh all of the evidence before reaching a decision or consensus.

The group structure must be stable. This stability must be founded on a sure knowledge that policies will not shift or change without proper discussion and dissemination of information. The membership must be constant and regular. This is absolutely essential for effective communication among its members.

A word of caution is in order. Stability and rigidity are not synonymous. Stability permits change, but it is orderly and systematically brought about. New policies, new personnel, are introduced when the work of the group demands them. Rigidity would fix both policies and personnel and permit no change. Stability is necessary; rigidity is to be avoided at all costs.

The group must recognize that it can solve problems by the group process. This may be a new idea for some members of the group. They will need to be led along gradually, until they are convinced of the power of this process.

A group to which this process is foreign will need to tackle and solve some small problems and experience success before they are conditioned to cope properly with larger problems. To use an old adage—it must "learn to walk before it can run." As the group begins to work together for the first time, the leader must constantly guide, counsel, advise, and suggest new ways of working, new sources of information, raise new questions, and, in every way, lead the group to its first feelings of success. The leader must never make decisions for the group and impose his authority upon it. The only way a new group unfamiliar with group attack upon problems can be convinced of the value of working together is by experiencing the superior solutions to problems that result from this method as compared to individual approaches.

The group must feel some concern for the solution of problems confronting it. Unless the concern is felt, no effective discussion can take place. Groups are given to seek solutions to their problems in very much the same way as individuals. When there is a need urgently felt by the group, it is willing, even anxious, to invest the time and effort necessary to seek its solution.

The group must feel and be able to see evidences of growth—its own growth toward maturity—as a vital, functioning unit. Any group, as it first begins to work together, will be immature and insecure. As it works together, it must sense its own growth and development toward maturity. Unless it has such a feeling, it will continue to be weak, insecure, and ineffective.

GOALS   No individual or group of individuals can be effective in its work without having some goal toward which to strive. It is a goal or series of goals that give purpose to all human endeavor, either individual or group.

Without them, activity is aimless, pointless, and ineffective. With clearly defined goals, activity has purpose, drive, direction, and effect.

Not only must the goals be set and clearly defined before a group's work can be effective, but the manner in which they are achieved and the degree of personal involvement are also of vital importance. Group goals must be set cooperatively, with all members of the group active in the process, before they can be effective. The process of setting goals often indicates possible solutions and possible lines of action.

The degree of concern the individuals of a group possess about the goals to be attained will govern the intensity of their activity toward those goals. Here again, human needs or drives, either individual or group, are the motivating influences toward intensive action. A group deeply concerned about the effectiveness of its teaching will be willing, even anxious, to spend the time and effort necessary to bring about its improvement. Without this concern, its efforts will be dilatory and without effect.

Individuals and groups of individuals are more zealous in pursuit of self-imposed goals than those imposed by someone else. A group of young people will eagerly clean up a house and yard for a party they are anxious to have. The same group, *assigned* the same tasks by their parents with nothing more than parental approval, will shirk, dawdle, grumble, and stop work as soon as the "authority's" back is turned. Groups of teachers working on problems "assigned" by the superintendent, principal, or supervisor, respond in exactly the same way. Tasks they set for themselves and in which they evidence great concern for successful completion are approached with eagerness and energy.

Goals set by a group to direct its efforts must be attainable. There is nothing so frustrating to a group or an individual as setting its sights so high or so unrealistically that they cannot be reached. Often, higher goals can be reached by a series of lesser goals as stepping stones. This process of setting and reaching goals gives a group the strength and power to reach ever higher and higher and be successful in attaining its objectives.

The efforts a group expends toward its goals must be felt to be of value to the group as a whole and to the individuals of which it consists. Even though they are concerned about the outcome of their endeavor and recognize that their goals are realistic, unless there is a sense of value felt in their work, the group will not function as effectively as it might. Groups and individuals soon weary of work that contains no sense of worthwhileness. The sense of value is one of the powerful energizing forces behind human endeavor.

WORKING TOGETHER   Each group, as it begins to work toward goals it has established, must agree upon the procedures it shall use as it works together. This *modus operandi* is important to the success of the group. First of all, it must be systematic. All of the activity of the group must be focused upon the end results or goals and bring the group closer to its objectives by every step of the process. System or organization in the activity of the group will prevent lost or wasted effort. There are many ways to proceed in attacking any problem, and undoubtedly much time will be spent in agreeing upon the procedures to be followed. This is time and effort well-spent, because the success of the group's efforts will be measured in large part by the effectiveness of the group's procedures.

The group process requires much discussion. It is important that all of this discussion be free and uninhibited, yet always directed toward the solution of problems confronting the group. Group discussions will never be useful and effective if the discussion is slanted or directed in a manner seeking the favor or sanction of a status leader—the principal, supervisor, or superintendent. The status leader must see to it that any fear of administrative disapproval or censure is removed from all group activity, and he must invite complete freedom in all discussion. This is not an easy condition to create, but it must be maintained if the work of the group is to be fruitful.

The procedures a group follows must be planned so that it feels success in moving toward its goals. "Nothing succeeds like success." This feeling of success is one of the strongest energizing influences in keeping a group actively in pursuit of solutions to its problems. As it works toward its more remote goals, its procedures should bring about successful attainment of minor goals on the way. A group must always have a sense of accomplishing things, if it is to keep its interest and drive at high pitch.

A group working successfully together must establish and maintain standards that are high and clearly understood by all of the participants. An opinion based upon conjecture must be challenged without loss of status within the group by the person expressing it. Proof or documentary evidence must be obtained for all suggestions made.

Group action is another area in which the six administrative functions discussed in Chapter 1 are clearly operative. There will be goals set—defining of purpose. There will be planning at all stages of the operation. Organizing will be apparent throughout. Directing will take place as possible solutions are tried. There will be evaluating all along the way, and a group that is earnest in its endeavor will be constantly improving its goals, its procedures, and the structure of the group itself.

The music director who can bring his staff to effective group action upon the problems confronting it is well on the way toward achieving the full purposes and bjectives of his work. The following sections outline some of the many ways he may use the group activity in doing the job expected of him by his superintendent, principals, school committee, and community.

STAFF MEETINGS The old-time faculty meetings were often deadly affairs; however, properly planned and executed, they can be made into powerful influences for teacher growth. When the staff group is working on a problem that each teacher has had a part in isolating and attacking, when each teacher is able to contribute his best talents and best thinking toward its solution, and when each teacher shares the weight of decision and responsibility, this device contributes mightily toward the professional growth of all members. It is necessary to get the group functioning as a democratic "we-centered" body.

When planning staff meetings and carrying them out, the following suggestions will be helpful.

1. Make certain that each meeting has a stated purpose clearly understood by all.
2. Have a planned agenda, preferably published and circulated in advance.
3. Stick to the agenda. Rule out or table for later meetings all irrelevant problems, even though they are important.
4. Give each meeting a definite starting and ending time, publish them, and stick to them.
5. Provide a summary of each meeting's accomplishments and distribute to all members of the group.
6. See to it that no one person, including yourself, monopolizes the discussion time of the group.

STUDY GROUPS AND COMMITTEE ASSIGNMENTS It is often desirable for smaller groups of the entire staff to work cooperatively on some problem of professional growth. These may be study groups brought together by a common interest or desire to study a certain phase of the teaching-learning process. Self-organized and self-directed groups are extremely desirable. The director of music should encourage the formation of such groups and assist in their planning when called upon to do so. He will also serve as a resource person or consultant.

Committees carrying out definite assignments and responsibilities are valuable. Membership in such groups should be voluntary, but in a wholesome democratic setting, such assignment will be eagerly sought. The director of music should work toward that end. The difference between a study group and a committee is that the study group is self-organized, self-directed, and works on its own problem, while the committee is charged with responsibility by the entire staff, studies a specific problem, and brings back a report to the larger body.

WORKSHOPS   This type of group attack upon an educational problem is similar to the previous two, but with certain distinguishing characteristics. Whereas the study group and committee tend to work on a single problem of rather narrow scope, workshops tend to deal with broader problems and issues, but focus the thinking of the entire group on separate contributing factors leading to the larger issue. Very often, the workshop breaks down into smaller groups or committees for detailed study and analysis of the problems under consideration.

Workshops may be set up within the school system or outside its sphere of influence. It is common practice nowadays for teacher training institutions to conduct workshops studying a host of problem areas. It is also rather common practice for school systems to establish workshops, for all their staff in the fall, just prior to the opening of school. No matter when, where, or by what means, they are organized, there should be an abundance of resource material and resource people available to make certain that the work done may be most beneficial to all participants.

The following suggestions are intended to be helpful to the person charged with the responsibility of organizing a workshop.

1. Be sure the area to be studied by the workshop is a live, burning issue for the people you hope to attract.

2. Secure the services of leaders in whom the expected workshop workers have confidence—those whom they will accept as so-called experts in the area to be studied.

3. Publicize clearly, widely, and completely. Use bulletins, brochures, news releases, correspondence, word of mouth, and all possible media of communication.

4. Inject some planned fun into the functioning of the workshop. Provide song fests, dances, picnics, parties, and other diversions. Make the workshop a social experience as well as a work session.

5. Make a written summary available to all participants.

6. Make certain that ample resources are available during the entire period the workshop is in session. Consider such things as published materials, book displays, visiting experts, and field trips.

7. Make certain that all physical facilities are conducive to the effective functioning of the workshop.

CLINICS   The conducting of clinics is a common practice in music education circles. They are usually sponsored by some professional organization or teacher training institution. It is entirely possible, however, for a clinic to be established within a large system and to be focused upon a particular need of that system. The clinic differs from a workshop in that the former is established with a preset focus on a particular area and usually involves the services of a so-called expert, demonstrating methods of dealing with problems as they arise, in a group of students assembled for that purpose. The expert is expected to show by demonstration and explanation the best approaches to problem areas in music education.

Band clinics, orchestra clinics, choral clinics, reading clinics, and other clinics, are common practice in music educational circles. It is conceivable that similar activities might be valuable avenues for growth in a large city or county school system. If such is the case and a music director plans to form one, he would need to keep in mind the specific suggestions already given for the workshop and adapt them to the clinic to be organized and executed.

All other things being equal, the workshop is the better avenue for teacher growth because it makes use, to a greater degree, of the actual participation by the teachers or the workshop members themselves.

BULLETINS   Although this device is usually thought of as a means of interstaff communication, if it is carefully planned and written, it can also serve as a device for the improvement of instruction. It must be brief and to the point, clearly and interestingly written, and attractively presented, in order to hold reader interest and attention.

In its function as a channel of communication, it also serves as a means of teacher improvement. It may be an indirect means, but adequate intradepartmental communication is vital to the establishment of an organization in which all of its members may grow and develop properly. If the bulletin aids in this, it becomes an agent for teacher improvement.

PROFESSIONAL CONFERENCES   The periodic meetings, conferences, and conventions, of the various professional organizations should be considered an activity leading toward professional growth.

Everything possible should be done to assist teachers in attending these meetings. If the meeting occurs on a day school is in session, teachers should be permitted to attend without sacrificing pay. It is also possible to provide all or part of the extra expenses incurred by attending such conferences. Social projects, concerts, and programs, can be scheduled so their preparation and presentation will not be impaired by attendance at these conferences.

Although it is difficult and often impossible for all teachers to participate in the large state and national conventions, there are always the regional, county, and local professional meetings that provide innumerable experiences for teacher growth. In truth, these smaller meetings are often more effective than the larger. The value of some conferences is sometimes lost because of the enormous size and complexity of the meeting. The greatest value in all of these gatherings lies in the opportunities afforded for professional discussions in small, often informal, groups, the inspiration derived from outstanding speakers and demonstrations, and the exhibits of educational materials and equipment.

In Chapter 2, reference was made to the music educator's personal contacts beyond the community in which he works. It was pointed out that this professional activity would reap benefit for the children of the local school. We have just shown that attendance at meetings of professional organizations is an important means for improving instruction. Up to this point, we have been concerned about the music educator and his staff participating in professional meetings that focus primarily upon music and music education. The paragraphs that follow will discuss the importance of the music educator's participation in professional activity outside his field of special interest.

The real leader, both musical and educational, will also become active in professional organizations that serve the total field of education as well as the field of his special interest. Depending upon the demands of his job and his own particular interests, the forward looking and thinking music educator will participate in such organizations as the National Education Association, the Association for Supervision and Curriculum Development, National Society for the Study of Education, and others.

Participation means more than belonging and attending. It means being a part of the organization and its purposes. It means accepting committee assignments and faithfully carrying them out. It means holding office, if the association so desires. It means writing for its professional journals. It means accepting clinic, workshop, and panel assignments. It means devoting as much time and energy to the work of the organization as local pressures and responsibilities will permit.

Obviously, the music educator's first responsibility is to the district that employs him. The local board of education and administration that hired him will expect him to devote a certain amount of time and effort in the cause of education at both the state and national level. It is only by this broader interest and effort that the music educator can truly become the artistic and educational leader his position requires.

A complete listing of professional organizations serving the cause of education and of those people working in, and interested in, education is not within the scope of this book. However, it is wise to pause long enough to give a brief description of the organization of the National Education Association and some of its affiliated groups in which the music educator should be interested and active to some degree.

Figure 17 shows graphically a summarization of the organizational structure of the departments of the NEA. This large and influential professional organization is singled out for special consideration because it contains the one

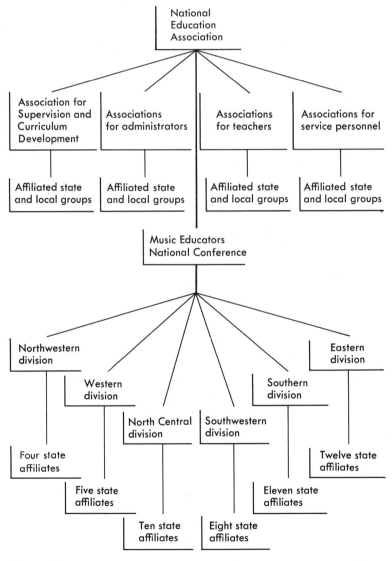

Figure 17   **PROFESSIONAL ORGANIZATIONS**

professional organization in which all music educators should be active—the Music Educators National Conference. There are many others that will stimulate music educator's professional growth, if given the opportunity.

There are thirty departments to the NEA, each with complete autonomy, yet contributing to and receiving assistance from the central body, the National Education Association. The various departments include associations for administrators (superintendents, principals), classroom teachers as well as teachers of special subjects (art, music, physical education, dance), and service areas (audio-visual instruction, research). Other departments cover special areas in education (Educational Secretaries, Adult Education, Higher Education). Nearly all of these groups have organizations at the state level; many have divisional organizations including two or more states; and several have units serving smaller areas such as individual, or groups of, counties.

Every music educator should be active in the Music Educators National Conference and as many of the other organizations as his time, energy, and job responsibilities, will permit.

With today's core courses and self-contained classrooms, the music director is more and more dependent upon non-music specialists for many of the experiences provided the pupils of his school. He will therefore be concerned with the improvement in instruction of these people as far as music is involved. All of the group and individual devices discussed in this chapter are pertinent for dealing with this problem.

Summary

One of the most important duties of the director of music is to see that his staff is producing the best possible kinds of learning situations for the children of his community. This assumes that each teacher is developing his professional capacities to their highest possible degree. It is the director's job to provide the environment in which this type of teacher growth is possible. This chapter suggests that a democratic environment is essential; that the process of curriculum development is a valuable avenue for teacher education; and that, in his role as a teacher of teachers, the music director must provide incentives for growth and furnish those experiences that make it possible.

Suggested Activities

1. Using a school district you know thoroughly, examine the supervisors' plans for improving instruction. How does their philosophy of organization and presentation follow the concepts developed in this chapter?

2. Plan a series of workshop meetings designed to help teachers become more expert in teaching music. Be specific and detailed in your plans.

3. Does your school system have a professional library for its staff of teachers? If so, study its catalog and suggest ways in which it could be strengthened. If not, prepare a catalog of 50 or 75 titles that could serve as a nucleus for developing such a library.

4. Make a list of the professional meetings, workshops, and clinics that will be held in your state, county, and community that could be expected to assist teachers in the following categories improve their competence in music:
   a. Elementary classroom (general music)
   b. Junior and/or Senior High School general music
   c. Instrumental music, all levels
   d. Choral music, all levels
   e. Supervisors

For Further Reading

Association for Supervision and Curriculum Development. *Research for Curriculum Improvement.* Washington, D.C., The Association, 1957. Chapter 8.

Claye, Clifton M. "Lola Gets What Lola Wants from Supervision." *Journal of Educational Research,* 56, No. 7:358–361, March, 1963.

Foshay, Arthur W. "Curriculum Improvement Through Action Research." *National Education Association Journal,* 46, No. 4:265–266, April, 1957.

Hammock, Robert C., and Owings, Ralph S. *Supervising Instruction in Secondary Schools.* New York, McGraw-Hill Book Co., Inc., 1955. Chapter 4.

Hartsell, O. M. "How Super is Your Supervision?" *Music Educators Journal,* 44, No. 5:40, April–May, 1958.

National Society for the Study of Education. *Basic Concepts in Music Education.* Fifty-seventh Yearbook, Part I, Nelson B. Henry, ed., Chicago, The Society, 1958. Chapter 6 and 7.

Smith, Mary. "Action Research to Improve Teacher Planning Meetings." *School Review,* 60, No. 3:146–150, March, 1952.

CHAPTER 5

Public Relations

THE CONCEPT OF SCHOOL-COMMUNITY RELATIONSHIPS has undergone marked change since the first public school opened it doors in this country. This change has been gradual, to be sure, and not always consistent. There was a time when educators took the position that the community should leave the school alone. Teachers did not want parents "meddling in their affairs" and felt that professional educators were the only persons competent for making judgements about the school. The community was expected to play no part in the school program except to provide funds and children.

Later there gradually evolved the "selling" type of approach to school-community affairs. This phase could more rightfully be called school publicity; it was a type of propaganda. Such a pattern of action made no great effort to inform the public about the real nature and purposes of the school. It was most often used in an attempt to sell the community on the terrific job the school was doing or to whip up public sentiment in support of a bond drive. There were occasions when schools resorted to this technique in an attempt to cover up, or gloss over, their shortcomings or mistakes. Experience has proved, however, that no amount of publicity can cover up or sell a bad program.

Definition of Public Relations

In reality, the school and community are co-partners in education. This pattern has been inherent in the public school system in this country from the start, but for many years has been handled badly. Years ago, one partner, the community, was expected to pay the bills and keep out of the way; by design, it was kept in the dark about the purposes, objectives, and accomplishments, of the organization while the other partner, the school, went along either ignoring its associate or intentionally keeping information from him, believing it to be none of his business. It is obvious that such a relationship could not exist for long.

The school-community relationship in support of education can be likened to that of a large corporation. The school is the corporation, the community the stockholders, and the product is education. The community has its faith and money invested in the school and confidently expects that the product will be of such quality that a profit will be realized at the end of the fiscal year. As stockholders, the members of the community expect to know what is going on in the corporation and, when profits are made, they expect their share; they also expect to have a part in forming major decisions of the joint effort, leaving the day-to-day decisions for the manager of the corporation and his assistants to make and carry out.

Out of this partnership concept of school-community relations, has emerged the belief that public relations is interpretation of the school to the community and the community to the school. Moehlman places so much importance on this operation that he gives it status as a basic executive function and defines it in these terms:

> Interpretation is the activity that keeps the public informed of community conditions and needs and provides organized, informational service to keep the people informed of the purpose, value, conditions, and needs of their educational program . . . Interpretation is an activity that permeates all phases of organization including the Board of Education, executive agents, and individuals, as well as groups within the total community.[1]

The sound public relations program today is seeking to bring about a closer understanding between the taxpayer and community, on the one hand, and the school and school personnel, on the other. This is known to be a vital necessity if schools are to perform the tasks to which they have been assigned. Public relations is the process by means of which a closer bond of understanding and cooperation is forged between the school and the community.

This chapter will discuss the two phases of public relations: the conditions necessary to carry them out and practical procedures that the music educator may put into operation as his contribution to the public relations program of the entire school.

Phases of Public Relations

UNDERSTANDING THE COMMUNITY AND ITS NEEDS — An important step is that of securing all possible data that have any bearing on the music program—

[1] Arthur B. Moehlman, *School Administration*, 2nd ed., Boston, Houghton Mifflin Co., 1951, p. 85. Used by permission.

close or remote. This begins with a study of the community's economy. What are its principal industries? Is it a community built around a single business or industry? Is it a suburban or independent community? Is it urban or rural? What are the principle occupations of its residents? What is its tax valuation and how does it compare with neighboring communities? What proportion of its taxes is used in support of its schools? All of these and many other questions will need an answer, before an understanding of the economic structure of the community can be developed.

The social structure of the community must be carefully studied. What national groups are represented in the community? What different races make up its population? What are the dominant national groups and races? What are the minority groups? How did the community vote in the last election? What is the religious composition of the community? What are the minority religions; which, the majority? What are the forces that draw the community together? What forces tend to divide it? Does it have an "exclusive" section? Is there an "across the tracks" section? What are the natures of the community factions, if any? These are but a few of the many questions to which the music educator must seek answers in his search for understanding.

Community attitudes and convictions are another important area to be studied. What does the community believe about public, private, parochial, higher, and music education? Are intellectual pursuits looked upon with favor or disfavor? Are the arts warmly received or neglected? What does the community feel about its young people? Are they considered good or are they considered delinquent? Does it provide social and recreational facilities for its young people outside of school, home, and church?

The educational resources of the community, especially for music, must be ascertained. Are the church choirs active and thriving? Is there a community concerts association? Are there community choruses, orchestras, bands? Is there a music club in the community? Are there music stores providing opportunities for the purchase of music, records, and instruments locally? Is there a local radio station or one near at hand? How about television? A long list of questions will need answers before the music educator knows enough about his community to be effective in launching a public relations program.

The understanding of the community and its needs, which is necessary for the establishment of the best public relations program, cannot be gained by the collecting of data alone. The music director and his staff will find it necessary to live, work, and play, in the community; they will need to identify themselves with the community, to become a part of it, to feel, to sense it as a social organism. It is only upon such close, intimate understanding that a truly effective public relations program can be built.

KEEPING THE COMMUNITY INFORMED — The second phase of interpretation, or public relations, is keeping the community informed of the purpose, value, conditions, and needs, of the school. Whether we consider the public relations program from the standpoint of the music department alone or that of the school as a whole, this phase is of vital importance. The public relations program operates on a two-way street; some activity goes from the school to the community, some in the reverse direction. One is as important as the other, and both lanes must be kept open and the traffic moving in both directions.

A word of caution is necessary at this point. The music educator must be constantly aware of his position in the larger structure of education and co-ordinate his public relations work with that of the school as a whole. He can-not go his way, oblivious to the remainder of the educational program and the direction in which it is moving. All parts must be kept in close unity and bal-ance, each unit or department making its special contribution to the whole in order that the best interests of education may be served.

All possible lines of communication must be used in this phase of inter-pretation. Face-to-face contacts, working groups, the spoken word, the printed word, demonstrations, displays, concerts, and all other possible ways of pro-moting better understanding between school and community, will have their role to play in the complete program. Many of these will be discussed in the final section of this chapter.

Necessary Conditions

Before a public relations program can operate effectively and accomplish the purposes for which it was created, certain conditions must prevail. The wise music educator will examine his position critically to be sure they do exist and are operating before he increases the tempo of his campaign. If any of the basic conditions are weak or inoperative, they must be brought up to peak efficiency before the program can move forward.

ACTIVE INVOLVEMENT OF SCHOOL STAFF — All school staff members, both professional and non-professional, must be concerned about, and actively in-volved in, school and community relations. This is something woven into the very basic fabric of their jobs, not something set apart to be used only when needed. The American Association of School Administrators supports this point of view.

The school administrator is not a superintendent or principal one day and a public relations agent the next. A teacher is not a teacher during the day and a public relations agent after school. They are educators and public relations agents all the time. Public relations is part of the educational process itself.[2]

The best type of public relations is developed when the product of the school is good; that is, when it has value and worth in the eyes of the public. The virtue of the product is determined by the established purposes of the school, as put into practice, and by the relationship of these purposes to those that the community has established for its schools. The schools that train children in the manner that the community expects will have the understanding, goodwill, and support, of its patrons. If the schools are doing what the community hopes they will do, their product is judged to be good, and the community willingly supports their work in all ways.

The staff of a school should be concerned primarily with the results achieved in changed lives of the children. This is true, in the first place, because the chief duty of the school is to educate the children and, in the second place, because this is the first step in developing good public relations, also a concern of the staff.

The chief and most active emissary of opinion about the school is the child. As a public relations agent, he is always on the job. He goes into the homes of the community day after day and, for better or worse, freely tells everyone within earshot how he feels about the school. The child who is happy and making progress carries good reports; the child who is unhappy and being pressed to do things he cannot do tells unfavorable tales. There is no escaping the fact that the children of our schools always have an opinion and are usually not unwilling to express it. What reports they carry into the home and community rest with the teachers, the principals, the supervisors; in fact, the entire staff.

When the child is recognized as the chief distributor of information about schools, it then follows that the school person closest to him, the one from whom he draws his deepest impressions—the teacher—is the most important single cog in the machine that shapes public opinion and creates public confidence in the schools.

Staff members who are public relations conscious will find other ways to

[2] American Association of School Administrators, *Public Relations for America's Schools*, Twenty-eighth Yearbook, Washington, D.C., The Association, 1950, p. 20. Used by permission.

carry their message to the community. They will participate in the life of the community, make their homes there, and be active in social, cultural, fraternal, and religious activities of the community. The teachers and other staff members will become known as persons rather than as teachers, or supervisors of this, or director of that, or principal of this school, or principal of that school. As the community becomes better acquainted with them as persons, as individuals, it begins to understand the school itself in its true light. The community begins to see the school as an organization of persons, just as the community is itself.

The very manner in which the school people move about the community, their very bearing, reflects the conditions at school. Are they happy in their work? Are they sold on their jobs, on the school, on the community? Are they fond of the children with whom they work? All of these things interpret the nature of the school to the citizens of the community. This personal, face-to-face type of public relations is most effective and most convincing.

The entire staff must be brought to understand the importance of its role as public relations agent and play its part accordingly, if the public is to be informed of the nature and quality of the schools in their community.

Sharing information with the public creates sympathy for the school's program and problems. Out of this sympathy grows cooperation, and cooperation is essential to good relations between people and their schools.

ABSENCE OF CONFLICT — The second condition necessary before a public relations program can operate effectively is the development of cooperative mutual understanding between the various groups within the school itself. The music department must understand that there are times when the physical education department has need for a campaign of interpretation that, at the moment, may be more important than that of the music department. The secondary program may need, for the time being, to take precedence over the elementary; the campaign for a new elementary building may be more important than new uniforms for the band. Throughout the school staff, there must be a realization that the good of the whole is more important than that of any of its parts.

It must be clearly understood that there are special problems and special needs within the music department that call for publicity or a place in the general public relations program of the school. They should be taken care of at the proper time and in the proper manner. The music director is the right person to provide the leadership for bringing them to fruition. He and his staff will be the energizing influence behind such a campaign, but, at the same time, they must see that what is done is in keeping with the school-wide plans for public relations.

The music department, because of the very nature of its program, is continually in the public eye. This puts it in an advantageous position for developing favorable public reaction and support to its program. However, it also serves as a public relations agent for the school as a whole and must serve as efficiently and graciously in this regard. As these special programs of public relations are carried out, they must be kept in balance with all other units of the school system. Cooperation must prevail at all times, at all levels, and among all departments and special services.

Cooperation of the sort called for here does not just happen. It must be planned for, directed, and guided, by some person or a group of persons made so responsible with sufficient authority to carry such plans to completion. The organizational means whereby this is done varies from school to school. A person may be appointed to the superintendent's staff with the sole responsibility for the public relations program. If the school system is large, he may have a staff working with him. Smaller systems may have a person who devotes part of his time to this work and the balance to teaching or administrative duties. It is also possible to have a committee appointed by the administration for carrying on this function. By whatever means it is provided, the music director must plan and execute his public relations activity in accordance with the pattern existing in his school.

LIAISON BETWEEN POLICY-MAKERS AND STAFF — The board of education is the policy-making body for the school system. It is the group that determines officially what the schools shall be, what they shall do, and how they shall do it. The board of education will have its own interests in the public relations program of the school; there will be times when a program of its own is imperative. Since the purpose of the process of interpretation is to create better understanding and support of the school system as a whole, the board of education must be kept informed so that all policies may be properly presented to the public. Also, the staff of the school must be kept informed of the policies and plans of the board so that they may be properly fitted into the developing scheme of public relations.

The superintendent of schools, in his capacity as executive officer of the board and administrative head of the school system, is the logical person to serve in this liaison capacity. There may be certain instances, however, that would cause the board of education and superintendent to decide to form a committee of staff members for making possible the necessary communication.

By whatever organizational device it is brought about, there must be this intercommunication and common understanding of purposes and procedures before the public relations program of the schools can be expected to operate effectively.

CONTINUING EFFORT — All too often, interpretation of the school's work and philosophies is permitted to be a sporadic affair. In such cases, it is used to build up public good will for some new project, a bond issue, or some other plan needing public support. It is frequently used as a plan to counteract some bad or faulty impression erroneously made. Although this type of program has its immediate goal and can be effective in attaining it, it can scarcely be called a public relations program.

To be most effective and live up to the true purposes of interpretation, the public relations program of a school system must be well planned, continuous, and of consistently high quality. The focus of such a campaign can change as needed, shift from one aspect of the school to another, and center its attention on those areas most needing the benefits of public knowledge and understanding at any given time.

It is obvious that such a program will necessitate long-range planning and constant close supervision, so that the required publicity can be handled on schedule and with maximum effectiveness.

The music educator, as he plans his own public relations activity and seeks to coordinate it with that of his school, will need to provide a continuous flow of activity in this area and be sure his staff is fully aware of the importance of its role in the entire process; he must work cooperatively with all other groups within the school system; he must use or develop some form of liaison between the board of education and his activities. Nothing worthwhile can be done without meeting these conditions.

Practical Procedures

When the music educator studies his responsibilities for public relations for the whole school as well as his own special needs, he will find many avenues for his activity. The music department is often referred to as the public relations bureau of the school because so much of its work is in the public eye. The very nature of its activities make it so; however, the other aspects of the school's program that need public understanding and cooperation must not be overlooked. The chief avenues by which the music educator assists in develop-

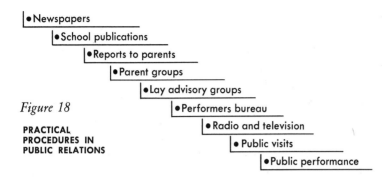

Figure 18

**PRACTICAL
PROCEDURES IN
PUBLIC RELATIONS**

ing good public relations for his school will be discussed in the section that follows.

PUBLIC PERFORMANCE — The concert appearances of school performing groups have been taken for granted so long that their function as public relations activities is frequently overlooked. The very nature of music demands that it be performed and that it be heard. Performing groups have not completed their full activity cycle until concerts and public appearances are presented for the community. Parents, relatives, and friends, of school musicians are always interested in the work of student concert organizations and eagerly await each opportunity for hearing them perform. This is exactly as it should be, and the school's performing groups become the crowning climax of the school's music program.

All too often, the worth of the entire music program of the school is judged in the eyes of the community by the public acceptance of the school band, orchestra, or chorus. This is an easy condition to create since these are the organizations of the music department that are constantly appearing before the public, but it can all too often lead to faulty conclusions and an erroneous concept of the true worth of the school's music program.

Let us look at School A. Its high school band is an excellent one. It is large, is completely equipped, plays and marches well. It makes frequent appearances in the community at parades and public programs; it presents concerts and plays at football games and other sporting events. Judged by the musicianship and excellence of this organization, the music program in School A is a flourishing one and commendable in every way.

By examining the total program carefully, however, the following facts are obtained: (1) There is no string program at all and consequently no orchestra. (2) The choral groups are small, poorly equipped, and receive tag ends of scheduled time and the music director's energy; thus, the morale of the groups is low. (3) There are no general music experiences provided at any level. In truth, the entire music program is centered in the band and the experiences that lead to its betterment.

Conditions such as these can indicate only that, taken as a whole, the music program is shortsighted, weak, unbalanced, and in general not suitable to the best concepts of democratic education. A music program of this sort is as bad as a mathematics program would be that taught only the processes of addition and totally excluded subtraction, multiplication, and division. It is presenting to the community and its children only one small part or phase of a music program.

In Chapter 3, a plea was made for considering general music as the base and core of the music curriculum. By its very nature, this is not a program that is frequently in the public eye, but the ingenious music educator can see that it comes in for its full share of performance and recognition. Not so very many years ago, a junior high school in Connecticut gave a concert version of the *Mikado* by Gilbert and Sullivan, produced and performed entirely by the general music classes of the seventh and eighth grades. Four or five perform-ances were given and each time to a packed house.

All these occasions where school performers appear before the public should be properly considered avenues for developing a greater degree of public understanding and acceptance of the school's purpose and work. This will include not only the formal concerts by major performing groups, but all other performances before the community as well. Such occasions will include appearances for community and different civic groups, service clubs, churches, parades, and even competition-festivals. All such programs must be considered a part of the public relations program, and all details of planning, organization, and executing, of them must be meticulously supervised.

The importance of the public performance of the smaller ensembles, the soloists, and members of the music staff, must be stressed. If the music educa-tor is properly considered the music leader of his community, then all of the musical performances for which he is responsible, either directly or indirectly, are important aspects of his relations with the public. By means of the smaller ensembles and soloists, even though they may be performing on their own initiative and without the official guidance of the school, the music director is able to reach other segments of his community in a closer, more personal way than he can with the formal concerts and performances of his larger ensembles. All public performances have high public relations value that should be capitalized upon.

Just recently, the writer heard of a band director who was rather boast-fully claiming ninety public appearances with his high school band in one year.

It is difficult to know where the line lies that separates public relations activity from exploitation of school performing groups. The danger of overburdening school performers with too frequent appearances must always be guarded against. One fact must be kept continually in mind: the school music program exists to furnish young people with experiences essential for their well-rounded development, *not* as a provider of "free" performances to suit the whims and fancies of the director or of the various influences in the community.

The music director who is anxious to develop the most cordial relationship with his community, give it the greatest service, and yet not be guilty of exploiting his student musicians, will do well to form a lay advisory committee to assist in making plans and decisions for his performing groups. This committee of parents and friends of the music program can suggest policies governing out-of-school performances and encourage their adoption by the board of education. They can caution the director when his commitments are overburdening the students or can advise other ways of presenting the musical groups to the community. These are but a few of the ways such a committee can be of assistance to a director of music.

Aside from being of invaluable assistance in this capacity, the committee is a very powerful public relations device in itself and will be duly discussed later in the chapter.

Public performances by school musicians have inherent worth in addition to their actual capacity for developing public understanding and acceptance of the music program and of the school as a whole. It is extremely unwise to consider them from the public relations point of view *exclusively*. Music performed by school orchestras, bands, choruses, and ensembles, is a most valuable community service. It is a means for adding to the cultural life of the community. Excellent music, carefully chosen and artistically performed, can have a profound effect upon listeners.

By carefully planned, artistically presented, school performances, the listening habits of an entire community can be changed. A school music program that has won the support of the community can be the means for raising the cultural level of that community. Music ignored on the radio, television, or in the concert hall, will be listened to and enjoyed when performed by an excellent school group.

Many communities have no concert organization other than those supplied by the school. In such instances, the personal intimate contact with music supplied by school performances carries a much greater impact than that of the radio or phonograph and is, therefore, a stronger force in developing desirable cultural habits.

A word of caution is necessary at this time. A most delicate balance exists between public acceptance of the music offered and a music director's attempts to raise the cultural level of his community. To be of any lasting benefit, the music presented must be accepted by the community. That is, the music performed must be a little above, but not too far above, the public's taste. The audience must accept and enjoy the music being performed. It is quite possible for a director to give a concert of musical masterpieces and still lose ground in public acceptance and support of his program, nullifying possible cultural advances at the same time. This is especially true if the community looks upon such music and its performance as a type of snobbery.

By no means should the caution just expressed be interpreted as an attempt to minimize the music educator's responsibilities for cultural leadership in his community and his efforts to encourage growth in these directions. It is mentioned only as a reminder that it is wise to "make haste slowly"; that public relations benefits and cultural growth are lost when the community does not understand and accept the performance. The music to be performed and the manner in which it is to be presented must be considered with great care, weighing all factors prudently.

The music director must be certain that all music performed is well performed. A good performance has tremendous value; a bad performance can do irreparable harm. It is better not to perform at all than to do it poorly. It is far better to play easy, simple music and play it well, than to tackle a work too difficult for the group and play it poorly. The standard of excellence must be kept high at all times.

The printed program, the advance publicity, the ticket selling campaign, if there is one, and the newspaper reviews that follow the performance, are all important parts of the public performance as a public relations activity. The advance publicity affords the music director an opportunity for highlighting and pointing up various aspects of his total program and the nature and purposes of the performing group or groups in particular. The way in which the ticket campaign is conducted speaks well or ill of the music program as a whole. The printed program placed in the hands of the audience on the night of the performance tells and shows the public what the school is doing musically and the way in which it is accomplishing its purposes. The published reports of the concert, if good, reflect with favor upon the music program of the school; if poor or indifferent reports result, the influence is negative. Possible after effects of the concert should concern the prudent music educator as much as the preparations beforehand.

PUBLIC VISITS — Inviting the public to visit school and observe the music program in action is a very useful and rewarding form of public relations.

Making parents and friends welcome at rehearsals of the band, chorus, and orchestra, is instructive and enlightening. The community is able to have a more vital appreciation of the contributions music makes to the lives of young people, when they see music in this setting rather than from the distance of the concert stage. Even though only a few avail themselves of this opportunity. they carry their observations to their friends and associates in the community. Quite possibly, no one will attend these open rehearsals at first, but the good-will that results from such an invitation is of tremendous value.

Music is an art in which participation is of great importance and of intense value. It affords a unique opportunity for parents and children, patrons and pupils, to share in the common experience of making music. Assemblies at Christmas time can be devoted, wholly or in part, to school children and adults from the community, singing the traditional Christmas music together. Adults may be invited, even encouraged, to bring their instruments to orchestra and band rehearsals and to join in making music with the student musicians. Such open rehearsals should be deliberately planned from time to time throughout the year. When the idea takes hold, portions of public concerts can be devoted to the performance of music by children of the school, joined by adults of the community. Many opportunities for the school and community to make music together will come to the attention of the alert music director, and he will eagerly seize upon them for the betterment of his school, his community, and his music.

RADIO, TELEVISION, AND PICTURES — In this day and age, there are many opportunities for reaching the public that supports the schools through these media—especially radio. It is not at all unusual for music groups to be called upon to prepare and present programs over the air; opportunities may be sought out for performing over the radio. For such occasions, the music director should study his entire program and, over a period of time, present all phases of it to the radio audience; the elementary, the secondary, the vocal, the instrumental, the general, and the special, should all be presented to the listening public at the proper time and in the proper setting.

All of the values inherent in the discussion of public performances in the previous section are present in radio performance but are, in many instances, even more critical. The audience is larger and covers a wider range of musical interests and more varied background; therefore, the program must be selected and presented with even greater care in order to make it appealing and to hold the listeners. In the concert hall, people are hesitant to walk out if they do not care for the program, but they have no inhibitions about turning the radio off or switching to another station when interest lags. The presence of young people on the concert stage is visually appealing; this appeal is lacking on the radio, and the music must speak through sound alone. The acoustical conditions of the studio are vastly different from those prevailing in the school auditorium and must be compensated for in the music and the performance of it, if the activity is to assume its greatest value as a means of public relations.

As yet, television has not opened its studios to school performances very extensively. With educational TV on the threshold of wider acceptance, there will be increasing opportunities for the use of this medium. The audience of this new type of mass communication also has its unique tastes, and it must be catered to if the message is to get through. The techniques of straight concert performances, even on commercial television, have not been sufficiently refined to make the concert vitally interesting. New techniques of program presentation must be worked out before the music director can make the most effective use of television as a means for developing his public relations program. As these techniques develop and opportunities for air time become more widespread, music educators will here find a fertile field for public relations activity.

The sound motion picture is coming into wide acceptance as a powerful and versatile medium for carrying the message of the schools to the community. Frequently, the making of such a picture is an activity of the public relations program of the school system as a whole. As such, the music department should receive its rightful share of footage.

The public has become accustomed to perfection or near perfection in the programs offered on radio, television, and in the motion pictures. In order for the schools to hold, entertain, and inform the general public, through these forms of communication, all performances must be of the highest caliber and above criticism in every way.

PERFORMERS BUREAU — One of the best ways to gain community goodwill and support is to provide a service that is wanted and, at the same time, makes a community's life more wholesome. Such a service can be the operation of a performers bureau. This bureau can be organized and operated by the students of the music department as a service to the community.

All communities, and the organizations and societies that are a part of the communities, have frequent need for performers at their meetings, banquets, and dinners. An active music program in the schools will have many students who desire and need such performance experiences, both solo and ensemble.

The performers bureau can help to bring musicians to the groups that need them and can operate to the mutual advantage of all concerned.

Although this is a wholesome activity and should be encouraged, it is not without its element of danger and possible harm. It is a known fact that some schools offer this type of service for the express purpose of providing additional revenue for the purchase of equipment and supplies for the music department. This is a deplorable situation. In the first place, it is contrary to the *Code of Ethics* agreed upon by the Music Educators National Conference and the Musicians Union. This activity, so carried out, could conceivably deprive some professional musician of a portion of his livelihood.

It is even more deplorable on a second count. It places a form of double taxation upon certain segments of the community. It jeopardizes the full public support of the school's total program by taxation. It also places a price upon a public relations activity that should be presented as a community service having educational value.

Aside from the deplorableness of this practice on purely educational grounds, it is fraught with danger in another way. It can lead a community to believe that the music department can be expected to be self-supporting, at least in part. This can cause the community to withdraw or deny its support from public monies for the music department and its activities. This could, and often does, retard the community's acceptance of its responsibility for supporting the entire program of the school on an impartial basis.

Undoubtedly, this is a policy decision, the responsibility for which rests with the board of education. The music director who takes the long view of his program and seeks to integrate it into the program of the school as a whole will provide his board of education with the information necessary to develop the policy most suitable for his community. Once this policy is made, it is the music director's obligation to support and execute it.

In the best interests of good public relations for the school and the music department, the music director must be certain that the performers who appear before the public under this plan are properly prepared and will, therefore, reflect good to the school.

LAY ADVISORY GROUPS — A valuable approach to the development of community understanding and support of the music program in its schools is the securing of as much lay participation as possible. This activity can take on a variety of forms—curriculum development, advisory committees for choir, orchestra, and band, and study groups for the development of general music activities. Whatever form they may take, the objectives are the same—better schools, better school music programs, better community support, better community understandings.

Not only is this type of activity valuable to participants, but it also serves as a link with the remainder of the public for developing better relations with the community as a whole. As lay and professional people work together on problems of mutual interest, they begin to understand each other's point of view much better. They can work together for better effect upon the lives of the children of the community.

PARENT GROUPS — Organized parent groups, on a system-wide basis as well as on a single school or unit basis, help foster a wholesome type of school-community relations. Such organizations will undoubtedly take on some form of parent-teacher association that may or may not be affiliated with National Congress of Parents and Teachers. Such an organization may vary from school to school and community to community, but the purposes and the public relations values for the music educator will remain constant.

In his contacts with such groups, the music educator will welcome opportunities for speaking before them, participating on committees, in study groups, panel discussions, and other activities. He will also provide performing groups for their meetings as the need arises. There will be times when such organizations will be carrying on projects in the interests of the work of the schools; the music director will lend his active support and assist in their promotion to the limits of his time, energy, and ability. This type of working together with parents interested in the welfare of the school and its program for the children of their community is a valuable point of contact for the promotion of desirable public relations.

It is possible to develop some type of suborganization for the express purpose of promoting or supporting the music program of the schools. In such cases, the plan used should be that of looking upon the larger organization as the parent body with the special interest group subservient to it. This is by far a better procedure, in terms of wholesome public relations, than the formation of independent organizations devoted to the exclusive interests of a single group, such as a Band Parents Club, Choir Mothers Club, or Orchestra Boosters Club. The latter type of organization tends to divide the parent group into special interest segments, whereas the former builds toward a unity of purpose and activity that is more wholesome for the school.

The music director will also work closely with the music clubs, community music orgaizations, and church choirs, in developing wider understanding and acceptance of the music program of the schools. Although these groups have no official connection with the school or any organization of the school, they do afford the music director an opportunity for carrying his message of school music to the organizations in the community most interested in music. This opportunity should not be overlooked.

REPORTS TO PARENTS — In a very real sense, this chapter in its entirety has been devoted to the topic of reporting to parents. However, at this time it is well to consider the problem of both formal and informal direct reports to parents.

The whole problem of reporting to parents has been under consideration by educators for a long time. Activity in this area has taken many turns through many channels. Perhaps the poorest type of reporting is the old-fashioned report card. There are schools that still use it, and some that still claim that Johnny is worth 85 in music and his neighbor Billy is worth 86. It is utterly impossible to discriminate finely between the influence music has had upon the lives of Billy and Johnny. The newer type of report card is better but still leaves much to be desired.

Some schools will find it valuable to prepare periodic bulletins to be sent to the parents of children in the music program, while others will find open letters to parents helpful. Some music educators will take advantage of opportunities for speaking before parent groups and give their reports verbally; others will seek opportunities for talking with parents individually. By whatever means the job of reporting is done, it must help get across the nature, the purposes, and the progress, of the music department, always in relation to the nature, purposes, and progress, of the school as a whole.

At one time in his teaching experience, the writer adopted the practice of sending to the parents a personal, written report accompanying the report card. At the time, he was primarily responsible for the instrumental program of the school, and these reports were sent to the parents of all band and orchestra members of the elementary, junior high, and senior high schools as well as all pupils receiving class instrumental instruction. These messages were entirely individual, critical but constructive. There were more than one hundred and twenty-five to be written and signed each marking period, causing a tremendous amount of work, but the benefits in parental understanding and cooperation were of such magnitude that the cost in time and effort seemed negligible.

SCHOOL PUBLICATIONS — The student publications of the school are more powerful as public relations mediums than most music educators realize. They offer an opportunity for keeping the student body informed of the goals, aspirations, and purposes, of the music program. When this is interestingly and attractively presented, it can serve as a means for promoting good public relations within the school, and, as pointed out above, this message is transmitted through the pupils to the parents at home. It is also surprising how many parents read the student publications and, in this way, receive the message directly.

The wise music educator will see to it that there is a music reporter for each school publication. He will tip off the reporter to forthcoming events that are newsworthy and in keeping with objectives of the publication and the music department. He will help the reporter write his articles interestingly and accurately, even checking them for content and style himself. He will assist in gathering necessary information, pictures, and copies of programs. He will make the music department a good source of news and welcome all opportunities for getting his message before the public through the school publications.

NEWSPAPER PUBLICITY — The local newspaper serving the community that supports the school, whether it be a daily or weekly publication, is a forceful medium for forming public opinion about the music department and its relation to the purposes of the entire school. The music director interested in developing the most wholesome community atmosphere for his musical activities will make a point of establishing good relations with the publishers and reporters of all the papers serving his community. Throughout the entire year, he will furnish them with newsworthy stories containing human interest and not confine his efforts to receiving news space at concert and contest times only. Pictures that will make the article more interesting and informative will be furnished with all news stories. Great care will be exercised in providing the newspaper with an accurate list of people participating, particularly those who play leading roles in any performance or activity. All news copy will be typed, preferably triplespaced, and presented to the proper person well in advance of the deadline.

It is advisable to remember that the editor makes the final decision on what and how much of the story submitted is to be used. He also determines its location in the layout of the paper. It is entirely presumptuous for the music educator to suggest the location in which he expects his story to appear and that he prefers it to be used without cutting. At all costs, he should not be offended if the story is shortened, placed on an inside page, or perhaps left out; in the editor's opinion, there may be other stories more newsworthy. At all times, he should show appreciation for the coverage given and ask for ways of helping secure stories of even greater reader interest and value.

Summary

Public relations is defined as the process by means of which a closer bond of understanding and cooperation is forged between the school and the community. It consists of a two-way system of communication; a continuing study of the community and its purposes and goals and the transmission of information about the school to the community. Its successful operation depends upon all members of the school staff being actively involved, conflicts among groups or club-interests being eradicated, the board of education and the school working in harmony, and the program being continuous rather than sporadic. The music educator has many practical procedures by means of which he can make his contributions to the public relations efforts of the school as a whole and his department in particular. Several of these activities have been discussed in this chapter.

Suggested Activities

1. Plan a public relations campaign for your school district using as many avenues of communication as is feasible.
2. Make a thorough study of your community and its needs for music and music education. What public relations activities are suggested by your study?
3. Write a radio or television script that will explain some phase of your school's music education program to the public.
4. Write a series of articles for the local newspaper which will explain some phase of your school's music education program to the community. Be sure to plan the types of illustrations such articles would need.
5. Prepare an announcement to the community informing them that a Performers Bureau will soon be established by your school. Be sure to include all of the information that an interested group would need to engage a performer from the Bureau.

For Further Reading

Fitzpatrick, Edward A. "Public Education Is Public Business." *American School Board Journal,* 126, No. 4:54–55, April, 1953.

Graham, Floyd Freeman. *Public Relations in Music Education.* New York, Exposition Press, 1954.

Ludeman, W. W. "Teacher's Public Relations." *Education,* 78, No. 6:337–338, February, 1958.

Morphet, Edgar L., Johns, Roe L., and Reller, Theodore L. *Educational Administration: Concepts, Practices, and Issues.* Englewood Cliffs, N.J., Prentice-Hall, Inc., 1959. Chapter 6.

Morrill, Charles L. "Better Public Relations." *School Executive,* 77, No. 1:74–76, September, 1957.

Music Educators National Conference. *Music Curriculum in Secondary Schools.* Washington, D.C., The Conference, 1959. Pages 29–33.

_____. *The Music Teacher and Public Relations.* Washington, D.C., The Conference, 1958.

Leadership in

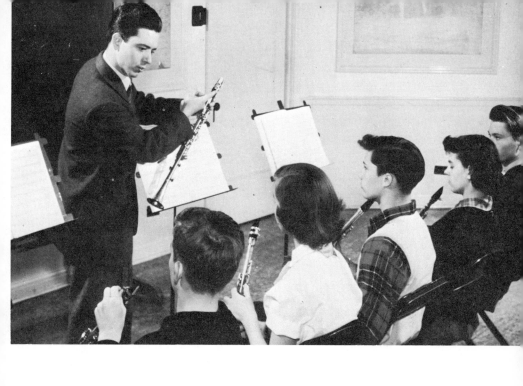

Operational Activities

CHAPTER 6

Scheduling

THE SCHOOL SCHEDULE is of vital interest to all educators, regardless of what their special field of endeavor may be. It certainly is a problem of great concern to the music educator; much of the success of his administrative duties will depend upon his insight into the nature and purpose of the schedule and the process by which it is built. Even though the chief responsibilities for schedule making rest with the principals of the various units in the school system, a music educator is severely handicapped when he does not understand the problems and procedures of the process. He needs these insights in order to be of most assistance when his advice and opinions are sought regarding the scheduling of music classes and activities. Without such understandings, he and the principals through whom he works cannot talk the same language. In such instances, the music program with its unique needs is not as adequately cared for as might otherwise be. The music administrator who is alive to his responsibilities as musical leader for his school and community cannot be ignorant of such an important phase of administration.

In addition to his capacity as advisor to the maker of the master schedule for any school or system, there are other aspects of the educational program where the music director must assume complete, or nearly complete, responsibility for schedule making. In order to be able to do this efficiently, he needs both a basic understanding and basic skills for scheduling competence.

After a discussion of the school schedule, what it is and what it expects to do, the various types of schedules will be explained and the scheduling process presented. Complete understanding can come only after considerable experience working with scheduling problems, but a desirable degree of initial competence can be attained as a result of a presentation of this type.

Schedule Defined

A simple definition of a schedule would be that it is an organization of time, facilities, and personnel, to meet the educational needs of the children for whom the school is responsible. This is undoubtedly an oversimplification of a complex instrument; however, it does deal with time, space, equipment, and people, and attempts to put them all into a functional relationship with each other that will bring about the best educational results.

Education is change moving through time. It is a living, progressing process of growth and development, beginning at birth and ceasing with death. The school is held responsible for the formal or planned training of children from approximately the fifth or sixth year through the seventeenth or eighteenth or longer, depending upon the community and the individual's personal desires and needs. This large block of time, covering a span of ten or twelve years, is broken down into smaller units for ease in handling and more efficient planning.

Each year is divided, traditionally, into a nine- or ten-month school session and a two- or three-month vacation. This block of time is further reduced to smaller units, such as semesters or quarters, and then into subdivisions of monthly, weekly, and daily units.

All of these various blocks of time must be in the minds of schedule makers as they organize the work of their school units. This chapter will concentrate upon the daily, weekly, and yearly schedules.

When education consisted of learning specific data and facts in organized bodies of subject matter and all areas were considered of equal importance, the schedule was a division of time to assure equality of emphasis in all fields. As the purposes of education have changed, schedules or divisions of time have of necessity changed. In other words, as the purposes and procedures in education change, the organization of time to meet these purposes must change. Although the form may be altered, the basic definition does not vary—the schedule is still an organization of time, facilities, and personnel, to meet the educational needs of children.

Responsibility for Scheduling

There must always be a clear-cut definition of responsibility for schedule making in any given school system. The general over-all schedule by which a school unit operates is usually made by the principal of the building. It would be extremely difficult to conceive of a person's being made responsible for all of the educational activity within his building and yet being denied the right to design the schedule by which the school will operate. In a school system containing more than one school unit, there would undoubtedly be some consideration given to schedule problems on a system-wide basis, but certainly the schedule by which a single unit will operate must be made by the principal.

The chief problem of the principal will be to make available to all children the full facilities and resources of his school in a proportion commensurate with each individual pupil's needs. What the principal believes the goals of education to be, what he believes to be the best way to arrive at those goals, what he believes to be important in the school's curriculum, will be reflected in the schedule he makes or approves. If he believes education to be an amassing of facts and skills, his schedule will provide a setting for this type of emphasis. If he believes it is the school's business to provide a stimulating, wholesome atmosphere in which children may grow and develop, his schedule will make such a setting possible. As music is contained in the schedule or affected by it, the music educator may advise, counsel, or persuade, but the final decision rests with the principal.

The importance of music in the lives of people is no longer debatable. This places music in a secure position as far as the curriculum of the school is concerned. The American Association of School Administrators in their Thirty-first Yearbook recognize the special contribution music makes to the developing lives of children when they say, "Music education is more and more thought of as one of the basic parts of the curriculum. It is definitely not a frill or a fringe subject."[1] Since music has won its place in the curriculum of the modern school, the efforts of all administrators should be devoted to bringing its benefits to all children.

The schedule makers are the persons who control, to a large degree, the amount of music, the kind of music, and the proportion of time for music, available to each child. It is within their power to place musical subjects and activities in a prominent place on the school's schedule, or they may relegate them to a place outside the regular daily program to an after-school time. This latter arrangement places music in a category outside and beyond the important events of the day. This is indeed unfortunate because music can give its best service when it is permitted to be a part of the daily mainstream of human experiences. The modern schedule places *all* music instruction and activity within the school day. General music, instruction in voice and on instruments, rehearsals of instrumental and vocal groups, courses in theory, musicianship, history, and listening, and all other musical activities, are given status in the school's curriculum by an equitable share of the school's time and facilities as reflected in the schedule.

---

[1] American Association of School Administrators, *American School Curriculum,* Thirty-first Yearbook, Washington, D.C., The Association, 1953, p. 180. Used by permission.

The amount of time and the proportion of the school's facilities to be devoted to music will vary from one school to another. A complete lack of time and facilities is too little, and a full use of both is too much. Somewhere between these two extremes, each community must discover the distribution that brings to its young people all of the benefits of music in a proper relationship to the remainder of the curriculum.

Although some consideration is given later in the chapter to special schedules and other ways of bringing music to children outside of regular school hours, they must all be recognized as makeshift arrangements. They are to be used only when the community, the school, and the administration, have not yet reached a full and complete understanding of the special contribution music can make to the developing lives and personalities of children.

As is very frequently the case when areas of instruction have been assigned to special directors or supervisors, the music educator will be fully responsible for certain types of schedules. In such circumstances, it is important to recognize that these special schedules are superimposed upon the master or general schedule and must, therefore, be made in such a way that the educational purposes and resources of the school are kept in balance. Understanding this, the music director will seek the advice and counsel of the principals involved to make certain that nothing in the special music schedule is in conflict with the efficient operation of the school as a whole.

The guiding principle that must be in the mind of any person making a schedule for any purpose is that it be possible for each pupil to be in the right room, with the right teacher, and with the right facilities, that allow him to participate in the experiences that contribute most to his normal, healthy growth and development.

Types of Schedules

DAILY-WEEKLY — Seldom will any school unit be operating on a schedule in which each unit of time in each sucessive school day is an exact duplicate of all others. Usually each week's schedule is a replica of the previous one. It must be understood, however, that in building a weekly schedule, each day must of necessity be considered separately. Since schedules are more frequently thought of in weekly units, the daily-weekly schedule will be discussed as a unit.

CONVENTIONAL SCHEDULE   The conventional schedule contains a pattern of time units of equal length throughout each day of the entire week. It is based on the concept that all subjects in the curriculum are of equal importance and must therefore receive equal emphasis in terms of the time allotted to them. The units of time are fixed, inflexible, unchanging, throughout each day and each week This type of schedule is found at all levels—elementary school, junior high school, and senior high school—and reflects the older, more traditional philosophies of education in practice.

At the elementary level, the conventional schedule sets aside a certain number of minutes each day for each subject. It is tightly compartmentalized with no subject permitted outside its allotted time. Music, in such a program, is frequently thought of as of lesser importance and therefore scheduled for fewer minutes each day than reading, writing, and arithmetic; in fact, it may not be scheduled at all.

Such a schedule forces all children into a common mold and pattern, ignoring the individual needs and growth patterns of the pupils. It is an entirely adult-imposed organization of time with no provision for teacher-pupil planning. Happily, this rigid, conventional type of schedule is rapidly disappearing from the elementary school scene.

In junior high schools using a schedule of this type, the pattern is the same as that of the elementary school, except that the periods are longer and the emphasis is upon the academic subjects. If special subjects, such as music, are allowed in the program at all, they meet fewer times per week (usually once or twice) than English or mathematics, for example, and frequently at the least desirable times of the school day. Special activities and activity groups must meet outside of the scheduled day or in a single activity period, if they meet at all. Although such a type of schedule is rather common at this level, a good number of schools are breaking away from its strictness and rigidity as newer philosophies of education come into practice.

Subject-centered senior high schools, especially those that place great emphasis upon preparation for entrance into college, still use the conventional schedule to a considerable extent. Music seldom finds its way into the daily program of this type of school on an equal basis with college preparatory subjects. It is relegated to the activities period or out of school hours.

The conventional schedule is retained at the senior high school level with greater persistence than in the junior high and elementary schools. One frequently finds a strictly conventional schedule in the senior high school in systems using a more modern type of schedule at lower levels.

The music educator serves only in an advisory capacity in schedule making of this type, with the principal taking the initiative, making all decisions, and bearing full responsibility. Although he carries no responsibility and authority for schedule making of this type, the music director must be familiar with its limitations and development, in case he is called upon to work in a system where it is in use.

MODERN SCHEDULE   The modern schedule in practice reflects a newer educational philosophy than does the conventional. Instead of the emphasis being placed upon acquisition of facts and skills contained in prescribed bodies of knowledge, the modern schedule provides an organization of time in order that large, interrelated areas of interest may be explored. It makes possible teacher-pupil planning and the development of a pupil-centered curriculum. It provides a setting in which pupils and teachers may organize their own sequences of work, channel their efforts into areas of concern to the pupils at the moment, and draw upon the full resources of the school and community. The modern schedule furnishes an organization of the school day and week that makes possible full employment of democratic principles and practices in the classroom. A school that believes that children grow and develop best when given freedom, under guidance, to practice democracy in their daily living, to explore their interests as they develop, and to reach out continually for new experiences, must of necessity operate under a less rigid time organization than that of the conventional schedule.

The modern schedule frees large blocks of time, often a full half day or more, in which teacher and pupils have freedom to plan their own day's work and to develop the curriculum of greatest interest and value to the group. This can be done even though it may be necessary for certain special subjects such as music, art, and physical education, and many elective subjects, to use the conventional type of schedule—one teacher, with one group, for one period.

The principals of the various schools will be charged with the responsibility for building this type of schedule, just as they were with the conventional type. There will be this difference, however: principals will be much more likely to consult and seek the advice of the music educator when building the modern schedule than when building the conventional. The difference is that the modern schedule is based upon democratically conceived goals of education, and the conventional upon authoritarian.

FLEXIBLE SCHEDULE   Because of the heavy pressures and demands made upon the schools by our society, many new and often radical approaches to scheduling problems are being tried. The most recent of these and the most frequently discussed is that of the flexible schedule. In both the conventional and modern schedules discussed above, once a time organization is established it remains relatively rigid for a semester or school year. The characteristic difference between these types and the flexible schedule is that the latter does not necessarily remain static, but rather changes from week to week and often from day to day. Each day of the week need not be an exact replica of the previous one, nor is each weekly pattern necessarily the same.

The motivating principles of the flexible schedule are fundamentally the same as those behind the modern schedule, but the primary emphasis is upon the needs, interests, and abilities of the individual student. Generally speaking, larger single blocks of time are devoted to those subjects which can be approached efficiently through lecture and demonstration, often by mass teaching devices such as closed-circuit television. Smaller discussion groups are assembled to clinch and extend the learning begun in the lecture sessions. Ample time is provided during the school day for each student to engage in individual projects and self-directed study. A schedule of this type frequently makes possible longer, more frequent rehearsals of performance groups when special needs, such as an important concert, arise.

It is not the purpose of this discussion to give all the details of all the various types of flexible schedules. Rather it is intended to inform the music educator of the recent emphasis upon this approach to scheduling. One who is confronted with a scheduling problem can begin exploring this field with the suggested readings listed at the end of this chapter. A music educator in such a position would do well to study the literature on flexible scheduling and discuss its merits with his principal.

SUPERVISORY SCHEDULES   Rather than organizing time and resources for pupils' work and activities, under this heading we are seeking an organization that provides for an equitable distribution of the work of a specialist. The music director should be responsible for building the supervisory schedules for himself and any other music specialists serving in this capacity. Since the supervisor works in the various school units upon invitation of the principals in charge, the supervisory schedule should be worked out in cooperation with the principals of the buildings involved and have their full approval.

The supervisory schedule is superimposed upon the schedules of the schools in which the specialist works. If the unit in which the supervisory work is to be done operates on a conventional type of schedule, the supervisory program must be constructed along similar lines. A freer, less restricted type of school program, making use of large blocks of time, will necessitate a supervisory schedule that will conform to it and complement its purposes.

When a person has supervisory responsibilities in different school buildings on the same day, or in various parts of the same building, it is essential to provide time in his schedule for travelling from one building to another or from one part of the same building to another. All too frequently, music supervisors punish themselves and create bad relations with the teachers with whom they work by setting up a schedule of appointments and not allowing sufficient time for the movement they must make between supervisory visits. If a room teacher is expecting the supervisor to meet with her and her children at ten in the morning and the music specialist does not arrive until ten-fifteen or ten-twenty, the efficient planning and operation of the room is placed in jeopardy, and the teacher's temper becomes ruffled—not without cause.

SPECIAL SCHEDULES   Since much of the music schedule, except regular classes and rehearsals, is superimposed upon the regular schedule of the school, it frequently becomes necessary to devise special types of schedules to provide for the need of the pupils and the music program. This is particularly true of special fields of activity, such as instrumental instruction and group re-

Figure 19

ROTATING SCHEDULE

SCHEDULE A — FIRST WEEK

Period	Time	Monday	Tuesday	Wednesday	Thursday	Friday
Homeroom	7:40–7:55	Homeroom	Homeroom	Homeroom	Homeroom	Homeroom
I	8:00–8:50	BAND	Beginning strings	Advanced strings	Beginning strings	Advanced strings
II	8:55–9:45	Beginning woodwinds	BAND	Advanced woodwinds	Beginning woodwinds	Advanced woodwinds
Nutrition	9:50–10:05	Nutrition	Nutrition	Nutrition	Nutrition	Nutrition
III	10:10–11:00	Beginning brass	Advanced brass	BAND	Beginning brass	Advanced brass
IV	11:05–11:55	Orchestra	Orchestra	Orchestra	BAND	Orchestra
Lunch	12:00–12:30	Lunch	Lunch	Lunch	Lunch	Lunch
V	12:35–1:25	Percussion	Free	Percussion	Free	BAND
VI	1:30–2:20	Beginning orchestra	Beginning orchestra	Beginning orchestra	Beginning orchestra	Beginning orchestra
Homeroom	2:25–2:40	Homeroom	Homeroom	Homeroom	Homeroom	Homeroom

hearsals, both large and small, in which pupils from several classrooms and several grade levels participate at one time.

The *rotating schedule* has been found to be a very practical solution to this problem. It is the type of program in which the class or rehearsal meets at a different time on succeeding days or weeks. In order for it to function properly, it must be carefully planned and thoroughly understood by all persons affected by it.

For example, let us suppose we are interested in scheduling the band rehearsal one period each day on a rotating basis. On the first week of the schedule, band could meet the first period on Monday, the second on Tuesday, the third on Wednesday, the fourth on Thursday, and the fifth on Friday. (See Figure 19.) The following week it could meet the first period on Tuesday, second on Wednesday, third on Thursday, fourth on Friday, and the fifth on Monday. (See Figure 20.) A similar rotation would occur the following three weeks until band had rehearsed each day of the week during all five periods. The sixth week of school would follow the same schedule as the first

Figure 20

ROTATING SCHEDULE

SCHEDULE B — SECOND WEEK

Period	*Time*	*Monday*	*Tuesday*	*Wednesday*	*Thursday*	*Friday*
Homeroom	7:40–7:55	Homeroom	Homeroom	Homeroom	Homeroom	Homeroom
I	8:00–8:50	Advanced strings	BAND	Advanced strings	Beginning strings	Advanced strings
II	8:55–9:45	Beginning woodwinds	Advanced woodwinds	BAND	Beginning woodwinds	Advanced woodwinds
Nutrition	9:50–10:05	Nutrition	Nutrition	Nutrition	Nutrition	Nutrition
III	10:10–11:00	Beginning brass	Advanced brass	Beginning brass	BAND	Advanced brass
IV	11:05–11:55	Orchestra	Orchestra	Orchestra	Orchestra	BAND
Lunch	12:00–12:30	Lunch	Lunch	Lunch	Lunch	Lunch
V	12:35–1:25	BAND	Free	Percussion	Free	Percussion
VI	1:30–2:20	Beginning orchestra	Beginning orchestra	Beginning orchestra	Beginning orchestra	Beginning orchestra
Homeroom	2:25–2:40	Homeroom	Homeroom	Homeroom	Homeroom	Homeroom

and continue through the rotation again. This rotation would continue thus throughout the entire school year.

In any given week, the band members would report to the rehearsal room for band rather than to the other classes to which they are assigned on the regular school schedule. Although pupils would of necessity miss one of their regularly scheduled classes each day, the fact that they would miss a different one each day would cause interference to their other work to be negligible. For example, if there were five periods needed to complete the rotation, they would miss any given class but once in six sessions if that class met five times each week. If a six- or seven-period rotation were used, they would be absent from each class even less frequently. Experience has shown that by this means the pupil gains an opportunity to participate in music activities without undue sacrifice to other work for which he is responsible.

Before such a schedule could be expected to operate efficiently and effectively, it would need to be clearly understood by administration, teachers, pupils, and parents. The experience of the writer has been that the pupils reach this understanding sooner than the other three groups.

It must be recognized that today some secondary schools operate on some form of rotating schedule for the school as a whole. In such cases, the same ends can be gained for music by operating music on a fixed schedule.

SHORT-TERM SCHEDULES   As the music educator does his work, he is frequently required to set up temporary, short-term schedules. This is particularly true when it becomes necessary to provide for special or extra rehearsals of performing groups. Usually they are provided for outside of the regular school day, or in activity or lunch periods. On other occasions, they may be held before school in the morning, after school in the afternoon or early evening, during vacation periods or week ends.

In preparing this type of schedule, it is equally important to work closely with the administrators of school units whose children are involved. All details must be cleared through them before the schedule is placed into operation. The same care must be used in its preparation as in any type of regular schedule covering a longer period of time. Since the special schedule is out of the ordinary, even greater care must be exercised in publicizing it and instructing those administrators, teachers, pupils, and parents affected by it.

YEARLY — The yearly schedule is usually referred to as the school calendar. It contains the date of the school's opening, the vacation periods, examination or testing periods, and school closing. All of the music program of the school must be built within this framework. The daily-weekly schedule provides for all curricular offerings, including rehearsals, for the large performing groups. However, since so much of the music department's work involves public performance, which must be prepared for over long periods of time and which uses the services of many pupils as well as the full resources of the school on occasion, it is necessary to plan a yearly schedule of events in order to avoid excessive concentration of activities in any one season of the year. This eliminates duplication of student effort and interests, spreads performance pressures more evenly throughout the entire school season, and makes possible the best use of the school-community resources and personnel, both pupil and staff. We shall consider this yearly calendar from four points of view—seasonal activities, general activities, special activities, and the extended school year.

SEASONAL ACTIVITIES   Many of the activities for which the music educator is responsible are seasonal in character—they confine themselves to certain periods of the school year and seldom occur elsewhere. The music educator considers the football shows the band stages, the Christmas concerts for the various vocal and instrumental groups, commencement programs, Memorial Day parades, and the competition festivals, as belonging to this category.

The wise music educator will schedule such dates early in the fall or, better yet, as much as a year in advance, if that is at all possible. These are more or less fixed, inflexible dates and need to be known before other general and special activities can be scheduled. By so doing, there is less likelihood of the intensive preparation periods overlapping to the detriment of all concerned.

GENERAL ACTIVITIES   Other activities, such as assembly programs, operettas, general concerts, and instrumental demonstrations, are not committed to any special day or season. They should be scheduled at times during the school year when seasonal activities are not pressing. In this way, it is possible to furnish more uniform motivation throughout the school year. It is also possible to avoid spurts of intense activity followed by lulls of unwholesome quiet, so that musical growth and development are more consistent.

SPECIAL ACTIVITIES   The music educator will expect and welcome opportunities for his performing groups and ensembles to appear before community organizations and their public meetings; service clubs will welcome his performers; frequently, church groups will request the music department of the school to furnish music for some public gathering. Even though these performances may involve only a few students in a small ensemble, they should be arranged as much as possible during the periods of relative quiet, as far as the yearly schedule of events is concerned.

A lull in performance activities is a good time to highlight the general music program of the school system. A display of notebooks and handwork might be scheduled. A concert version of an operetta; a varied program of folk songs, dances, and games; a field trip to a music store, youth concert, or church organ loft—each or all might be included in a schedule of special activities. It will serve to bring the general music program to the attention of the administration and community and, at the same time, make more real educational experiences for students.

All seasonal, general, and special activities should be placed on a large wall calendar so that locating activities can be done at a glance. Major events will demand a period of from four to six weeks of intensive preparation. Special activities should be kept at a minimum during these times.

EXTENDING SCHOOL YEAR   There has been a marked trend toward making greater use of the school's plant and facilities outside of the regular school day and year. In addition to adult education programs, many communities are extending the school year by the introduction of planned activities for their young people during the summer months. Many music departments have been doing this for a number of years, and the practice is becoming increasingly common.

The instrumental program has often been merged with the community band for the summer months, necessitating regular rehearsals and a regular schedule of concerts. Frequently, a daily program of instrumental instruction is carried on. Some communities provide such an activity as part of their summer recreational program; others, as a part of their summer high school. By whatever administrative device the school year is extended to include a summer program of music instruction and rehearsals, a schedule to organize the various activities must be constructed. The director of music will usually have a freer hand and bear more responsibility for such a schedule than he will during the regular school term.

Scheduling Process

As stated earlier in the chapter, complete competence in handling the scheduling process comes only after a great deal of experience in working with such problems; however, the new director of music needs some information and a pattern of action that will equip him with enough initial competence to build his first schedule. This section of the chapter is presented for that purpose. A series of steps that must be taken in order to construct a schedule will be presented and discussed. These steps will vary only slightly according to the type of schedule being developed. These variations will be discussed in their proper setting and sequence.

BASIC INFORMATION — There are certain facts that must be at hand before the schedule maker begins his work. It is extremely important that all of these facts be verified and accurate, because mistakes at this point will cause drastic errors at the later stages and will consume much wasted time in correcting them. Careful caution at the beginning of the process will make the later stages easier, and a better schedule will result.

LENGTH OF THE SCHOOL DAY   The exact times at which each school day begins and ends, as well as the lengths of periods or units of time into which the master schedule divides the school day, must be known. When the director of music works on a system-wide basis he must know the differences in opening and closing times between the various school units, if such differences exist. If the lengths of periods differ from school to school, he must also know that. When part of the music program is conducted outside of the regular school schedule, the music schedule maker must know the amount of such time available to him. In school systems transporting children to and from school, he must know the arrival and departure times for all busses. In other words, he must know the over-all schedule for the entire school system and for each separate school unit involved in his planning for the schedule.

FACILITIES AVAILABLE FOR USE   This music director who is about to prepare a schedule for his program must have exact information about all facilities available for his use. He must know the rooms, the auditoriums, practice rooms, and rehearsal rooms, that may be used in carrying out his plans. He must also know whether all special equipment is available in the right place, at the right time, and in sufficient quantity, in order to carry out his proposed program.

PERSONS INVOLVED   Accurate information must be obtained about the persons involved in the program being scheduled. The music director must know the number and needs of the pupils for whom the schedule is being constructed. If the schedule is for instrumental classes, he must know the number expecting to take violin and how many are beginners, how many in their second year, how many in their third year. He must know the number of teachers available to do the work. If some teachers are assigned other duties in addition to their music work, he must know the exact times of each day they are available for his program. He must also know the commitments of other teachers and staff members, pupils, parents, custodians, and clerks, if they are in any way involved with the schedule he is building for the music department. All of this information must be clearly in mind or recorded accurately.

CONSTANTS   The music-schedule maker must also know those aspects of the school environment or master schedule that are unalterable. This will include such items as the fixed homeroom periods, all-school assembly periods, or any other conditions that absolutely cannot be changed or altered, in order to provide time or facilities for the music program.

VARIABLES   The variable factors of the school environment must also be known to the schedule maker. If it is possible to shift the weekly school assembly from Tuesday to Thursday, that fact should be known. The dramatics class is scheduled in the auditorium on Friday, the last period, but if necessary it could be changed to Thursday, the same period. In other words, all of those factors appearing on the master schedule that can, if necessary, be shifted to accommodate other parts of the total school program should be known.

BUILDING THE SCHEDULE — The actual process of building the schedule should not begin until all of the above factors are known and recorded in a form that can be understood and used. The process to be used will be determined by the type of schedule being built. The various types of yearly schedules, since they are the simplest, will be discussed first.

It has already been suggested that yearly events be placed upon a large wall calendar. Many business houses will provide these for the school's use if they are asked to do so. The constant information should be recorded first: the opening date of school in the fall, the exact day and time when school is dismissed for the various holidays, the dates school resumes after the holidays, the examination periods, the dates of home and away football games, the senior play, and all other information of this sort. After this is done, tentative dates for the annual band concert, the spring festival, the all-state concerts, and other events, are recorded to be verified as the year progresses. Tentative dates should be recorded in pencil so they may be changed easily, but as soon as they are fixed they should be recorded in ink, signifying that they are fixed

Figure 21

WORK SHEET — MUSIC SCHEDULE

Period	Time	Monday Room 112	113	114	Tuesday Room 112	113	114	Wednesday Room 112	113	114	Thursday Room 112	113	114	Friday Room 112	113	114
Homeroom	7:40 7:55	Homeroom			Homeroom			Homeroom			Homeroom			Homeroom		
I	8:00 8:50															
II	8:55 9:45															
Nutrition	9:50 10:05	Nutrition			Nutrition			Nutrition			Nutrition			Nutrition		
III	10:10 11:00															
IV	11:05 11:55															
Lunch	12:00 12:30	Lunch			Lunch			Lunch			Lunch			Lunch		
V	12:35 1:25															
VI	1:30 2:20															
Homeroom	2:25 2:40	Homeroom			Homeroom			Homeroom			Homeroom			Homeroom		

149

and unalterable. In larger school systems, the music director should keep a yearly calendar showing all of the special music activities of all schools. Unless this is done, there is danger that he may find himself scheduled to attend two PTA meetings at opposite sides of the city on the same night!

Conventional, modern, flexible, supervisory, rotating, short-term, and summer schedules can be handled by similar processes and will therefore be discussed as a group. The problem is to put the variable factors of the schedule in relation to the fixed factors in such a way that the best educational ends may be served.

After all basic information has been gathered, a large cardboard or tack board is ruled off to make a large chart upon which to work. The days of the week, with the teachers involved and space available, are placed at the head of the vertical columns, while the time units into which each day is divided are placed on the left at the head of horizontal columns. When lines dividing these columns are extended the length and width of the chart, a checkerboard effect results. It is helpful to use a different color of ink or a heavier line to set apart the days of the week in the vertical columns and the major divisions of the school day, such as opening time, lunch dismissal, afternoon opening, and school closing. This makes it easier for the eye to fall quickly upon a particular block of time on any particular day, thereby increasing efficiency and accuracy. (See Figure 21.)

The basic information that is variable is placed on cards, preferably cut to the same size as the squares on the work sheet. The nature of this variable material will depend upon the type of schedule being constructed and the purposes it is to serve. Let us assume, for example, that a schedule for ABC Junior High School is being built. There are three full-time music teachers assigned to this building: Mr. Buzzie Lipps, a brass man who will direct the band; Mr. D. String, a violinist who will direct the orchestra and string ensemble; and Miss I. Singsweetly, who will handle the vocal groups. All will teach some general music classes. (See Figure 22.)

Figure 22

DESCRIPTION OF AVAILABLE TEACHERS

Mr. Buzzie Lipps	*Miss I. Singsweetly*	*Mr. D. String*
Instrumentalist	Vocalist	Violinist
Brass specialist	Choral groups	Wants orchestra and string ensemble
Prefers band	Wants some general music	Will take some general music
Will take general music		

The ABC Junior High School building has three rooms in which this work will be done; two general music classrooms and a rehearsal hall for the larger performance groups. (See Figure 23.)

Figure 23

DESCRIPTION OF AVAILABLE ROOMS

Room 112	*Room 113*	*Room 114 (rehearsal hall)*
Seats 35	Seats 35	Seats 90
Chairs: 35 tablet arm	Chairs: 35 tablet arm	Chairs: 90 straight
		Stepped floor: 3 levels
Equipment:	Equipment:	Equipment:
Piano 1	Piano 1	Piano 1
Phonograph 1	Phonograph 1	Phonograph 1
Projection screen 1	Projection screen 1	Projection screen 1
Projection table 1	Projection table 1	Projection table 1
Music stands 4	Music stands 10	Music stands 45

In all, twelve sections of general music, general chorus, beginning band, advanced band, string ensemble, orchestra, and concert choir, must be accommodated. (See Figure 24.) The school operates on a six-period day. Each period is fifty minutes in length, and five minutes is allowed for passing time between classes. There are two homeroom periods of fifteen minutes each and the usual lunch and nutrition periods.

With all of the fixed and variable information now assembled, the schedule maker is ready to begin the task of actual schedule making. With the worksheet before him and each class and organization described on separate cards cut to fit the vacant squares, the game of checkers begins. The result may look something like Figure 25.

Another example may prove helpful. This time let us assume that a supervisory schedule is being built for elementary schools whose general schedule is of the modern type. The principal of the building wants the music supervisor to meet in the classroom with each of his teachers once each week. He and his teachers expect that, of necessity, the supervisor must use a conventional schedule for his visits, even though the general schedule pattern of the school is flexible. There are some cadet teachers assigned to this school so that each room teacher is free to have a ten-minute conference with the music supervisor immediately following the classroom visit.

The length of the supervisory visit and the conference period that follows is known, so that exact time for beginning and ending each visit and its

Figure 24

DESCRIPTION OF CLASSES AND ORGANIZATIONS TO BE SCHEDULED

7A General music	*7A General music*	*7A General music*
Daily	Daily	Daily
35 pupils each section	35 pupils each section	35 pupils each section

7B General music	*7B General music*	*7B General music*
Daily	Daily	Daily
35 pupils each section	35 pupils each section	35 pupils each section

8A General music	*8A General music*	*8A General music*
3 days weekly	3 days weekly	3 days weekly
Alternate with Art 2 days	Alternate with Art 2 days	Alternate with Art 2 days
30 pupils each section	30 pupils each section	30 pupils each section

8B General music	*8B General music*	*8B General music*
2 days weekly	2 days weekly	2 days weekly
Alternate with Art 2 days	Alternate with Art 2 days	Alternate with Art 2 days
30 pupils each section	30 pupils each section	30 pupils each section

General chorus	*Beginning band*	*Band*
Daily	Daily	Daily
Unlimited number	Unlimited number	Unlimited number
	Prerequisite:	Prerequisite:
	instrument class or	beginning band or audi-
	audition by instructor	tion by instructor

String ensemble	*Orchestra*	*Concert choir*
Daily	Daily	Daily
Unlimited number	Unlimited number	Unlimited number
Prerequisite:	Prerequisite:	Prerequisite:
beginning string class	string ensemble or	audition by instructor
or audition by	audition by instructor	
instructor		

Figure 25

COMPLETED SCHEDULE — ABC JUNIOR HIGH SCHOOL

Period	Time	Monday			Tuesday			Wednesday			Thursday			Friday		
		Room			Room			Room			Room			Room		
		112	113	114	112	113	114	112	113	114	112	113	114	112	113	114
Homeroom	7:40 7:55	Homeroom			Homeroom			Homeroom			Homeroom			Homeroom		
I	8:00 8:50	7A	8A	Band	7A	8B	Band	7A	8A	Band	7A	8B	Band	7A	8A	Band
II	8:55 9:45	7B	7A	String ensemble	7B	7A	String ensemble	7B	7A	String ensemble	7B	7A	String ensemble	7B	7A	String ensemble
Nutrition	9:50 10:05	Nutrition			Nutrition			Nutrition			Nutrition			Nutrition		
III	10:10 11:00	7A	7B	General chorus	7A	7B	General chorus	7A	7B	General chorus	7A	7B	General chorus	7A	7B	General chorus
IV	11:05 11:55		8A	Orchestra		8B	Orchestra		8A	Orchestra		8B	Orchestra		8A	Orchestra
Lunch	12:00 12:30	Lunch			Lunch			Lunch			Lunch			Lunch		
V	12:35 1:25			Concert choir			Concert choir			Concert choir			Concert choir			Concert choir
VI	1:30 2:20	8A	7B	Beginning band	8B	7B	Beginning band	8A	7B	Beginning band	8B	7B	Beginning band	8A	7B	Beginning band
Homeroom	2:25 2:40	Homeroom			Homeroom			Homeroom			Homeroom			Homeroom		

conference is placed on the left side of the work sheet at the head of the several horizontal columns. It is also known that it will take one full day and half of another in order to visit all of the teachers in this particular building. (See Figure 26.)

Figure 26

SUPERVISORY SCHEDULE WORK SHEET

Time	Monday	Tuesday
9:15–9:45		
9:50–10:20		
10:25–10:55		
11:00–11:30		
11:35–11:50		
Lunch	Lunch	Lunch
1:15–1:45		
1:50–2:20		
2:25–2:55		
3:00–3:15		

With all of the basic information secured, the next step is to record the variable data on appropriate cards. The name of each teacher to be visited, the number of pupils in the room, the grade level he teaches, and any other necessary material, is placed on the cards cut to fit the open squares on the working schedule. (See Figure 27.) With these steps taken, it is possible now to fit each teacher into an appropriate time niche on the schedule. As this is being done, the director of music keeps in mind the location of each teacher's room in the building. He will schedule his supervisor (or himself, if he is doing the work) so that his movement from one room to another will be as efficient as possible. He will avoid, for instance, asking his supervisor to travel from a classroom at the south end of the first floor to another at the north end of the third floor. He will arrange the schedule so that no valuable time is lost in making excessively long moves between classrooms. (See Figure 28.)

The advantage of having the fixed portion of the schedule inked in on a large work sheet and the variable factors on cards is that it makes it easier to handle the variables without error; it is much faster and more accurate

Figure 27

SUPERVISORY SCHEDULE

TEACHERS AND CLASSES TO BE VISITED

Grade 1

35 pupils

No piano

Phonograph available, 30 copies *Sol-Fa Music Series* available

Teacher: Miss Flat, does not sing well

Grade 2

34 pupils

Small piano

Phonograph available, 31 copies *Sol-Fa Music Series* available

Teacher: Helen B. Sharp, does a great deal with music

Grade 3

36 pupils

No piano

Phonograph available, 35 copies *Sol-Fa Music Series* available

Teacher: Mr. Aiken Bones, ex-football player who thinks music is a waste of time

Grade 4

32 pupils

No piano

Phonograph available, 31 copies *Sol-Fa Music available*

Teacher: Miss Bea Quiet, has charge of school library and cannot be visited before 10 A.M.

Figure 28

SUPERVISORY SCHEDULE

FICTITIOUS ELEMENTARY SCHOOL

Time	Monday	Tuesday
9:15–9:45	Third grade (1)	First grade (1)
9:50–10:20	Third grade (2)	First grade (2)
10:25–10:55	Fourth grade (1)	Second grade (1)
11:00–11:30	Fourth grade (2)	Second grade (2)
11:35–11:50	Principal	Principal
Lunch	Lunch	Lunch
1:15–1:45	Fifth grade (1)	
1:50–2:20	Fifth grade (2)	
2:25–2:55	Sixth grade	
3:00–3:10	Principal	

Given time is beginning time in each room. Thirty minutes is to be devoted to demonstration lesson, observation, or conference. Five minutes is allowed for traveling to, and beginning work in, next room at the proper time.

than the pencil and eraser method. Undoubtedly there will be some shifting of the variables until the best possible schedule has been made. The cards make it easier to do so without "losing" a teacher.

The process for making a rotating type of schedule is the same. In some ways, it is easier to make than other types because conflicts are ignored. That is, its very operation depends upon administrative approval and staff cooperation for permitting pupils to miss classes on the regular schedule, when they conflict with the rotation of the music classes.

There is one further step in completing the rotation schedule. After it has been worked out by the same method described above and it has been checked for errors and omissions, it is necessary to work out the entire cycle of rotation and publicize it with the dates of the specific school weeks during which each schedule is to be operating. For example, a six-period rotation would demand six complete schedules in order to show each class or rehearsal in its six possible positions. Each schedule could be named or numbered, and a brief study of the school calendar will make it possible to indicate the exact weeks in which each will function. (See Figure 29.)

Figure 29

SYSTEM OF SCHEDULE ROTATION

FALL SEMESTER

Week of	Schedule	Week of	Schedule
September 16, 19—*	A	December 2, 19—	F
September 23, 19—	B	December 9, 19—	A
September 30, 19—	C	December 16, 19—	B
October 7, 19—	D	December 23, 19—	Vacation
October 14, 19—	E	December 30, 19—	Vacation
October 21, 19—	F	January 6, 19—	C
October 28, 19—	A	January 13, 19—	D
November 4, 19—	B	January 20, 19—	E
November 12, 19—	C	January 27, 19—	F
November 18, 19—	D	February 3, 19—	A
November 25, 19—	E		

* The date designated is the first school day in the week.

EXPLAINING AND PUBLICIZING — It is always wise to publicize and explain any schedule before it is placed in operation. This is particularly true of a schedule that differs from the master or basic time pattern of the school. It is essential that all concerned with it, administration, teachers, custodians, clerks, pupils, and parents, clearly understand it and its purpose and functions. This necessitates a program of explanation and information that can best be done in a setting where questions may be asked and answered, and where a full critical discussion may be had.

The principals of the buildings affected by the schedule can offer valuable assistance in spotting conflicts and inconsistencies in the proposed schedule. Even though their help may not be needed, it is absolutely necessary for them to understand the schedule and approve it before it is publicized and put into operation.

Certain easily understood schedules may be mimeographed or duplicated and circulated in tentative form to test the reaction of the persons affected by them. This should be done well in advance of the time when the schedule is to be placed in operation, in order to allow sufficient time for study, questions, and possible revision in the light of suggested improvement.

PLACING IN OPERATION — After all of the previous steps have been taken and the schedule is as satisfactory as it can be made, the date upon which it is to go into effect is announced. Often this date coincides with the opening day of school, in which case the entire process must have taken place prior to that date, possibly the spring before, or during the summer months.

Frequently, special music schedules do not go into operation until two or three weeks after the opening of school. When this is the case, the director of music must be absolutely certain that the starting date is clearly publicized and understood.

Supervisory schedules involving service to several schools on a bi-weekly or tri-weekly basis also need to be clearly publicized, worked out in detail, duplicated, and sent to all teachers affected. In every instance, the administration must be fully informed. Any schedule that is to operate smoothly must be clear in every detail with nothing left to doubt.

By carefully following the various stages of the scheduling process just discussed, the beginning music director can expect to build a schedule that is workable, efficient, and effective in meeting the educational needs of the children of his school system.

Summary

The music director's responsibilities for scheduling are partly advisory and partly operational. In his position as musical leader for his school and community, he must be familiar with the processes by which schedules are built and with the factors that influence the decisions that must be made in constructing them. This is necessary in order for him to advise properly those who are responsible for the creation of the school's master schedule. As administrative head of his department, he must be able to develop the type of schedules that place the right people with the right facilities in the best possible relationships for the musical growth of his school and community. This chapter has explained what is meant by a schedule, discussed the various types of schedules with which the music director must be familiar, and presented a sequence of activities that leads to the construction of a successful schedule.

Suggested Activities

1. Visit a nearby junior high school and study its master schedule. Try to determine whether it has been built by the conventional approach or with flexibility in mind. Are the music classes and performance groups scheduled advantageously? What portions of the schedule are constants? Which are variables?

2. Obtain the schedule of a music supervisor from a nearby school. Does it contain planned conference periods with each teacher being supervised? Is time planned for travel from school to school? For moving from room to room?

3. Recall the schedule in use when you attended high school and evaluate it on the basis of the principles of proper scheduling set forth in this chapter.

4. Ask the director of the choir, band, or orchestra in which you are now performing if you may make out, under his guidance, a short-term schedule for some special concert, tour, or program for which extra rehearsals are necessary.

For Further Reading

Bush, Robert N., and Allen, Dwight W. "Flexible Scheduling." *The Bulletin,* National Association of Secondary School Principals, 47, No. 283:73–98, May, 1963.

_____. "Flexible Scheduling for What?" *Journal of Secondary Education,* 36:346–353, October, 1961.

Ellis, U. Berkley, and Dick, Stanley B. "Scheduling the Practical and the Fine Arts in the Large Junior High School." *The Bulletin,* National Association of Secondary School Principals, 46, No. 273:36–41, April, 1962.

Hills, Arthur C. "A New Schedule for a New School." *Musical Educators Journal,* 48, No. 5:50–52, April-May, 1962.

Music Educators National Conference. *Music Curriculum in Secondary Schools.* Washington, D.C., The Conference, 1959. Pages 19–21 and 104–108.

National Association of Secondary School Principals. *Focus on Change.* Chicago, Rand McNally & Co., 1961.

Trump, J. Lloyd. "Flexible Scheduling, Fad or Fundamental?" *Phi Delta Kappan,* 44, No. 8:367–371, May, 1963.

_____. "Developing and Evaluating a Class Schedule To Help Each Pupil To Learn Better." *Journal of Secondary Education,* 36:338–345, October, 1961.

CHAPTER 7

Equipment, Materials,
and Supplies

A GREAT DEAL of physical paraphernalia is needed in our schools today in order to bring the learning processes to complete fruition. Many years ago, the teacher was the chief educational resource of the school, and little more was needed than a few books, a slate, and a place in which to work. As the curriculum has broadened, particularly in recent years, there has been increased demand and need for more and more equipment, materials, and supplies with which to provide children the learning experiences expected by the school and community. The type of activities and experiences a school plans for its children will govern the type and amount of paraphernalia necessary for carrying out its program. Science has its special needs, industrial arts has its particular requirements, and certainly music has its unique essentials. This chapter will deal with these essentials, their accountability, their procurement, their storage, their service and repair, and their useful life and replacement.

Types of Physical Paraphernalia

In order to make the following discussion clear, it will be necessary to define and categorize the paraphernalia of the music department in terms of their use and the length of their useful life.

PERMANENT — There are certain things used in the music department that have a period of usefulness extending over many years. This group includes such items as band and orchestral instruments, pianos, band uniforms, choir robes, tape recorders, and phonographs. Chairs, risers, blackboards, and similar items, are considered part of the building equipment, although used by one department almost entirely. For the purposes of this book, those permanent

items that are portable and used exclusively, or nearly so, by the music department will be referred to as *equipment.*

SEMI-PERMANENT — Basic music books, band music, orchestra music, choral
music, records, films—those things that have a relatively shorter life than
equipment, but which may be used more than once before their usefulness is
ended—will be referred to as *material.*

EXPENDABLE — Those items whose serviceable life is exhausted after using
once, such as chalk, staff paper, mending tape, will be referred to as *supplies.*

Purchasing

The administrator of the music program has a substantial amount of responsibility for purchasing, or making decisions leading to the purchase of, equipment, materials, and supplies. Even though curriculum development and the
study of needed resources for its activities has, properly, been the process of
group action, the final decision is often the responsibility of the music director.
The decisions, whether group or individual, must always be based upon the
educational objectives of the school, the best procedures for carrying them
out, and the necessary equipment, materials, and supplies for reaching them.

ESTABLISHING NEED — No administrator is justified in spending public money
unless it is absolutely necessary in order to achieve the educational goals the
community has set for its schools. The essential needs for the achievement of
these goals must be determined by a process of thorough study. Such a study
will demand the cooperative effort of school staff, both professional and non-
professional, parents, and pupils.

The first step to be taken is the establishment of the minimum needs for
the department, those things that are absolutely essential for maintaining the
music program without retrogression or falling short of objectives. In times
of depression or when, for other reasons, a curtailment of the school budget
is required, it may be necessary to be content merely with maintaining the
status quo.

In better times, music educators, as well as all other educators, must
think in terms of desirable facilities and accoutrements for moving beyond

the *status quo* and for leading toward the improvement of education, society, and democracy. The latter point of view considers desirable goals and assumes educational leadership in the area of purchasing needed equipment, materials, and supplies, for the fulfillment of these desired ends. This is one of the primary functions of educational administration as discussed Chapter 1. Such an obligation cannot be ignored if the music director is to serve his school and community properly.

It is important to develop a sense of timing in establishing the urgency for the purchase. It is also important to seek to determine how far beyond the present status of music education the community is willing to move and how much it will support with its interest and money. No rule of thumb can be given for building such insights, but as the music director works with his staff, his pupils, and his community, and as he keeps his finger on the pulse of public thinking and action, he grows in his ability to understand the direction in which his community wants to move and its willingness to support its schools and their program of music.

By establishing minimum essentials and determining the desired requirements for a forward looking program, the music director is furnished with the only proper basis for making decisions. No purchases should be made unless such needs are clearly and definitely established.

CRITERIA — The music director should follow some criteria in deciding which articles to buy. With so many manufacturers providing products for the school market, it becomes his responsibility to select the best ones for use in his school. Eight criteria will be offered to assist him in choosing from the multitude of articles on the market those that will be best for his particular school.

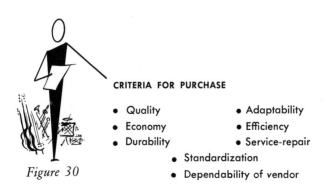

CRITERIA FOR PURCHASE

- Quality
- Economy
- Durability
- Adaptability
- Efficiency
- Service-repair
- Standardization
- Dependability of vendor

Figure 30

QUALITY   The prudent administrator will seek to receive the most value from each school dollar spent. This value must be determined in terms of the item or items in question. If all other factors are the same in a group of products from which a selection is to be made, the educational worth of the article must be the deciding factor. The one that will do the greatest good for the educational program and the children of the community is the one that will have the greatest value and be of the highest quality. Public money should never be spent for articles of inferior quality or of inferior educational worth.

ECONOMY   It is doubtful whether any music department has unlimited money to spend; certainly most departments want far more than they have. One way to stretch each dollar is to be certain that, all other things being equal, each item purchased is obtained at the lowest possible price. A word of caution is necessary, however; the cheapest item is not necessarily the most economical when all other factors are taken into consideration. It must be remembered that economy is but one of eight criteria that must be taken into consideration when decisions are made. The music educator should seek to supply the requirements of his department with the greatest economy, when it is possible to satisfy the other criteria as well.

ADAPTABILITY   An article must be adaptable to the educational goals of the music department as it serves the school and community. Rather than being usable in performing one task only, it should be serviceable in a variety of ways, all of which will further progress toward educational goals. Such questions as the following must be raised and answered about each item to be purchased. Does the French horn being considered possess those qualities that will make it useful in both the band and the orchestra? Will it be useful in small ensembles? Will the music for the a cappella choir serve for the spring concert as well as the festival to be held at a later date? Will the tape recorder be as useful in the vocal program as in the instrumental? How will it adapt to the classroom? With most music departments short of equipment and materials for reaching even the minimum requirements, it is unwise to spend money for items that cannot be adapted to a variety of uses.

DURABILITY   Is the useful life of the contemplated equipment or material long? Will it stand up and continue to serve educational goals effectively even though used continously and hard? Will it last longer than a similar item being considered? Any article a music director purchases for his school must have lasting qualities and remain useful throughout its active life.

EFFICIENCY   Any item of equipment or material or supply must be able to do its expected task better and faster than any other. Will its proper use speed up the attainment of educational goals? Will it do so without loss of time or motion? The results it produces must be better than those of any other such item. It must be efficient in doing the job it is expected to do.

SERVICE AND REPAIR   Even though the equipment, materials, or supplies, to be purchased prove themselves to be durable and efficient, there will be times when most of them will demand service and repair during their useful life. In order for an article to stand high under this criterion, it must be possible to secure such service and repair quickly, reasonably, and economically. After service and repair, will the item function as efficiently as when new? Is it so constructed that repairs can be easily and economically done? Will it be expensive in terms of time and money to keep in active use? If it is not easy to service and repair, any item should be put aside in favor of another that meets these requirements.

DEPENDABILITY AND HONESTY OF THE SELLER   The consummation of any business transaction depends upon faith, trust, and confidence. All other things being equal, the businessman with high business and moral integrity should be favored when purchasing equipment, materials, and supplies, for the music department.

There are many unscrupulous business practices and many unscrupulous businessmen. This is by no means an indictment of the commercial world as a whole, nor does it imply that such practices are confined only to business; it is intended only as a statement of fact and as a word of caution to music educators responsible for spending the public's money wisely.

The music director will more probably receive full value for the money he spends and thus serve his school and community better when he buys from a firm known to be honest and reliable. Such a concern is much more likely to stand behind its goods and business promises and much more likely to give the type of service the music administrator desires. The prudent music educator cannot afford the risks involved in doing business with a person or a firm that is even suspected of being undependable and dishonest.

STANDARDIZATION   In larger school systems, particularly, it is often advantageous to effect some standardization. Such a practice will usually lead to better prices when supplies are ordered in quantity, thereby stretching the value of each dollar. Standardization will also make it possible to move equipment, materials, and supplies, from school to school and have them function as efficiently and effectively in all music situations. It will also make their service and repair easier and more economical.

The quality of educational excellence, the economy, the adaptability, the durability, the efficiency, the ease of service and repair, the dependability and honesty of the seller, and the standardization of the item, serve as guides in helping the music administrator make the best decisions when purchasing for his schools. Without such criteria for judging the value of the product under consideration, the music director may be guilty of spending money foolishly.

ETHICS — A word about the music educator's personal and professional code of ethics is in order. Any member of the education profession is a public servant. Since the schools are an agency of our society, operated for the welfare of the entire community and supported by public taxation, all who work for this organization and receive their compensation from public funds must not be guilty of using their position for private gain or otherwise securing advantage for themselves.

There are those business firms that will solicit business for themselves by insidious forms of bribery. This malpractice takes many forms and is often carefully shielded, but it is bribery nonetheless. The percentage "kickbacks" on instrument purchases, the expensive "gifts" at Christmas or other times of the year, are but two of the more common forms of this evil. The music educator is perhaps in a more vulnerable spot for this type of temptation than workers in other areas of the school's employ. He must not permit himself to fall into such a trap. More than a few otherwise competent school musicians have been discharged from their positions, when this type of dishonesty became known to the school authorities and communities. Often these persons have been unable to find re-employment in the profession and have been forced to earn their livelihood in other types of work.

Just as serious a moral and ethical error is committed when the music educator accepts a "commission" from a dealer who supplies individuals of the community with music equipment—instruments, for example. Some persons attempt to justify this practice on the grounds that public funds are not involved. A public employee who uses his office to secure private gain is just as guilty of bribery or malpractice when private monies are used as he would be if public funds were involved. The school musician who accepts these "commissions" is indulging in a vicious practice because his act is keeping the cost of such equipment high, thereby denying the children of his community the best equipment at the lowest possible price.

Still another practice that is contrary to a desirable ethical code is that of using one's position to build up a large number of students for private instruction. The writer is not condemning the music educator for attempting to teach his specialty on a private fee basis during those hours when he is free of responsibility to his position at school. What he is condemning with all possible vigor is the exclusion from school music activities of those who do not study privately with him. He is also condemning the practice of accepting so much private instruction outside of school hours that his effectiveness and efficiency on the job is impaired. Believe it or not, these things do happen. These types of behavior are unethical and a misuse of one's position for private gain.

The National Education Association, of which the music educator is a part through his affiliation with the Music Educators National Conference, in its *Code of Ethics* makes a clear statement on the above practices in its Fourth Principle. "Members of the teaching profession have inescapable obligations with respect to employment" and in fulfilling these obligations will "accept no compensation from producers of instructional supplies when one's recommendations affect the local purchase or use of teaching aids." Also, the music educator will "engage in no gainful employment *outside of his* contract, where the employment affects adversely his professional status or impairs his standing with students, associates, and the community." [1]

The music educator who is motivated by a desirable code of ethics will also hold sacred those published materials protected by the copyright law. The laws of our country have clearly established that the works of one's mind are as much his property as his house, his automobile, and other personal property. The music educator who copies, or causes to be copied, works protected by a valid copyright is as guilty of thievery as the person who steals another's wallet or automobile. Using such illicit material for educational purposes is no more excusable than the unauthorized use of a fellow townsman's car to transport musicians to a concert or festival.

BUSINESS PRACTICES — All schools, in their purchasing of equipment, materials, and supplies, will follow some pattern of established business practice. The nature of this practice, the processes by which it is carried out, the provisions for protecting the public's money, the means for protecting each individual from suspicion, will be established by the board of education and

---

[1] National Education Association, *NEA Handbook*, Washington, D.C., The Association, 1958–59, pp. 62–63. Used by permission.

the superintendent of schools. The director of music, as he accomplishes his tasks, must become familiar with the patterns of the business operation of the school system in which he is working. In his best interests and the best interests of the community he serves, he must conduct the business affairs of his department in a way that adds to the good name of the school as a whole.

There should be checks and balances operating that will make it impossible for a school administrator to use any public money, or his public position, for private gain. Ordering will be done by requisition, invoices will be expected from all suppliers, bills will be paid by check; only in this way can proper audits and adequate accounting of the expenditure of public funds be made. The music director must at all times remember that he is responsible for the spending of public money; he is in a position of public trust and, because of this, must exercise extreme care in seeing that all funds are spent wisely and are strictly accounted for.

Large school systems may have a business office charged with the responsibility for conducting all business affairs of the school. Where this is the case, there will undoubtedly be a purchasing department, or at least a purchasing agent, and the music director must do all purchasing for his department through this office. Smaller systems will handle all business matters through the superintendent's office. The music director must know, understand, and follow, the purchasing practices in the school system that employs him.

Some school systems may require music directors to supply specifications for the equipment, materials, or supplies, needed for their departments so that bids may be secured from several firms in order to secure the best possible price. In this case, the music director must prepare such specifications well in advance of the date the equipment is desired so that sufficient time is allowed for the necessary advertising, receiving of bids, and resulting purchase. This must be done so that all firms may have an equal opportunity for bidding, and the price most favorable to the school obtained. Smaller systems may not require bids, but certainly shopping around in order to satisfy all criteria is the ethical responsibility of the music director.

In writing specifications for any equipment it is extremely important to be complete, accurate, and clear in all details. The following points, at least, should be covered in all specifications:

1. Design
   a. Mechanism
   b. Dependability
   c. Ease of maintenance
   d. Unique features

2. Construction
   a. Materials used, including seasoning, durability, acoustical properties, finish, and so forth
   b. Manufacturing details
3. Musical characteristics
   a. Tone
   b. Ease of playing
   c. Evenness of scale
   d. Intonation
4. Accessories to be included
5. New or used merchandise
6. Inspection privileges
7. Delivery date
8. Guarantee period

Quite frequently, a musician finds the writing of detailed specifications an irksome task; it is tedious to say the least. The task becomes less irksome and tedious when one realizes that, by exercising careful diligence in writing precise specifications, he is assuring himself, his department, and the children he serves, the best possible equipment for the money he has to spend. Without such specifications, it is possible for the unscrupulous vendor to include inferior items when filling the order.

When such specifications must be submitted through a purchasing agent of the school's business office, great care must be taken to write them in language that is meaningful to the layman, the nonmusician. One of the difficult tasks of the music educator is the communication of musical values to the non-musician. The writer was confronted with just such a problem recently when some pianos were to be purchased for his school. An inferior grand piano, both musically and mechanically, was judged (by the purchasing agent) to be the equal of one of the acknowledged leaders in the field. The business agent saw the three legs, the eighty-eight keys, the exterior dimension, and the difference of $300, and decided to save the money because the pianos were the same. It was with extreme difficulty that the business agent (a non-musician) was brought to understand the difference, musically, between the inferior instrument and the acceptable one. Out of this experience was developed the discussion, "Some Basic Concepts for Judging Piano Quality," contained in Appendix B, page 263.

The music director must not permit himself to become irked at the red tape of the established business practices in his school system. When it is understood that this so-called red tape is necessary for his own protection, it can be more easily tolerated. Anyone responsible for the spending of public funds is open to suspicion, and the prudent administrator sees to it that all business matters are conducted in such a way that any suspicion is groundless.

Receiving

The music educator's responsibilities for following sound business practices do not end with careful selection and purchasing; in fact, this is only a beginning. The next step in the process is taken when the goods have been delivered to the school. Usually all such deliveries are made in one central office. It may be the superintendent's office, the principal's office, or a central receiving office associated with the purchasing department.

As soon as shipments arrive, they must be carefully checked. Each article should be unpacked with care and examined for possible damage; all items must be counted in order to be sure the full order for which the school has been billed has been received. The invoice or packing slip that accompanied the shipment should be compared with the original order or requisition to determine whether a full or partial order has been shipped. In other words, all shipments should be checked to make certain that all goods are definitely in good condition when received, in proper quantity, and conform to the specifications of the order.

The music director will have varying responsibilities for the goods after their arrival, depending upon the pattern of practice in the particular school system in which he works. A large system may have a receiving clerk who does this work for all departments of the school; a small system may require that the music director himself do the job. No matter who does the work, it is the music director's responsibility to see that all items ordered are received and that they have arrived in good condition. He may be able, in time, to train someone else to do the job, but he is still responsible for seeing that it is done properly. This is another step in safeguarding public money and its proper expenditure.

As soon as goods are checked and found acceptable, they should be clearly identified as the property of the school. Books and music will be marked with the school stamp and full descriptive information recorded on proper forms (which will be discussed later); then they will be assigned and delivered to the proper building, teacher, or activity. Uniforms, choir robes, orchestra jackets, and other items, will be marked, recorded, and either stored properly or assigned to the individual pupils who will use and care for them. Serial numbers and all other information for keeping accurate accounting will be recorded for instruments, phonographs, and tape recorders. Supplies will be accurately counted, sent to a storage room where they will be protected against damage or deterioration, and where proper checks and balances can be put into operation to assure their economical use.

Accounting

Good business practice demands that a strict, accurate accounting of all equipment, materials, and supplies, assigned to the music education department to be kept. This is not a useless chore, but another means of protecting a public investment. It also furnishes much valuable information for building future budgets. Since each category differs from the others, accounting practices for equipment will be discussed first, followed by those for materials and supplies.

EQUIPMENT — A record should be kept of all school-owned equipment. Appropriate forms for this information can be obtained from music supply houses or instrument companies; however, it is the writer's belief that it is a better practice for each school to develop its own form—the one that best suits its own needs. The school's duplicating department or print shop can reproduce these forms in sufficient quantity at a minimum cost. Standard 4x6 or 5x8 cards should be used so that file drawers may be used to keep the information protected and readily available. A little experimentation will determine the best size to use, and thereafter it should be consistently followed. It is extremely difficult to develop an efficient file of records when the card size used is not the same for all items. The card should be sufficiently large to record all descriptive information about the piece of equipment, a cumulative repair record, and the individual room or organization to which it has been assigned. (See Figure 31.)

BAND AND ORCHESTRA INSTRUMENTS The form for all school-owned band and orchestra instruments should provide space for recording the name, make, and manufacturer; the serial number; the date, price, and dealer from whom purchased; and a list of accessories included. It should allow for a record of the person to whom assigned, with the date, condition, and date of return. The repair record, kept on the same form, should also show the nature of the repair, the date, and the cost. All of this information is vital for the annual inventory and future budgets.

When a school-owned instrument is loaned or rented to an individual, a contract stating in detail the conditions of the loan, the date it is to be

Figure 31

EQUIPMENT RECORD CARD

(*Front*)

CALIFORNIA STATE COLLEGE
at Los Angeles
Music Department   Equipment Record
Item_____Serial No._____State Tag_____
Manufacturer_____Vendor _____
Purchase Date _____Purchase Price _____
Accessories:

USE RECORD

Date	Location	Use

(*Back*)

SERVICE RECORD

Date	Work done	By whom	Cost

returned, the condition of the instrument, and its value at the time it was assigned, should be executed. (See Figure 32.) This contract should be signed by the pupil, his parents, and the music director, *before* the instrument leaves the school.

Figure 32

INSTRUMENT LOAN CONTRACT

ALLEBREVE PUBLIC SCHOOL

Music Department

INSTRUMENT LOAN CONTRACT

I, _____, accept full responsibility for _____ _____, serial number _____. I will return it for inspection promptly when called for and return it on or before _____. I understand that the approximate value of the instrument at the time loaned to me is $_____.

I agree to keep the instrument in sound playing condition and pay for any repairs made necessary by my misuse, negligence, or carelessness. I further agree to use this instrument for school or private functions only and will never use it for performances for which I am paid.

Date: _____

_____
Student

_____
Parent

_____
Music Director

The adoption of such practices will avoid a condition that confronted the writer several years ago. He started a job in a school system that had not kept any record of the instruments owned. When the principal was asked about the number and kinds of such equipment, he said, "I don't know exactly. The school does own quite a few, but what they are, how many there are, and who has them now, I really don't know." After frantic pleas in homerooms, school assemblies, and on bulletin boards, the writer began to get an idea of the nature and amount of equipment owned by the school. About Christmas time, a rather sheepish student came to his office saying,

"Here is a school oboe. I've had it since last year sometime and no longer wish to play it. I have just forgotten to bring it in." Until that moment the writer had not known that the school owned such an instrument!

PIANOS   The accounting forms for school-owned pianos will record the make, manufacturer, serial number, style, purchase date, price, and the dealer from whom bought. In addition, they will show the school and room in which located, and the date, nature, and cost of all tunings and repairs. (See Figure 33.)

ELECTRONIC EQUIPMENT   Radios, record players, and tape recorders, will be properly accounted for on forms showing information similar to instruments and pianos and containing space for any items that are unique to such equipment.

Figure 33

PIANO RECORD CARD

(Front)

CALIFORNIA STATE COLLEGE at Los Angeles		
Music Department		Equipment Record
Make _____ Model _____ Serial No. _____ State Tag _____		
Manufacturer _____ Date Purchased _____ Price _____		
Vendor _____ Accessories _____		
USE RECORD		
Date	Location	Use

(Back)

TUNING AND SERVICE RECORD			
Date	Work Done	By Whom	Cost

UNIFORMS AND ROBES   Since equipment of this sort does not normally come stamped with a serial number or some such distinguishing characteristic, it will be necessary to assign each article a particular number so that it may be identified quickly and easily. When two or more pieces make up the complete robe or uniform, each one should be given the same identifying mark. The details of purchase, cleaning, repair, and assignment, should be made a matter of record as with any other form of equipment. (See Figure 34.)

MISCELLANEOUS EQUIPMENT   Music stands, risers, autoharps, bar bells, and all other items of equipment in the music department, should be accounted for, and a proper form containing all necessary and useful information placed on file in the office of the music director.

In larger school systems, where the director of music is a member of the central office staff, it may be necessary to have these forms filled out in duplicate. The director of music should have a complete and accurate record of all the equipment in the music department of the entire school system, and the teacher in each separate unit should have a complete record on file in his office. It is by keeping such records that the music director will be able to know with certainty the cost, amount, and condition, of all equipment for which he is responsible. He is able to know those items that are expensive to maintain and should therefore be replaced. He is able to know the location of any piece of equipment by referring to his files. He is able to take better care of all of the equipment in which the community has invested its money.

Figure 34

ROBE AND UNIFORM RECORD CARD

(Front)

CALIFORNIA STATE COLLEGE

at Los Angeles

Music Department   Robe and Uniform Record

Item _____ Identifying Number _____

Manufacturer _____ Price _____

Vendor _____ Date _____

Description: Size _____ Length _____ Color _____

Material _____

USE RECORD

Date	Location and/or User

(Back)

SERVICE RECORD

Date	Work Done	By Whom	Cost

MATERIALS — Accurate records should also be kept for each item of published music in the department. For this work, it is desirable to develop forms for recording the information most useful to the particular school system in which the music director is employed. Such forms should show the title, author or composer, publisher, publication number, copyright date, date of purchase, cost per item, and the dealer from whom purchased. It is also helpful to have information about an item's possible uses—elementary, junior high school, beginning band, girls' trio—as well as the school or group to which it has been assigned. The information should be so complete and accurate that the music director can tell in a matter of minutes the exact location of each item of material and the amount in usable condition. (See Figure 35.)

All items of material should bear the school stamp or some other identifying characteristic and be provided with a code or serial number, so that each piece of choral octavo music, or each march book, can be clearly and promptly

Figure 35

MATERIAL RECORD CARD

(*Front*)

CALIFORNIA STATE COLLEGE		
Music Department	at Los Angeles	Material Record
Author or Composer _____College No. _____		
Title _____Publication No. _____		
Publisher _____Copyright _____		
	Purchase	Unit
Vendor _____Date _____Cost _____		
No. of Copies _____Description _____		

USE RECORD		
Date	Location	Use

(Back)

USE RECORD (Continued)		
Date	Location	Use

SERVICE RECORD			
Date	Work Done	By Whom	Cost

identified. This information is extremely useful when conducting the annual inventory, which will be discussed later.

Strict accounting, as well as proper care in purchasing, storing, and handling music materials, can save many dollars on the annual cost of operating a music department. The music director is responsible for assuming this leadership.

SUPPLIES — It is quite possible that music supplies, especially those used in elementary school classrooms and general music classes, will be kept in the principal's general supply room. In such circumstances, the principal and his staff are more likely to keep an accounting of them, issue them in accordance with their general supply policies, and consult with the music director when ordering is necessary. Even so, the music director should know quite specifically what supplies are available in each school, how they are issued, and the purpose for which they are intended.

The music administrator can do much to assist in conserving supplies and avoiding waste. Every dollar saved, which through carelessness might have been lost, is available for use elsewhere.

INVENTORIES — The accounting and record keeping discussed in the preceding paragraphs have been leading in the direction of a permanent inventory. It has already been stated that the music director should know all equipment, materials, and supplies, assigned to, and used in, his department. A system of records like the one just described gives him this information at his finger tips. At the end of each school year, a complete, stock-taking inventory should be conducted.

Just as all businesses take inventories at least once and usually two or more times each year, all schools and all departments of all schools should take stock. All items should be located, their condition checked, their useful life estimated, shortages discovered, overstocking noted, and plans made for an improved inventory one year hence.

Although the annual inventory will take time and effort on the part of the music director and his staff, it will undoubtedly prove its worth in protecting and accounting for the investment the community has made in its music program. The location of a bassoon that might otherwise have been lost or the detecting of necessary repairs on a grand piano before serious trouble develops will more than repay the music director for the cost of his leadership in this area.

Storage and Filing

Not enough attention is being given to plans and facilities for filing and storing the valuable materials and equipment used by the music education department. These items must be protected from damage and loss but, at the same time, readily accessible when needed. This section of the chapter will discuss the facilities necessary for storage and the process involved in filing; the construction problems of such facilities will be discussed in Chapter 9.

ROBES AND UNIFORMS — Space must be provided for hanging choir robes and band uniforms so that they may be kept clean and well-pressed. It is also important that they can be checked out to pupils quickly and efficiently. As a rule of thumb, it is better to keep such equipment at school and issue it to the students just prior to each concert or public performance. Robes and uniforms can be more consistently cared for and protected, when kept in the school storeroom where there is less likelihood of moth damage, loss, and damage through carelessness or neglect.

INSTRUMENTS — Any school that has an active instrumental music program will have a tremendous amount of money invested in band and orchestral instruments. It is merely exercising sound common sense to provide adequate facilities for storage. Cupboards, shelves, and lockers, should be provided for all school-owned instruments. The humidity or the room should be controlled so that woodwind, percussion, and stringed instruments, will not become excessively dry or excessively moist. Such measures can often be the cause of saving costly and unnecessary repair bills.

The storage facilities should be large enough, and accessible with sufficient ease, to make it possible for students to keep instruments protected during the school day and yet be able to secure them quickly and easily at rehearsal or dismissal time. Even privately owned instruments should be kept in the school storage room during the day and not in the student's hall or homeroom locker. Every year, in schools all over the country, instruments are stolen or damaged because of careless neglect.

The music administrator must see to it that all instruments both privately and school-owned, are protected against theft and fire loss by adequate insurance. If the school's general insurance policies do not give this protection, then the music director, with the help of the superintendent of schools, should make plans for securing adequate coverage.

School-owned pianos are, for the most part, located in classrooms, practice rooms, rehearsal rooms, auditoriums, and gymnasiums. Care must be taken, however, to keep them as free from moths, dust, and careless damage, as possible. Pianos located in auditoriums and gymnasiums are especially vulnerable to careless damage, and all possible precautions should be taken without curtailing their service and usefulness. Under certain conditions it may be necessary to place them under lock and key, but it is earnestly hoped that all members of the student body take pride in their school's equipment, so that such drastic measures are unnecessary.

MUSIC, BOOKS, AND RECORDS — A great amount of public money is spent each year on music materials. It is outrageous to see these books, records, octavo music, and instrumental arrangements, so inadequately cared for that the rate of loss is high and the useful life short. Each school should provide enough shelves to accommodate all bound books when not being used by students—over the summer vacation, for example. Vocal music, instrumental music, and unbound books should be properly indexed, placed in manila covers, and stored in steel files. Records and other audio-visual material should be clearly indexed and properly filed in order to be protected from loss and damage and yet be ready and accessible for use.

In most schools, it will be necessary to have such materials stored in several places throughout the building. This is good practice—to store them close to the rooms in which they will be used—but it is imperative that they be as adequately protected as if placed in special quarters designed for that purpose alone.

MUSIC LIBRARY — The music educator has a special problem of filing music for his performing groups. Most schools have hundreds, if not thousands, of dollars invested in materials of this sort. Frequently, it is so poorly stored and organized that the only way a number can be located is by searching through pile after pile of music on dark, dusty shelves. The development of a catalog and filing system is the best solution to this problem.

Without an organized library of music, it is difficult, if not impossible, for the music educator to keep in mind all of the music available to his performing groups. This is certainly true when a new director takes over the responsibilities of a music department that has been in existence for some time.

If the material in a music library has not been catalogued and properly filed as it has been purchased, it is a difficult but not insurmountable task to develop some system that is workable. The librarians of the various performing groups can be trained to carry out such a project to completion with a minimum of guidance. If there is a great deal of uncatalogued material, other volunteer student help can be enlisted. Students who take pride in their musical organizations and feel that they have a share in their operation will welcome such opportunities for aiding the welfare and efficiency of the entire group.

It is possible to purchase prepared catalog cards with a descriptive code for filing, but it is better for each director to work out a system, possibly with the assistance of the school librarian, that will best fulfill the special needs of his department. Anyone with an understanding of the functioning of a library catalog can build one of his own that will serve the purpose.

In general, each item should have a card that gives full bibliographical information and the number one needs to identify it. This information will include the title, composer, arranger, publisher, publication number, style (march, overture, sacred, secular, and so forth), and the performing group for which it is written and arranged. (See Figure 36.)

Figure 36

LIBRARY CATALOG CARD

	File 3
BREAK FORTH, O BEAUTEOUS, HEAV'NLY LIGHT	Drawer 4
("Christmas Oratorio")	
Bach, Johann Sebastian	
Chorale	
SATB	
Christmas Season	
E.C. Schirmer Music Co., Boston, Pub. No. 302	
9/55 Number of copies ——————— Cost per copy ———————	

	File 3
BACH, Johann Sebastian	Drawer 4
Break forth, O beauteous, heav'nly light	
("Christmas Oratorio")	
Chorale	
SATB	
Christmas Season	
E.C. Schirmer Music Co., Boston, Pub. No. 302	
9/55 Number of copies ——————— Cost per copy ———————	

Figure 36 (continued)

File 3

CHORALE   Drawer 4

Break forth, O beauteous, heav'nly light
    ("Christmas Oratorio")

Bach, Johann Sebastian

SATB

Christmas Season

E.C. Schirmer Music Co., Boston, Pub. No. 302

9/55 Number of copies ――――― Cost per copy ―――――

File 3

MIXED CHORUS― SATB   Drawer 4

Break forth, O beauteous, heav'nly light
    ("Christmas Oratorio")

Bach, Johann Sebastian

Chorale

Christmas Season

E.C. Schirmer Music Co., Boston, Pub. No. 302

9/55 Number of copies ――――― Cost per copy ―――――

File 3

CHRISTMAS SEASON   Drawer 4

Break forth, O beauteous, heav'nly light
    ("Christmas Oratorio")

Bach, Johann Sebastian

SATB

Chorale

E.C. Schirmer Music Co., Boston, Pub. No. 302

9/55 Number of copies ――――― Cost per copy ―――――

Each item should be cross-indexed, at least by composer, title, style, holiday-seasonal use, and performing group. Each card should be coded to show the exact location of the music; for example, the file number, drawer number, and location within the drawer. It is amazing how much time the conductors of performing organizations can save when their music is catalogued into a functional library.

In a large school system, it may be desirable to build a central library of music from which all schools may draw for their needs. Certainly, the least the music director could do would be to have a central office catalog of all material owned by the school system, indicating the particular school building in which it is located. By such a method, schools could borrow from each other and avoid duplication of numbers in several schools. This would make possible the saving of a great deal of money and, in the end, build a larger, more diversified library for all of the performing organizations in the school system.

Each folder or envelope in which music is filed should show the number of copies available or the instrumentation provided. This makes it possible for the director of any performing organization to determine in a very short time whether or not there are enough copies or sufficient instrumental parts to supply his group. Any music lost or damaged during the time it is in use should be replaced or repaired before being filed away. In this manner, a permanent inventory of all music is built up and maintained.

Some provision should also be made for recording the date, occasion, and group performing, as each piece of music is used. It should also be noted when material was used for sight reading or study but not performance.

TEXTBOOKS — A complete catalog of all of the textbooks and bound materials available in the system should be set up in the central office of the music director. Such a file will give complete bibliographical information on each book in the system and be cross-indexed to show author or collaborator, title, type of work for which the book was designed or level at which it is best used, and topic, such as vocal, instrumental, general, or reference. School systems having two or more units at any one level could profitably have a central library from which the individual school would be able to draw books for auxiliary and resource material.

RECORDS, FILMS, AND TAPES — The modern program of music education is demanding more and more use of phonograph records, sound motion picture films, and magnetic tape recordings. Possibly this type of material will be catalogued and filed in the audio-visual department. Even though this may be the case, the music director should know what is available and where it is located. The handiest, most flexible way to assemble this information is on 3x5 cards, as in a library catalog.

This type of material should be cross-indexed in the same manner as in the music library. Undoubtedly the audio-visual department of the school will have done this for the school as a whole, but the music educator needs this information about musical audio-visual materials at his finger tips—in his office. He may work out his own system or follow that already adopted by his school's audio-visual department. (See Figure 37.)

Figure 37

CATALOG CARD—AUDIO-VISUAL MATERIAL

	Call or
TITLE	Location No.
Composer, Author, or Compiler	
Performers	
Medium (tape, record, film, film strip)	
Subject	Time of Performance _____
Recording Co.	Record No. _____
Date Added to Library	Unit Cost _____

Service and Repair

The nature of most musical equipment necessitates periodic service and occasional repair in order to keep it functioning at peak efficiency. Generally speaking, it is better to have equipment checked and serviced at frequent intervals than to postpone such attention until the cost is almost prohibitive.

Many smaller service and repair jobs can be handled by school personnel—custodians, staff, or students, but larger and more complicated jobs must be handled by skilled craftsmen. When it is necessary to seek the services of a skilled repairman, it is best to send the work out to the shop that has the best facilities and workmen for doing a thoroughly competent job; work skillfully and accurately done will last longer and be more economical in the long run.

INSTRUMENTS — All instruments used in producing music will demand service and repair from time to time. Rhythm sticks may need repainting, a clarinet may need repadding, a crack in a violin may require glueing, the auditorium piano with a cracked sounding board may call for attention, to mention but a few possibilities by way of illustration. The director of music must see that these repairs are made as skillfully, promptly, and economically as possible.

PIANOS   The grand pianos in auditoriums probably represent the largest single dollar investment in musical equipment in school systems, yet all too frequently they are not protected by adequate tuning and care. It is well understood that conditions vary greatly from school to school, but a good minimum policy calls for all pianos owned by the school to be carefully tuned twice each year, with the auditorium pianos and those in classrooms used most frequently given additional tunings when needed.

The first tuning should be given soon after school opens in the fall, preferably after the heat has been on two or three weeks. In warmer climates where buildings are not heated until quite late in the season, it may be necessary to alter this schedule to fit the conditions of the climate. The second tuning should be made about three or four months before the close of school in the spring. Special tunings should be given each piano throughout the year for emergencies and for special concerts.

All pianos should be checked for necessary repairs at least once each year by the regular tuner as he makes his rounds, and the nature and probable costs of such repairs reported to the director of music.

After each tuning or each repair job has been completed, the music director, or some competent person delegated by him, should check each instrument before accepting the work and authorizing payment of the bill in order to assure the best possible workmanship from the tuner.

In a community where there are several tuners and piano mechanics available, it may be necessary to try the services of each one. After deciding upon those who will do the tuning regularly, an annual tuning schedule and agreement should be drawn up. Such a schedule assures tunings at the proper times during the year and often leads to a better price for the work.

The annual piano tuning agreement should state clearly the serial numbers, makes, and locations, of each piano to be serviced, the dates by which the tunings must be completed, and the unit tuning price. It is wise to put in a clause making the tuner responsible for notifying the music director when the job is finished and the instruments ready for inspection. The agreement should be signed by the tuner, the music director, and the superintendent of schools, and copies given to all three signees.

BAND AND ORCHESTRA INSTRUMENTS   All instruments in this classification will need expert service from time to time. Generally speaking, under normal usage, woodwinds will demand more frequent attention than the brasses, and strings more frequent attention than percussion. It may be possible and wise to arrange for such service on an annual contract or agreement basis, in the same way that was recommended for piano tunings; however, it is less likely that service and repair of band and orchestra instruments will conform to a pattern, such as is the case with pianos.

The music director will probably find it prudent to try out all available repair services until the ones are found that do the best work, give the best service, and keep the cost low. Whenever the work is sent out, the music director, or someone delegated by him, should inspect the instruments upon their return so that the quality of the work may be verified before payment of the bill authorized.

No instrument should wait for service until it is in very poor condition. Not only does this cause the repair bill to be greater, but the efficiency of the instrument is impaired, and the effectiveness of the music program reduced. As suggested earlier in the chapter, an accurate repair record should be kept on each instrument, showing the nature of the work done, the date, and the cost. When an instrument gets in such condition that it is frequently in the repair shop and the cost of maintaining it is excessive, it should be replaced with a new one.

All brass instruments will need periodic overhauling for the purpose of cleaning inside and out, removing dents, sterilizing, and tightening braces and joints. With proper care, this should not occur too often, but carelessness and neglect may necessitate frequent trips to the shop.

Many emergency repairs, such as stuck slides, stuck mouthpieces, minor dents, and loose joints, can be made by the music director, instrumental teacher, students, or custodians, if they are at all handy with, and have, the proper tools. When it is possible to take care of such minor repairs by the services of school personnel, a great deal of time and money can be saved.

Many of the above jobs require only a few minutes to perform but might take days in a repair shop waiting until the service man finds time to do them.

A woodwind instrument will need more frequent aligning and adjusting than a brass instrument. The mechanism is so intricate and critical that the slightest deviation from its proper setting will cause it to function poorly or not at all. With a little practice, the music director, or someone he has trained, can perform many of these minor adjustments; however, there will be many times when the services of an expert repairman are necessary.

Minor and emergency repairs such as replacing pads, straightening keys, and recorking joints and keys, can often be done by students or other school personnel, thereby saving much time and money in the course of a school year.

With proper care, stringed instruments will need overhauling less frequently than the brass and woodwinds. When repairs are necessary, it is absolutely essential to have the work done by a skilled craftsman. Repair work on stringed instruments is highly specialized; setting bridges, closing cracks, fitting pegs, all require special tools and a special knowledge of the instrument and its musical properties.

Stringed instruments require that repair work be taken care of promptly so that more difficult and expensive jobs may be prevented. For instance, an open crack will tend to increase in size the longer repairs are delayed. A large crack is more difficult to close, demanding more glue, more splicing, and thereby risking the possibility that the instrument may become permanently weakened and its musical qualities impaired.

The great variety of instruments in the percussion group causes service and repair problems not found in the others. With proper care, they should not need frequent attention, except for occasionally replacing drum heads. Promptness in caring for service requirements will keep costs low.

Many small instruments such as rhythm instruments, autoharps, and flutophones, are relatively inexpensive to purchase and therefore little money is invested in them. When they do need repairs, it is wise to examine critically the cost of such repairs and determine if the remaining useful life of the instruments is sufficiently long to be worth the cost; it may be more economical to purchase new ones.

UNIFORMS AND ROBES — Band uniforms, choir robes, operetta costumes, orchestra jackets, and other equipment, can be kept serviceable over a longer period of time when given proper care. Money thus spent is protecting the community's investment in education.

All items of apparel, such as those just mentioned, should be thoroughly cleaned at least once each year. A good time to have this work done is during the summer vacation period, when there is little or no need for having the garments readily available. It also makes it possible to begin each new school year with clean robes, uniforms, and costumes. Garments that are clean before being stored are less likely to be damaged by moths during their months of idleness. It is quite possible that the music director can secure a better price for this service during the summer months and thereby save the school many dollars.

At the time uniforms and robes are to receive their annual cleaning, they should be inspected carefully for minor repairs that have not been made during the school year. It has already been suggested that all school-owned garments be kept in the school storeroom and issued to the pupils prior to each performance and for that appearance only. Uniforms and robes receiving such care will be less likely to become damaged, soiled, or moth-eaten. Even when they have the best of care, there will be times when repairs are necessary. If they are not made promptly when needed, more costly ones are likely to appear, and the garments will need to be replaced sooner.

It may be possible to handle cleaning and repair on an annual contract basis with a local cleaner and tailor. Usually, such a practice reduces the cost of this service and repair by a noticeable amount.

ELECTRONIC EQUIPMENT — Care and repair of radios, phonographs, tape recorders, and similar items, may be the responsibility of the audio-visual department; however, since these pieces of equipment are used so much by the music department, the director of music must take the responsibility for seeing that they are properly cared for. Careful handling, frequent inspection, periodic overhaul, and prompt service when trouble appears, will keep costs down, efficiency up, and the useful life long.

BOOKS AND MUSIC — The employment of care in handling, storing, and filing, books and music will reduce the costs of repair to an almost negligible amount. After years of use, some books may need rebinding in order to extend their useful life; music may possibly need to be bound by some type of hinged tape. It is an economical practice to make such repairs rather than to plan to buy new materials, particularly if the repairs are to books that are still of value to the music education program and if they have not become outdated.

Minor repairs, such as mending torn pages, can easily be done by student librarians in the school; binding and hinging must be done by commercial repair services, however. The cost of the repairs, compared to the amount of time the useful life is extended, must be the basis for deciding between having material repaired or replacements purchased.

SCHOOL REPAIR FACILITIES — Continual reference has been made throughout this section to the possibility of performing certain service and repair operations within the school. The wise music director will secure the basic tools and equipment for making such minor repairs as padding, corking, and adjusting woodwinds; setting soundposts, closing minor cracks on the strings; removing dents, stuck slides, and mouthpieces, on the brasses; sewing buttons and tears on garments; and repairing books and music. There are several repair manuals that can be obtained to help the music director learn or train others in the skills necessary for making such repairs. A little practice in the development of such skills can save many costly repair bills and keep the equipment in use by avoiding the time and cost involved in sending the work out to professional service and repair shops.

The school's woodworking and metalworking shops can often be of considerable help in performing certain service and repair tasks. Frequently, the instructors of such courses are willing and anxious to have their classes work on such real and practical problems. Sewing classes can often be called upon for making minor, and possibly major, repairs on uniforms and robes. School custodians are frequently willing to make repairs and give service to the equipment used by the music department; they consider it a part of their jobs. Parent groups can also be formed that are willing and anxious to help in this work, when given an opportunity. The students of the several performance organizations can also be mobilized and trained to assist in certain types of repairs.

The music director who shows his administrators, his pupils, and his community, that he is doing all in his power to reduce the costs of his department and is actively concerned about protecting the public's investment in equipment will be assured of the unqualified support of the school and community.

Replacing Equipment

No matter how carefully equipment is treated, there comes a time when replacement is necessary. The wise music director will carefully study the useful life of each item and, before its educational returns have been reduced below minimum efficiency, will lay plans for having it replaced.

USEFUL LIFE OF EQUIPMENT — There is need for objective studies giving factual information about the useful life expectancy of the various items of equipment used by an active department of music education.

The life expectancies of the various types of equipment vary considerably. Generally speaking, pianos have a longer life than brasses and woodwinds. Each item must be closely observed and studied to determine the point at which it becomes too expensive to maintain in good repair; at such time, it should be replaced.

PURCHASE SCHEDULE — Whether a music department is well equipped or working toward a minimum level of supply, it is a good policy to build a long-range plan of purchase to maintain or improve facilities. By this means, it is possible to spread the costs of purchasing new, or replacing old, equipment over a longer period of time, avoiding heavy expenditures in some years and having little or none in others.

Summary

As an administrator, the director of music bears a great responsibility for wisely investing the public's money in the paraphernalia necessary for carrying out the program of music education desired by the community. Not only must this money be spent wisely, but the investment protected by proper care of equipment, materials, and supplies, after they reach the school.

This chapter has presented eight criteria for assisting the music director in selecting the items for purchase. It has also suggested ways of accounting for the physical accouterments of the music department and discussed problems associated with filing, servicing, storage, and repair.

Suggested Activities

1. Write detailed specifications for one instrument of each family of the orchestra for the following grades of instruments:
   a. Artist performance quality
   b. Middle grade for beginning instrumental instruction
2. Write detailed specifications for a concert grand piano for a high school auditorium. Do the same for upright pianos for an elementary school classroom and for a practice room.

3. Write a justification for an instrument needed by a music department you know. Address this justification to the principal or school superintendent and assume he is not conversant with musical terms or values.

4. Visit a school and become familiar with its business practices for purchasing music for performing groups. Also discover the procedures used for music equipment, instrument stands, files, and so on. Try to trace the steps and offices through which a request must travel from the order by the music teacher until the material or equipment reaches the music classroom and is put into use.

5. Prepare a list, including a realistic cost estimate, of all the tools, equipment, and supplies you would need to establish a school repair center for minor service and repair of band and orchestra instruments.

6. Prepare a purchase schedule of instruments and equipment for a new music department in a junior or senior high school. Indicate the instruments necessary to get started and those to be added year by year until a full orchestration is achieved.

For Further Reading

Moore, E. C. *How To Write a Woodwind Specification*. Kenosha, Wisconsin, G. Leblanc Corporation. 8 pp. Pamphlet.

Music Educators National Conference. *Music Curriculum in Secondary Schools*. Washington, D.C., The Conference, 1959. Pages 38 and 39.

Pascucci, Vito. "Improving School Bid Specifications." *Music Journal*, 21, No. 5:48 ff., May, 1963.

CHAPTER 8

Budget and Finance

THE DIRECTOR OF MUSIC in any school system is expected to furnish leadership in all activities that contribute to the success and well-being of his department and the school. The annual budget, its formation, administration, and appraisal, as well as enough financial support to make it operative, are extremely important concerns of the music educator. The music director must be sure that enough money is supplied for operating his department in the way the community expects and that every dollar spent returns its full value in goods and services. Such a responsibility cannot be taken lightly.

In order to help the music educators better understand the budget of the school as a whole, their departmental budget in particular, and the processes by which it is developed and administered, this chapter will discuss the nature of the budget, patterns of budgetary operation, the sources of financial support, and the processes of budget building.

The Nature of the Budget

BUDGET DEFINED — A school budget is a plan for estimating the cost and the proposed expenditure of funds in support of the educational program that the community desires for its children. Earlier in the book, it was shown that planning was one of the six basic functions of school administration. The budget is one of the phases of this planning that deals primarily with the financial support of the school and its program. It is not a first step, but it is a vitally important step in sound school administration. Waste of public funds and inefficient management of school money inevitably result when plans are not carefully developed or day-to-day financing procedures used.

While understanding that the budget is a plan, it must also be remembered that there must be a purpose underlying and undergirding such a plan.

The educational program of the school is always the primary objective. Collecting, safeguarding, and expending school funds are important, but only as they serve or make possible the educational program. One does not, therefore, make out a school budget until educational objectives have first been established.

It is quite possible for a person with a pocket full of money to go shopping for clothes and buy whatever his fancy dictates. With a purchase plan of this sort, it is unlikely that a well-balanced, unified, useful wardrobe will result. In terms of a practical, functional set of garments, he has wasted a great deal of time and a lot of money. It is never advisable for educational institutions to indulge themselves in the same type of aimless, purposeless spending. People entrusted with public money cannot afford the luxury of unplanned spending. Only the extremely wealthy, with money to squander, can do this. Education is not yet in the wealthy class.

No budget can be built and made operative unless the community wholeheartedly supports what the school is trying to do. It is, therefore, sound practice to make certain that the public is kept informed of the purposes of the school, the program within the school, and the cost of maintaining all phases of school operation. What the public knows about, and wants for its children, it is willing to support. The budget, then, expresses the amount the community is willing to pay in order to buy the type of educational program it wants.

PURPOSES OF THE BUDGET — Mort and Reusser[1] identify five well-defined purposes served by the school budget. Although these purposes refer to the financial plan of the school as a whole, as the discussion moves forward, it will be seen that they also apply to the portion of the budget that concerns the music education department.

PROJECTION OF SCHOOL PROGRAM INTO FUTURE   As school plans are laid for the future, it becomes necessary to provide the financial support needed for carrying them out. The budget is the underwriting of the school program as accepted by the board of education and the community, projecting it into the future for at least one year.

ESTIMATION OF EXPECTED REVENUES   In the American school structure

---

[1] Paul R. Mort and Walter C. Reusser, *Public School Finance*, 2nd ed., New York, McGraw-Hill Book Co., 1951, pp. 161–62. Used by permission.

of today, the funds used in support of the school's program come from several sources. The budget anticipates and estimates the amount of money to be obtained from these various sources.

ESTIMATION OF EXPENDITURES   After the educational plan for the school has been developed and the costs estimated for putting it into operation, the budget allocates the amount to be spent in support of each of the various parts of the educational program, as well as for the system as a whole.

DETERMINATION OF AMOUNT TO BE RAISED   After the anticipated school income is known and the expenditures in support of the program estimated, the budget will show the amount of money that must be raised by other means when the expected income is not as great as the proposed expenditures. For example, in planning its school program, a community may decide that a new building is necessary. The expected income from all sources is not enough to operate the existing plant, pay salaries of personnel, and in all other ways support its program and construct a new building as well; therefore, additional funds must very definitely be obtained through increased taxation, by borrowing, or by some other means. The budget brings to light the amount of money that must be raised by the community in support of its schools.

AID TO OPERATION OF SCHOOLS   The budget accepted by the board of education and the community reflects the emphasis they wish placed upon the various parts of the school plan. If they allow three thousand dollars for the athletics program and two thousand dollars for the music program, it is obvious that they wish to buy a greater amount of athletics than they do music. This type of information gives the administrator a clear course of action for conducting the schools according to the plan the community accepts and supports.

As the music educator thinks about the school budget and makes his contribution to it, he must keep in mind that there is, first of all, a budget for the school system as a whole. This is truly an area of concern for all members of the school staff, although the superintendent is directly responsible for it, unless it has been delegated by him to another officer of the system. Teachers and supervisors might easily feel far removed from this large over-all budget. They must guard against such a feeling, for it is out of this budget that their work, whatever it may be, is financed. If the necessary funds for their particular work are not appropriated and contained in the school budget, their program will be limited and hampered throughout the entire period of time covered by the budget.

The total school budget is made up of many smaller, or sub-budgets. The financial plans for the various departments of instruction, such as history, English, art, physical education, and music; those of individual school units, such as each elementary school, the junior high school, and high school; those of the special services, such as transportation, food services, and guidance— are all sub-budgets, which are a part of the over-all school budget and contribute to its formation and final structure. The music director is most directly concerned with the sub-budget pertaining to his special program and any other phase of the small or large budget that concerns his work.

Whether we think of the total budget or the sub-budgets, the purposes, the processes, the expected results, are the same. The discussion throughout this book will center upon the budgetary problems of the music director as he provides leadership in his special sphere of influence, always keeping in mind the relationship of the music budget to the budget of the whole school.

Patterns of Operation

There are four general ways in which the requirements of the music department may be fitted into the total budget of the school. Each will be discussed separately, with the strengths and weaknesses pointed out as they appear.

DEPARTMENTAL BUDGET — Under the strictly departmental budget, the director of music is responsible for estimating the needs of the entire music department, assembling a budget that meets these demands, and submitting the document to the superintendent of schools or his designated budgetary officer. In an operational plan of this type, the work of the music department is conceived as a unit. It cuts across the separate school lines and all the various kinds of musical activity. This budget would include provision for *all* musical activities at the preschool, elementary, junior high, senior high, junior college, and adult education levels.

Such a plan makes it possible for the music director to unify his entire program and guards against the dangers of overemphasizing one level or phase to the detriment of another. It has the possible danger of setting music too much apart and not permitting it to function as a part of the total educational process. This danger could be surmounted by careful planning and close cooperation with other department heads and the principals of the various school units.

Autonomous School Budget — Although the school system as a whole may have a director of music, his department may be supported by the budget of each separate unit to the degree that the program is active at the school. The director of music, or the teacher assigned to that building, must make his recommendations to the principal who, in turn, includes them in his budget, which is then transmitted to the superintendent of schools.

This plan of operation has the danger of causing the music program to become uneven and uncoordinated, when considered system-wide. It means that the music budget is designed for each school as an independent unit and should, therefore, fit the special requirements and program of that particular school better than does the departmental budget. Although this is valuable in terms of the school staff, it could be detrimental to the over-all music program. Some schools would undoubtedly make ample provision for the support of music in their budgets, while others would make little or none. The music director would be powerless to assist the schools with the weaker programs, except by attempting to persuade the principal and parents to provide greater support than they might otherwise give.

It could also be argued that, even though the director of music had full budgetary control, he would be unable to provide an improved music program in a school where parents and principal did not wish it. Although this is true, he would be in a stronger position to persuade when possessing financial power to support his desired program.

This plan of operation also poses a difficult problem when the music department of the school must seek part of its support outside of the regular school budget. The parents of some schools will be willing to provide this outside support to a greater extent than others. It could result in some schools being "rich" as far as funds for music are concerned, while others in the same system could be "poor." This problem will be discussed more fully later.

Split Music Budget — The split music budget provides a separate financial plan for the vocal, instrumental, and possibly the general music program. Each phase of the music curriculum arrives at its budget independently of the others. This plan may operate in either or both of the two previous plans, but it is basically weak because it splits the unity of the music program itself. No school should have a vocal music program, an instrumental music program, and a general music program. All should have a *music* program, which includes all possible avenues of activity and experience.

It is wise to be realistic enough to be aware of the fact that there are school systems that do operate in the manner just described, and the music director may have no other immediate course open to him than to prepare his budget along these lines. All the time he is doing it, however, he should be working with his superintendent and principals to bring about improved conditions for music organization and finance. Together, the staff and the public must decide what it is they expect from the music program and provide the organization and support that will realize these expectations.

NO BUDGET — This fourth plan, if indeed it may be called a plan, assigns the music department no regular, fixed place in the over-all budgetary planning; each need must be met as it arises, and the principal or superintendent allots whatever funds he has at his disposal to meet it, if he approves of the music director's proposal. This practice reduces the stature of the music department to that of begging for its very existence. Sad to relate, there are schools that attempt to operate a music department in this fashion.

Sources of Money

In order to work intelligently with problems of budget and finance, the music director must have a clear understanding of the sources of revenue that supply the funds for operating the schools. There are three such sources—taxation, special funds, and gifts. Each will be discussed with particular reference to financing the music department.

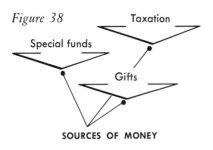

Figure 38

SOURCES OF MONEY

TAXATION — Since the advent of free public education in the United States, schools have been supported by some form of taxation. Schools were, and still are, the responsibility of the local community, and each is required by law to maintain a school for the education of all children at public expense.

The original purpose of the school tax was to provide a program of education in which all children could share equally; this purpose still remains. When one studies the socio-economic structure of any community, he can easily see that if each family were forced to pay tuition for the education of each child, great inequalities would exist. Children from families of wealth and means would be adequately cared for, while children from the lower end of the socio-economic scale would be denied education. Our democratic society decided early in its history that schools were to be *publicly* supported. To that end, each community is given authority by the state to levy a tax to support its schools. This tax is usually in the form of levy on real estate and continues to be the base of tax support for schools, in spite of the fact that through the years the structure has changed considerably. For the purposes of the present discussion, there is no need for greater detail than a simple statement of this basic truth.

As the various states observed that all districts were not able to support schools equally well, various forms of state aid were established to raise the level of all districts to at least a desirable minimum. Even this is none too high in some states today, although great gains are being made.

With the passage of the first Smith-Hughes Act giving aid to schools offering training in agriculture, home economics, trades, and industry, the federal government has assisted in the support of education. Since the original enactment in 1917, subsequent bills have extended this aid and also assisted in supporting vocational guidance programs.

Today, public schools still receive their greatest financial support from local taxation, a large but lesser amount from the state, and a very small amount from the federal government.

Very frequently, directors of music are forced to seek funds outside of their regular budget for operating their departments. An article in the *Kentucky School Journal* in May 1951 contained this statement:

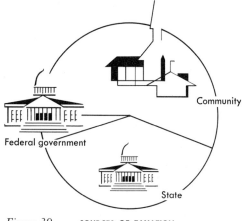

Figure 39   **SOURCES OF TAXATION**

More often than not, the supervisor of music in the public schools must find ways of supplementing his budget if he is to develop and carry on the various activities inherent in a modern program of education. The amount of aid required from extra budgetary sources will vary, of course, but usually a community will respond quite liberally to an appeal for additional funds if it is carefully and properly approached.[2]

The article then goes on to suggest ways in which money for the necessary operation of the music department can be raised by methods such as the conducting of tag days, bake sales, bridge parties, and booster days. If anything is degrading to the high calling of music educators, this is!

The most unfortunate part of the entire situation is the fact that such practices are entirely contrary to the basic concepts of public education in the United States and nullify the theory of equal sharing in the financial support of the public schools and equal opportunities for all children. In effect, those who support the music program by these "outside the budget" campaigns are being taxed twice, once by the community and once by the music department.

Public education started out to give all children equal opportunities for learning, including all of the various experiences and activities of the schools; it was based on the premise that the rich and the poor alike should have equal opportunities for education. The people taxed themselves so that the support of the schools should be shared in proportion to each family's means. If schools and communities decide that music has value in the curriculum, or outside it, they are honor bound to support it, in and through the school budget.

The best educational thinking supports this view. Chamberlain and Kindred say, "It would be better if the entire extra curricular program were underwritten by the board of education. . . . This would be in keeping with the educational values claimed in justification of the extra curricular program."[3] French, Hull, and Dodds, discussing the guiding principles in the administration of student activities, say:

> Participation in student activities should be equally available with restrictions related only to competency and interest in the given activity.
>
> When activities require more than nominal cost for participation, equality of opportunity likewise becomes more theoretical than real. . . . Keeping fees for clubs at a very nominal rate, providing general tickets that cover most or all activities and that by one device or another are available to all students, such as that needed in musical and recreational activities, are among the methods used to equalize the economic factor.[4]

[2] LeRoy Weil, "Financing a Program of School Music," *Kentucky School Journal,* 29:26, May, 1951. Used by permission.

[3] Leo M. Chamberlain and Leslie W. Kindred, *The Teacher and School Organization,* 2nd ed., Englewood Cliffs, N.J., Prentice-Hall, Inc., 1949, p. 376. Used by permission.

[4] Will French, J. Dan Hull, and B. L. Dodds, *American High School Administration,* rev. ed., New York, Rinehart & Co., 1957, pp. 247–49. Used by permission.

Simpson and Lake, in reviewing procedures that are generally recognized as good budgetary practice, say, "A good budget includes all aspects of a financing program, curricular and extracurricular."[5]

In the light of this evidence, it scarcely seems possible that communities would still expect their school music departments to finance themselves outside of the regular school budget, but the fact remains that many music educators are still called upon to promote fund-raising activities in support of their own program, charge rental fees for instruments loaned, and collect tuition fees for instruction given under the school's auspices. Music directors must take steps toward educating the public to full acceptance of its responsibilities for giving financial support to the music program of its schools out of the funds raised by the public taxation method.

SPECIAL FUNDS — Although it is impossible to defend the financing of a school music department, wholly or in part, outside the framework of public tax support for all of education, a realistic point of view indicates that it is still sometimes necessary, at least temporarily. There are some possibilities for income of this sort that can be mentioned at this time.

Asking the public to purchase tickets of admission for school concerts and programs is a rather universal practice. When this policy is adopted, it must be based upon sound educational principles. If concerts are considered as a means for reporting to the community, as discussed in Chapter 5, the established price must be in keeping with this purpose. The public is entitled to this report and should not be asked to pay an exorbitant price to receive it.

Many school systems create some sort of activity fund with all activities contributing their special proceeds to it and drawing proportionately from it. If the various musical organizations are classified as activities, they should be expected to contribute their concert proceeds and other special income to it and, at the same time, draw from it on an equitable basis with the other activities of the school.

Frequently the athletics fund is established outside of the activities fund. With the school bands playing such a prominent part in sports activities by means of their football shows, performances at basketball games, and pep rallies, many music directors expect and receive annual appropriations from this fund.

[5] Alfred D. Simpson and Ernest G. Lake in *Problems and Issues in Public School Finance*, R. L. Johns and E. L. Morphet, eds., National Conference of Professors of Educational Administration, New York, Bureau of Publications, Teachers College, Columbia University, 1952, p. 340. Used by permission.

The conditions surrounding the conducting of fund-raising drives, such as tag days, bridge parties, and dances, have been referred to in the previous section. In communities where this pattern of practice has been well established and expected, it will undoubtedly be necessary to continue such activities, at least for a time. The music director should lead his community to the acceptance of its full responsibility for supporting the music program through the regular school budget.

Some schools permit student organizations to perform for programs, parades, and other events, for private organizations expecting (possibly requiring) a "donation to the music fund." Some go as far as quoting the size of the "donation" expected, even to the extent of creating a price scale for the band, another for the orchestra, another for the choir, and still others for ensembles and soloists.

These special funds or sources of income are all unnecessary when the school and community assume their full responsibility and support the music program by making provision for it in the regular school budget.

GIFTS — There are times when genuinely unsolicited gifts of money come to the music department from local clubs, organizations, or individuals. Many times, these are given to the school for the specific and exclusive use of the music department. When such occasions arise, the music director should accept them graciously and put them to use in the best interests of the music program as it serves the children of the community.

If possible, the donors of such gifts should be encouraged to give them in an unrestricted manner, to be used at the discretion of the music director, with advice, possibly, from the superintendent or an advisory committee. It is frequently embarrassing to the music director, the school, and the music program, when a gift is made for a specific purpose and that purpose is contrary to the plans and goals of the school. It would be far better if gifts of this nature were presented so that they could be used as the music director and his advisory committee see fit.

Budget Building

ORIENTATION — Earlier in the chapter, the budget was referred to as a plan for estimating the cost and the proposed expenditure of public funds in support of the educational program the community desires for its children. This not only implies that it is a document, but a process by which those concerned with the education of children develop their plan and find ways and means for supporting it.

Those who are to work with the budget and within its limitations must have a certain voice in shaping it. Wide participation is absolutely essential; the budget, rather than being built by the superintendent of schools or his deputy, should grow out of the joint efforts of the entire staff, the public, and the pupils.

Ultimately, the budget must be supported by the people of the community. It is positively essential that they understand the educational plan to be financed, their part in building it, its application, and its support.

In order to create this understanding, lay committees will be formed to work with the music director and his staff in studying the musical desires of the community and its children. A plan for meeting these needs will be formulated, and the costs necessary for making it operative will be estimated. The same committee, or another, will work with the finance committee of the board of education in developing ways and means for securing the funds necessary to underwrite the plan.

There is also a place for pupil participation in the budget building process. This practice is not widely accepted as yet, but many schools are finding that, given an opportunity, students make valuable contributions to the work and, at the same time, are learning good citizenship by experiencing the democratic process in action. Student officers of choirs, bands, and orchestras, can prepare budgets for their own organizations to be fitted into the total music budget. Student committees can develop plans for economics in departmental operation; they can help secure information upon which decisions will ultimately be made; they can offer suggestions for improving and refocusing the purposes of the music department in the lives of young people. They are willing and anxious to help and can be of invaluable assistance when given the opportunity.

American education has frequently been criticized because there appears to be so little agreement as to its ultimate aims. Under local control, with each community establishing its own aims and purposes, it is easy to see how this seeming lack of accord has come about. Properly conceived, education must serve not only local needs, but develop national interests as well. Although local needs may differ in kind and degree, national interests are similar, if not identical, for all. Community participation in the budgetary process is an excellent place to initiate studies aimed at the reconciliation of these two apparently divergent points of emphasis.

One of the purposes of education in this country is to establish and make secure a social framework in which each individual can fully develop his personal resources and thereby improve society as a whole. If this social policy is to be implemented, it must be reflected in the budget. This can come about only when budgeting is recognized as a continuous process, with the people of the community involved in the planning and being permitted, even encouraged, to seek, through gradual development, the achievement of those social goals established by the group. In this light, the school budget can be seen as an expression of broad social policy.

The budgetary process is a continuing affair. It is not an activity that can be dispatched in a flurry of activity prior to the close of the fiscal year and ignored until the next fiscal season rolls around. Educational planning is a continuous, ceaseless action. It must constantly look to the future, always planning better and better purposes for educational structure and organization. The music director is a part of this process as it develops the plans for the school as a whole; he is the leader of the process as it affects the work of the music department.

**STAGES IN
BUDGET-BUILDING**

 ● Formulating program

   ● Translating program into policy

     ● Estimating cost

       ● Organizing for presentation
          A. *Cover letter*
          B. *Budget summary*
          C. *Proposed expenditures, anticipated receipts*
          D. *Supporting information*
Figure 40   E. *Presentation and adoption*

STAGES IN BUDGET BUILDING — There are four fairly well-defined stages in the development of a budget.[6] It makes little difference whether one is concerned with the large over-all budget for the school as a whole or a smaller sub-budget for one of the departments; the processes, the stages, and the forms, are similar if not exactly alike. The present discussion is focused on the music director and the budget building for this department.

PREPARATION This stage of budget building contains four separate steps. The first two have been treated in earlier chapters of this book and touched upon in the previous sections of this chapter; therefore, they will be

[6] This section is freely adapted from Mort and Reusser, *op. cit.*, pp. 168–183. Used by permission.

but briefly summarized at this time. The third and fourth steps will be discussed in detail.

1. *Formulating a program*   The program of music education should be in keeping with the educational plans of the schools as a whole. This step is curriculum development as discussed in Chapter 2. It was also discussed in the present chapter, in the previous section, as orientation to the process of budget building.

2. *Translating the program into policy*   No school or department policy can be operative until the superintendent and board of education officially adopt it. The process of policy formation leading to official adoption calls for wide participation by many people, including the music staff, the general staff, the public, the pupils, and the administration. The chapters on personal relationships, curriculum, and public relations, have touched upon this phase of the budget building process.

3. *Estimating finances and services*   At this time, the music director must determine the number of teachers needed for carrying out the instructional phases of the plan and how much it will cost to pay their salaries. It will be necessary to know the demands the program will place upon the existing school plant and the space available for placing the plans in action. Every item of goods, services, and facilities, necessary for the complete activation of the music program will have its price tag. It is at this point in the budgetary process that these requirements are determined.

The music director needs some method for determining whether or not the money he proposes to spend is in keeping with the amount spent by other departments of the school. There is need for research that will give him this guiding information.

The writer knows of only one recent study that has attempted to determine this relationship between instructional costs in music and other subjects of the curriculum.[7] The results are of limited worth because only teachers' salaries were used to determine the cost; such items as equipment, materials, supplies, housing, and a proportionate share of plant operating expenses, were ignored. It is interesting to note, however, that even on this limited basis, music is less expensive than English, arithmetic, social studies and science,

[7] Frederick J. Batorski, "The Costs of Music Instruction in Four Public School Systems as Compared with the Costs of Instruction in Other Subjects of the Curriculum," Unpublished Master's Thesis, Boston, College of Music, Boston University, 1949. Typewritten, unpaged.

health and physical education, and recess and recreation, and about on a par with art and writing in the elementary schools.

The secondary level was found to be more expensive than the first six grades. This is not surprising, since there are many studies that have shown this relationship. Again, in the junior and senior high schools, music was found to be one of the low cost subjects, on a par with guidance and physical education; industrial arts and household arts were found to be the most expensive, all others falling between these two extremes. This study computed the cost per pupil by dividing the teacher's salary by the amount of time devoted to the subject and dividing that result by the number of pupils with whom the teacher came in contact each day.

Each director of music will find it necessary to make a study of the cost per pupil of maintaining his music program. He certainly must do this before he can hope to secure more financial support for an expansion of his program. Undoubtedly, the superintendent of schools, or his budgetary officer, will have determined the amount of money per pupil that has been, or is being, spent by the school as a whole. He may also have developed unit costs for other departments and phases of the school's operation. If a study of the cost of the music program has not been made, the music director will find it helpful to do so; he must be certain, however, that the formula he uses in arriving at his cost per pupil is the same as that used by the superintendent of schools, or there will be no valid basis for comparison.

The simplest way to compute the unit cost of the music program is to determine the number of pupils in average daily attendance and divide the total cost of the music program by that figure. The result is the cost per pupil of the music department. The average daily attendance figure can usually be obtained from the superintendent's office or from the principals of the various schools throughout the system. Certainly the attendance officer will have the figures necessary for determining it.

It is helpful to know the amount of money per pupil the school as a whole expects to spend in order to finance its total operation. This figure will vary from school to school and will differ when various parts of the country are compared. Knowing what his school spends per pupil for its budget will give the music director a better idea of what he can reasonably expect to spend in support of his program.

In the absence of reliable information on a reasonable proportion of the school's entire budget that should be spent for music, the music director must use his own best judgment and the counsel of his administrators, his staff, and his advisory committee.

Let us consider an example in order to help clarify this entire procedure.

A small school will be used in this illustration in order to keep the process as clear as possible and the figures low.

The school at Budgetville, U.S.A., is building its financing plan on 1685 pupils in average daily attendance. The superintendent has informed his staff that the over-all budget is to be based upon spending $200 for each pupil. This amounts to $337,000 for the total budget and, by definition, is to exclude fixed charges, plant operation, debt retirements, transportation, and capital outlay. These items are to be covered by an additional amount per pupil, but are excluded here because they normally fall outside the area of responsibility of the music director.

The staff has been informed that special departments, such as music, are to figure their budgets on the basis of 5 per cent of the cost per pupil for the school as a whole. This means that the music director can figure on $10 per pupil for his music budget or a total of $16,850. The staff of the music department consists of the director, whose salary for the following year is to be $5,600, and his assistant, who will receive $4,200. By deducting the total of these salaries from the gross amount, the music director determines that he will have $7,050, more or less, for purchasing equipment, materials, supplies, and providing for any other needs of his department.

It is at this point that the director of music with his staff and advisory committees must decide what is needed in the way of goods and special services to put their program into action in the best possible manner. As he reports these requirements to the superintendent, he must be very specific when stating the net cost of each item and the place or places where they may be obtained for that amount. For example, if he needs five French horns, he must be sure he can buy all five of them for the price quoted in his budget and that the Toot & Scrape Music Company on Huffanpuff Street will supply them at that figure. Vagueness in submitted estimates will almost always be cause for having the item stricken from the budget, when it is presented to the superintendent of schools.

4. Organizing information into a budget document The precise form a final budget document will assume depends upon the superintendent of schools in charge of this operation. The basic structure, however, will be very much the same from school to school. The music director should plan to work within the framework expected by the administration of the school system in which he works. The form presented here will serve to familiarize the music educator with the major elements that any budget will probably assume.

A *covering letter,* or written statement reviewing the aims toward which .

the budget works, a summary of the budget needs, and an explanation of how the expenditures called for will bring desired results, should accompany the budget when submitted to the superintendent of schools. It is highly essential that this be done in writing because it gives the superintendent something tangible upon which to base his decisions. An oral presentation can be too easily forgotten or confused. A clear, concise, convincing statement in the language of the layman is the best policy to follow when preparing a covering letter to accompany the budget.

The *budget summary* should contain the anticipated revenues and proposed expenditures arranged in such a form that they may be easily and conveniently compared. The following items should be included:

1. Expected revenues from all sources.
2. Proposed expenditures for all purposes.
3. Increases or decreases by major items of expenditures a year or two in the past, if such information is available.
4. Enough explanatory materials accompanying estimates to make each item clear.

The third section of the budget should give detailed information on *proposed expenditures* and *anticipated receipts,* so arranged that they may be easily compared. This information should be sufficiently detailed to make it possible for the superintendent or the board of education to follow up any item of cost if they care to do so.

It is also important to follow the classification of expenditures the superintendent will use in his final budget. If code references are used in the final school budget, they should also be used here in the departmental budget.

Any *supporting information* the music director can offer in defense of his budgetary requests should be presented in this section of the form. Detailed analyses of equipment, materials, and supplies, their present status and future needs, comparisons with similar systems doing a like caliber of work—all descriptions such as these serve to strengthen the budget and give the superintendent and board of education a more secure basis for their decisions.

PRESENTATION AND ADOPTION   After the budget has been prepared and organized into a budget document, it is presented to the proper budgetary officer for review and inclusion in the complete financial plan of the school. It is at this stage that the superintendent, or any other officer with the necessary responsibility and authority, studies the budget and its demands in the light of the music education program and policies already adopted. He may accept it as it stands or suggest certain revisions or alterations to make it conform to school policies, the educational program, and the community's ability to pay. It is entirely possible that he might reject the budget entirely, return it to the music director with instructions to restudy the entire problem, and report back with a more or less completely new budget document. This latter possibility is less likely to occur when the budget has been built as the result of wide participation by staff, community, and pupils, and presented in good form.

As a practical matter, it is wise for the music director to understand that his departmental budget must be completed at an earlier date than that of the school as a whole. This must be done to assure the superintendent of schools sufficient time for studying all departmental or sub-budgets and incorporating their recommendations into his own.

ADMINISTRATION   After the budget has been adopted and the funds secured for its operation, it must be administered throughout the fiscal year it covers. Even the best budget will fail to achieve its purpose if it is not properly administered. It is the superintendent's responsibility to administer the budget for the school as a whole, but the music director will undoubtedly be called upon to assume his share of the responsibility as far as the expenditures of his department are concerned. He should know at all times throughout the year the status of his budget accounts. In all probability, the bookkeeping and accounting for the school will be done in the superintendent's office or business office. The office may adopt the policy of sending periodic summary statements to the various department heads informing them of amounts spent and funds still available. Whether they do this or not, the prudent music director will keep himself informed at all times as to the balances in his various accounts and see that they are not withdrawn.

Every budget should have a contingency fund of considerable size. It is impossible to anticipate all needs a full year or more in advance, and some monies should be available to the administrator of a budget for meeting these unanticipated needs or emergencies without unnecessary delay.

It is unwise to administer a budget so that accounts are overdrawn because, by doing so, some other deserving portion of the program will be denied its rightful share of the available funds. It is also unwise to carry over large amounts of unspent money from one fiscal year into the next, since future appropriations are likely to be reduced.

APPRAISAL   Throughout the fiscal year covered by the budget, the music director will keep a critical eye on all phases of his program and the expenditures that support them. He will be concerned to see whether the established aims are being satisfied, whether goals are being reached, and whether the public's money is being spent most advantageously.

It is a good practical policy to keep a file of observations about the budget and its operation. As ideas, thoughts, and suggestions appear, they should be written out and placed in the budget file so they may be studied and, if judged worthy, be incorporated in the budget for the following year. It should be made the music director's constant purpose to improve the budget, its process, and the program it supports, from year to year.

Practical Suggestions

Budgetary responsibilities might very well seem demanding and difficult to the already overworked music director. The following suggestions are offered to assist in easing the burden of budget making and accounting.

CITIZENS ADVISORY GROUPS — When specific needs arise calling for clear community understanding and support, it is often helpful to form a citizens committee to study the problem and bring in recommendations. This committee should be charged with a specific task and released when that task has been completed. The music educator and his principal or principals should decide which problem needs this type of study and determine the community groups that should be asked to furnish representatives.

It is a good idea to think of the person from each group that could be reasonably expected to furnish the type of assistance needed. With this planning done in advance, the president or chairman of the group solicited for representation is much more likely to appoint the person suggested by the music educator and principal. This assures the appointment of a group that is known, will work well together, and can be depended upon to give its best thought and energies to the assigned task.

MINIMUM AND DESIRED BUDGETS — It is often helpful to prepare two budgets. First prepare a *minimum* budget containing those sums of money absolutely needed to operate the department one more year on the same level as at present; this budget would permit no advance or improvement, only a continuation of the program on its present basis. Then prepare a second budget that would permit some growth in desired directions; this is the desired budget. Confronted with these two budgets, the superintendent, school board, and community, must decide how far they are willing to go above the minimum toward the desired. Experience has shown that most communities will move quite a distance away from the minimum in the direction of the desired, when the advance is reasonable.

INVENTORIES — At some specified time during the school year, probably the month of March, ask each person in the department (if the music educator is a one-person music department, he will end up doing it himself) to take a complete inventory of all equipment, material, and supplies, in his room or the area in which he works. After the inventory is made and before it is turned over to the director of music, ask each person to make requests for additional equipment, quantities of materials, and supplies, for the following year. With the inventories and requests, the director can confer with his staff and the principals of the various school units and construct a budget that is reasonable for the community and equitable for all concerned.

BUDGET ACCOUNTING — As a method for keeping the entire staff aware of budgetary problems throughout the entire year, it may prove helpful to prepare at regular intervals and present to all concerned a summary showing the amount allocated for each item on the budget, the amount spent, and the amount still available. The cooperation of all personnel is sought for keeping within the amount budgeted.

BUDGET FOLDER — Some music educators keep a folder in their file in a conspicuous place for the ensuing year. As ideas occur to them or suggestions are made by staff, patrons, pupils, or administration, they are jotted down and placed in the file. When budget preparation time occurs, these suggestions form the basis for requests. It is a good practice to keep such a written record throughout the year, so that suggestions will not be forgotten or overlooked.

BUDGET CALENDAR — Since financial planning is a continuous process with several deadlines to be met in the course of a year, it is wise for the director of music to make a budget calendar as an aid in scheduling year-round activities in the development of the budget. Assuming a fiscal year that begins on July 1, such a calendar could take on a form similar to that appearing as Figure 41. This could easily be made into a wall calendar as a constant reminder to the music director and his staff of the current phases of operation.

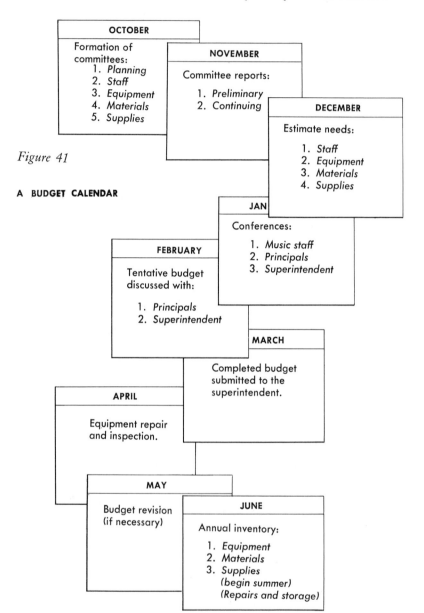

Figure 41

A BUDGET CALENDAR

OCTOBER

Formation of
committees:
1. *Planning*
2. *Staff*
3. *Equipment*
4. *Materials*
5. *Supplies*

NOVEMBER

Committee reports:

1. *Preliminary*
2. *Continuing*

DECEMBER

Estimate needs:

1. *Staff*
2. *Equipment*
3. *Materials*
4. *Supplies*

JAN

Conferences:

1. *Music staff*
2. *Principals*
3. *Superintendent*

FEBRUARY

Tentative budget
discussed with:

1. *Principals*
2. *Superintendent*

MARCH

Completed budget
submitted to the
superintendent.

APRIL

Equipment repair
and inspection.

MAY

Budget revision
(if necessary)

JUNE

Annual inventory:

1. *Equipment*
2. *Materials*
3. *Supplies*
   (begin summer)
   (Repairs and storage)

Summary

This chapter has discussed the financial planning that supports the program of music education in the public schools. The music director has a very important part to play in the development of the budget that provides the money for the musical activities of the whole school. The more clearly he understands the process by which budgets are built, the more actively he can enlist the participation of his staff, colleagues, and community; the better budget document he can assemble, the more likely will adequate financial support for the music program be forthcoming.

Suggested Activities

1. Obtain the annual budget of a nearby school district as presented to the Board of Education or Taxpayers Meeting for adoption. Study its details and makeup. Try to determine what proportion of it is devoted to the support of the music program. How does this amount compare with other special areas of the school's total program? How is it organized for presentation to the adopting body?

2. Secure the budget of the music department of a school with which you are familiar. From what sources does the money come which supports the music program? What type of budget is it? Truly departmental? Autonomous? Split?

3. Assist in the preparation of a budget for some organization of which you are a member, such as a social club, a fraternity or sorority, a church, or a Boy Scout or Girl Scout group. Does the preparation follow the stages suggested in this chapter? Would it be a better budget if it did? How is it organized for presentation for adoption?

4. Assist in the annual inventory of the music department of your college, or of a school district with which you are familiar. Evaluate the process in terms of the discussion in this chapter.

For Further Reading

Andrews, Frances M., and Cockerill, Clara E. *Your School Music Program.* Englewood Cliffs, N.J., Prentice-Hall, Inc., 1958. Pages 229–231.

Avery, Frank D. "A Building and Departmental Budget System." *American School Board Journal,* 135:47–48, September, 1957.

Eggert, C. Lee. "Make Budget Planning a Faculty Affair." *School Executive,* 73:42–43, September, 1953.

Leeder, Joseph A., and Haynie, William S. *Music Education in the High School,* Englewood Cliffs, N.J., Prentice-Hall, Inc., 1958. Pages 248–255.

Singleton, Ira C. *Music in Secondary Schools.* Boston, Allyn & Bacon, Inc., 1963. Pages 171–172 and 356–363.

CHAPTER 9

Space and Housing

THE NATURE OF THE MUSIC PROGRAM is such that it places special demands upon those who provide space, housing, and equipment, for its needs. For many years, most music departments have been forced to use makeshift facilities that have seldom been properly adapted to the particular demands of music. With the attention now being given to new construction, the music director has an unusual opportunity for serving his school and community through the development of proper facilities in new buildings, additions to existing structures, and remodeling old plants. It is well to understand that there are hazards in attempting to standardize music facilities. They must be tailored to suit the special requirements of each particular school and community. Trained consultants, such as architects and sound, heating, lighting, and ventilation engineers, can offer valuable services if supplied with educational specifications by school authorities. The music director is expected to show leadership in this activity.

Music is well established in the curriculums of schools today, and communities and boards of education are becoming more and more alert to the special necessities of the music department. Evidence of this is contained in the following statement from the Twenty-seventh Yearbook of the American Association of School Administrators. "The music program in good schools is no longer simply classroom choral work. It consists of bands, orchestras, a variety of choral groups, and individual instrumental work. The modern music program needs acoustically treated rooms planned to accommodate these important activities." [1]

French, Hull, and Dodds also recognize the necessity for adequate facilities for the work of the music department.

[1] American Association of School Administrators, *American School Buildings,* Twenty-seventh Yearbook, Washington, D.C., The Association, 1949, p. 17. Used by permission.

Specific areas planned for the music program are essential in the modern secondary school. In the small school this may mean merely arranging for built-in wall cases and adequate storage room for equipment near the auditorium, which can be used as the music room. In large schools, at least one separate room large enough for band, orchestra, or chorus, is essential. Desirable also are small rooms for small ensemble work and practice rooms for as few as six or eight students in instrumental and vocal classwork.[2]

Needs of Music Department

The music class is different from all others. The volume of sound expected is greater than that found in normal classrooms, thus the classroom requires more space for dissipation, diffusion, and absorption. A great deal of special equipment is used that requires adequate facilities for its proper storage and protection.

Since so much of the music work results in performances in assembly and concert, the music rooms need to be placed near the school auditorium in order to simplify transporting equipment and personnel from rehearsal room to auditorium stage. It is also desirable to locate the band room near the athletic field for very much the same reasons.

Special ventilation is essential. The amount of air inhaled and exhaled in the normal performance of both instrumental and vocal music rapidly reduces the oxygen content and increases the carbon dioxide in the air; it therefore must be replaced with a continuing supply of fresh air. The temperature and humidity must be controlled at constant levels in order to furnish the best protection for instruments, as well as to provide conditions in which proper intonation is possible.

Lighting presents special problems. Normal seating arrangements for choruses and instrumental groups make light coming from a single source unacceptable. Music rooms are normally used at night a great deal, and adequate artificial lighting is absolutely essential.

Music facilities must be located in relation to the remainder of the school so that sounds from rehearsal rooms and classrooms will not disturb other groups at work. An active music program will provide many opportunities for community groups to use school music facilities. They should be so arranged that they may be entered directly, without keeping

[2] Will French, J. Dan Hull, and B. L. Dodds, *Administration of the American High School*, rev. ed., Rinehart & Co., 1957, p. 490. Used by permission.

the entire school building open, unless it too is used for adult groups.

The music library is as vitally important to the music program as the school library is to the school as a whole. Facilities must be provided for proper storage of music, easy access, and efficient cataloguing and handling.

The development of adequate music facilities is truly a school-community program of the first magnitude. It is an ideal activity in which to foster lay activities in the study and development of plans toward the provision of proper housing and necessary equipment. Only by school authorities, competent architects, music educators, and interested citizens working together, can school music departments be properly housed and equipped. Cooperative planning of this sort will also help eliminate costly errors.

With the preceding discussions as a background, this chapter will discuss the location of music rooms, the types of music rooms, acoustical problems and treatment, illumination, heating and ventilation, and equipment. Every effort will be made to avoid technical terminology and specific recommendations; rather, the chapter will concentrate upon a general treatment of the stated topics in order to familiarize the music director with the problems confronting him and with possible approaches to their solution. When exact specifications are needed for a specific problem in a certain school, the music director will do well to consult experts in that particular field after he, his administrators, and his community, have clearly established the musical purposes and goals that the facilities are to serve.

Appendix F, page 293, gives several drawings and photographs of typical music facilities. They illustrate how some communities have solved their problems of space and housing for the music department.

Location of Music Rooms

The location of music rooms in relation to the remainder of the school plant is extremely important. There are four factors that deserve special consideration when decisions are to be made about such placement.

Music rooms should be conveniently placed in relation to the auditorium stage and other classrooms. Vertical travel should be avoided in transporting heavy and expensive equipment, unless an elevator is provided.

The music wing, or portion of the building housing the music department, should have a direct outside entrance that facilitates community and evening use as a separate unit and makes it easier for the band to assemble out-of-doors for marching practice, football games, and parades.

All music rooms should be situated close together to make it easier to coordinate and supervise work going on at the same time and to share equipment that may be used in common by several classes or organizations.

The music department should be physically isolated as much as possible to avoid disturbing other classes as well as to lessen the intrusion of outside noises that detract from music and its study. Proximity may be compensated for in construction by proper air conditioning, use of acoustical materials, and soundproofing.

There are several possible plans to follow in locating music rooms. They will be arranged in this discussion from what is considered to be the best to the poorest. It is understood that innumerable adaptations, variations, and combinations, may be necessary to satisfy local conditions.

The ideal solution to the placement problem is the construction of a separate building, located near the school auditorium and possibly the athletic field.

A good plan provides for a separate wing of the school building to be used by the music department. This should be located near the auditorium and be accessible from the outside by a direct entrance. It should be insulated from the remainder of the school and air-conditioned so that windows need not be opened, thereby sealing in all sound.

One possible plan might locate the music rooms on the same floor of the school building as the auditorium stage, with the storage room and music libarary between. Proper soundproofing must be provided as well.

Circumstances may demand that the auditorium stage be used as the music room; in this case, ample storage and library facilities must be built within easy access. This plan has the serious disadvantage that other worthy activities may limit the use of the auditorium.

Types of Music Rooms

The number of types of music rooms needed by any school will be governed by the greatest number and variety of courses ever to be offered in the music curriculum, as well as the greatest number of pupils expected in each course. This section will discuss common types of such rooms and general considerations concerning them.

REHEARSAL ROOMS — The rehearsal room is the nucleus of the entire music performance program. It can be built in various shapes and sizes, and can be made to serve various purposes. The balance between these factors will determine the actual construction details. Only general, broad specifications will be discussed in this chapter of the book.

CHORUS   The chorus rehearsal room should be about double the size of the average classroom, providing a minimum of fifteen square feet of floor space for each person to be accommodated. It should be wider than it is deep, and permanent semi-circular risers from six to eight inches high and from thirty to thirty-two inches wide should be placed from wall to wall in one half the room facing the center. There should be ample space in front of the risers for a grand piano, the director's stand and podium, radio, phonograph, and tape recorder. The wall opposite the risers should contain a large chalkboard, part of it permanently ruled with music staves, ample cork composition bulletin boards, and provisions for a projection screen. Electrical outlets should be placed at frequent intervals around the room, but especially at the front and the back. There should be ample space for a projection table at the rear of the room and audiovisual blinds for darkening the room when necessary.

ORCHESTRA   The orchestra rehearsal room should be spacious enough to accommodate the largest orchestra ever expected by the school. Each player requires twenty square feet of floor space and approximately 260 cubic feet of air space. The amount of cubic space can be lessened somewhat by the use of acoustic materials in construction and adequate mechanical ventilation.

The general plan of this room is similar to that of the chorus room except that the risers must be forty-eight inches wide, at least, in order to accommodate player and stand. The highest riser should be at least seventy-two inches wide in order to provide room for the larger instruments, such as the string basses, tympani, bass drum, and harp. There should be three or four risers in all, ranging from six to eight inches in height and stretching from wall to wall.

The furnishings are also similar to those in the chorus room. Electrical outlets should be placed about six feet apart on each riser as well as the front, rear, and sides, of the room in order to accommodate stand lights and certain electrical instruments like the vibraharp and electronic organ.

It is possible to construct some storage facilities around the edge of the room and in the corners, but a separate room nearby is better. The acoustical treatment should be in keeping with the needs of the orchestra.

BAND   The band room differs from the orchestra room only in the greater amount of air space or sound absorption material needed to accommodate the greater tonal volume of the band.

COMBINATION   Smaller schools may need to consider a combination orchestra-band room. This can be successfully done by means of careful planning and by striking a happy medium between the acoustical and physical demands of the various groups using it. It is obvious, of course, that such necessities cause less freedom to the schedule maker.

BROADCAST CONTROL BOOTH   Many schools have an intercommunication system that would make possible broadcasting from the rehearsal room to all other rooms in the building. Also, some schools make much use of the tape recorder, while others may be able to make arrangements with local radio stations for broadcasting programs directly from the rehearsal room. In any of these events, it would be extremely valuable to have a control booth for monitoring the program, which could be placed in one of the rear corners of the room. This booth should be completely soundproofed so that no sound is transmitted from rehearsal room to booth or vice versa. It could be so constructed and arranged that it would also serve as an individual or small group rehearsal room.

CLASSROOMS — In order to provide for the complete program of music instruction that an active music education program includes, a variety of classrooms must be considered. They require some special treatment and equipment in order for them to serve as suitable quarters for furnishing desirable and effective musical experiences for the children of the community.

GENERAL MUSIC AND THEORY   Rooms in which general music and theory classes are to be held should be the same general size as the ordinary classroom accommodating thirty to forty students. They should be acoustically treated and sound insulated so that optimum conditions for music instruction will result. They should be provided with movable chairs with tablet arms. Space should be provided for a radio, phonograph, recording machine, sound film projector and screen, teacher's desk, music cabinet, and bookshelves. The walls of the room should provide ample bulletin and chalkboard space. A closet should be provided for storing extra equipment and materials. It should be located near the other music rooms in order to make sharing of equipment and materials with other teachers easy. This room can also be used for other purposes, such as small ensembles, class instruction in voice and instrument, and certain types of dramatic rehearsals.

INSTRUMENTAL AND VOCAL CLASS INSTRUCTION   A classroom for instruction of this type can be slightly smaller than a general classroom, but it is wise to avoid building it too small and thereby causing it to be unsatisfactory for sectional rehearsals and small ensemble practice. It should be acoustically treated for maximum sound effectiveness and insulated from other rooms. It should be near the other music rooms, especially the storage room and music library. Good straight chairs affording proper posture should be provided.

PIANO CLASS   A room for class piano instruction can be much the same as for instrumental or vocal instruction, but preferably equipped with multiple pianos—one for each member of the class. There should be space enough for the teacher to use a grand piano, and the others placed so pupils may see the teacher with ease. The usual chalkboard, bulletin board, and other such equipment, should be provided at the front of the room.

It must be recognized that the above statement expresses the ultimate, the desirable, the strongly recommended. Pianos are costly items of equipment, and to delay introducing piano classes into the music curriculum until one may be provided for each student would postpone this important activity too long. Valuable learning can take place when only one instrument is available for a piano class. Inexpensive or handmade cardboard keyboards or silent keyboards help make the class environment more functional until the program is established and multiple pianos can be provided. In other words, one piano in a classroom with a competent, enthusiastic teacher is all that is needed to begin and carry out a successful program of class piano instruction. The work can be improved and extended as more pianos are provided.

LISTENING ROOM   It is very desirable to have a room equipped with several record turntables with sets of earphones for private record listening. This room may be a part of the music suite, the audio-visual center, or the school library. It should be placed near the record library so that pupils may use its facilities for free and independent or directed listening.

PRACTICE ROOMS — For the development of the best music program, small practice rooms are quite necessary. Some may be small enough for one instrumentalist or vocalist without a piano. Others will be large enough for an upright piano and one or two instrumentalists with chairs and music stands. A few should be equipped with two pianos and others should be large enough for trios, quartets, and small ensembles.

Practice rooms may be built in a series along the side of another music room or a corridor. They should be equipped with soundproof double glass windows so they may be supervised from some central place without interruption. They should be acoustically treated for maximum tonal comfort and insulated against sound transmission.

STORAGE ROOMS — The special and expensive equipment of the music department demands special storage facilities. All storage rooms should be placed so that they are conveniently located near the rehearsal, practice, or classrooms, in which the equipment is most often used.

INSTRUMENTS   The instrument storage room should be large enough to accommodate all school-owned instruments and those privately owned instruments brought to school for use in the building. They should be equipped with oversized doors, preferably more than one, so that traffic in and out may flow uninterruptedly at peak periods without damage to instruments. Lockers may be built all the way to the ceiling, with the higher spaces reserved for instruments and equipment infrequently used. A special ladder should be provided for reaching the higher storage space.

This room should be well ventilated, with humidity and heat carefully controlled and regulated for the best protection of the instruments. It should be located close to the rehearsal rooms and auditoriums. If possible, it is desirable to have it open off the rehearsal room directly, as well as the hall.

Steel lockers equipped with locks give the best protection and are generally the most serviceable. Lockers made of wood or plywood are also practical, but open shelves invite risk of damage by falling and offer less protection from thievery. Lockers should be of various sizes in order to accommodate the many different instruments. Generally speaking, the band instruments require larger lockers than do the orchestra instruments. Special racks should be provided for string basses, cellos, sousaphones, and similar items. Smaller instruments should be provided with separate lockers.

It is possible to build some storage space in the rehearsal room itself. For many schools this has worked very well, but as a general rule, a separate room affords better protection and control.

UNIFORMS AND ROBES   Storage space may be provided in a special portion of the instrument storage room or along the wall of the rehearsal room. In any case, enough space must be provided to permit the garments to hang without excessive wrinkling and mussing. This space should also furnish protection from moths, dirt, and theft. It should be closed with wide doors or removable panels so that the garments may be removed quickly and easily when being checked out for a public appearance and returned afterwards just as easily. Shelves may be built above the racks to accommodate uniform hats, stoles, and other small equipment.

LIBRARY Preferably, the library should be separate from the instrument or garment storeroom. It may conveniently open off the rehearsal rooms, but certainly should be located near them. It must be large enough to accommodate filing and storage space appropriate for the music being stored. If the usual business drawer files are used, the room must be wide enough to accommodate rows of such files, both legal and letter sizes, along each side, with plenty of room in the middle for passage even with some drawers open on both sides. Enclosed shelves may be built to the ceiling above such files. This space may be used for materials that are seldom used, and a ladder should be provided for reaching all such shelves easily.

Some schools have found that the newer, vertical files used by business firms can be adapted to the needs of storing music, eliminating the necessity of leaving the wide aisles which are necessary for operating drawers, and therefore using less floor space. Since such files are typically higher than drawer files, more music can be stored in less space.

There are also products now on the market that are especially designed for the unique problems of efficiently storing music of varying sizes. Certainly it should no longer be necessary for music to be stored haphazardly in inappropriate spaces around the building. However, it does take foresight and planning to obtain enough space for this purpose and to use that space most efficiently.

In any event, in planning new construction, enough space must be provided to enable a music department to expand its library through the years without undue crowding. There should also be enough space for placing sorting racks, work tables, card files, and desks in the library itself.

REPAIR SHOP The repair shop may be a small room, but it must be big enough to handle the largest instruments with ease. It should contain a work bench with a rack above it for tools and clamps. Ample cabinet space should be provided for storing extra parts and materials. It should have gas and electric outlets as well as a sink with running water.

OFFICE — It is quite essential that a comfortable, attractive, efficient office be provided for the director of music, at least, and preferably for all members of the music staff. The number of conferences with parents, meetings with student committees and lay groups, expected of the modern music educator requires this space for these important meetings.

The size and equipment of these offices depend upon the size of the school and the scope of the music work. It should contain at least a desk, two or three chairs, files, cabinets, and other special equipment. If at all possible, it should have a telephone for intraschool communication and a direct line to the community exchange as well.

COMBINATIONS — For reasons of economy, it may be necessary to combine various rooms and facilities. When this is done, care must be taken to make certain that no one function is called upon to make too great sacrifices, thereby impairing the efficiency and effectiveness of the music program.

Elementary schools may not be able to provide more than an all-purpose music room. The nature of the work at this level, with its self-contained classrooms and little emphasis upon special performing groups, would hardly make necessary any other space devoted more or less exclusively to music. In any event, it should be well planned and constructed in order to serve the purposes of the school and community well.

Junior high schools and senior high schools may need more appropriate music facilities in order to accommodate the specialized instrumental and vocal work typically offered at these levels.

Acoustics

THE IMPORTANCE OF ACOUSTICS — Music is the art of controlled and patterned tone. All that can be done to improve its performance and hearing should be brought about. Modern science, architecture, and engineering, know a great deal about sound, how it behaves, what it takes to control it, and how to build music rooms so they may serve the art of sound better.

The space in which music is performed is itself a musical instrument. The acoustical conditions of that space affect the way in which the music reaches the ears of the listeners from its originating sources. A room with too much reverberation causes tones to die out too slowly; thus succeeding tones are interfered with and the music sounds garbled. Rooms containing materials that absorb too many of the higher frequencies cause the music to lose a great deal of its brilliance. Rooms permitting too much unwanted sound divert the attention of the listeners, and the full impact of the music is lost. Too much sound absorption material in a room causes the room to be acoustically dead, and the music suffers. Even the most artistic performance will sound mediocre in a room where the acoustics are not right for the music.

When acoustical treatment of music rooms is an integral part of the planning before the building is constructed, proper sound conditions can be obtained with little, if any, additional cost. It is always more expensive to make such additions as an afterthought. Better results will be obtained at less expense by consulting acoustical engineers when such construction is planned.

FACTORS TO BE CONSIDERED — Two general purposes are served by architectural acoustics. First, it seeks to provide a satisfactory acoustic or sound environment, and second, it seeks to provide good conditions for hearing. Similar techniques are involved in achieving the two aims, but it is important to understand the significant differences between them.

ACOUSTIC ENVIRONMENT   The intensity or strength of all sounds existing in a given space and the manner in which these sounds are prolonged or spread within that space determine the acoustic environment. This type of environment needed is determined by the function the space is to serve. A room to be used as a library for reading, study, and research, requires an entirely different sound environment from a woodworking shop. The sound factors in the two rooms must be treated quite differently.

HEARING CONDITIONS   Satisfactory hearing conditions within a room of any type require the *background noises,* which are made up of sounds carried from the outside into a room and the incidental sounds created within the room, must be kept to a certain minimum. *Adequate separation* of sounds, both for music and speech, must be provided in order to prevent blurring, or one sound interfering with another. A certain amount of reverberation is necessary, however, to permit music to blend properly and to reinforce speech. The design and structure of the room must be such that all desired sounds may be *properly distributed* throughout the entire room without creating any dead spots, echoes, or distortions, at any point. This statement also implies that not only should the quality of sound be evenly distributed, but also the intensity as well, without distortion or interference. The sound must be *sufficiently loud* at all parts of the room so that even the softest passages of music may be readily heard and appreciated.

This need for sufficient loudness frequently requires sound amplification in large auditoriums. When this type of equipment is installed, however, expert help must be obtained in order that, from all locations within the room, the sound may appear to come only from its originating source.

ACOUSTIC PROBLEMS   The factors that bring about proper acoustic environment and hearing conditions are quite well known and fall into more or less definite classifications. Some principles have been reduced to formulas and results can be predicted with considerable accuracy; others can be treated only in a general way. It is not within the scope of this work to go into technical detail. The reader who needs such information can secure it by consulting acoustical engineers or referring to works on the subject.

It must be realized that understanding and successful application of these criteria depend upon technical skill, training, and experience; the novice is likely to bungle and make costly errors. By all means, it is better to consult an expert than risk costly failure. The purpose of this section is to point out three acoustical problems that must be met and solved, if a satisfactory acoustic environment and good hearing conditions are to result.

First, each room has its special function; everything in it and about it should be focused or controlled so that this special function may be served in the best possible manner. Activity going on in or near the room may result in undesirable, unwanted noise. This *background noise* should be controlled so that it does not interfere with the work going on in the room. In a radio or television studio, such sounds must be eliminated, but in a classroom or auditorium some of them can be tolerated. If, however, they become too strong and persistent, they will interfere.

Second, sounds within the enclosure of a room will bounce back and forth between walls, ceiling, and floor, until the sound energy dies out. Certain room conditions permit sounds to bounce around for a long time, while others cause them to fade away rapidly. *Reverberation control* is important because it influences the separation of successive sounds. Reverberation time is defined as the time in seconds for the sound to die away to one millionth of its initial intensity. Different rooms require different reverberation times; large ones will tolerate longer times than smaller ones; classrooms and auditoriums permit longer reverberation periods than libraries. The reverberation time of any room should lie within certain limits. Too long a time makes hearing difficult and the acoustic environment uncomfortable, while too short a time creates an unnatural, oppressive feeling.

Third, sound should be equally diffused throughout the entire room; it should receive *proper distribution.* It should be as easy to hear in the rear of the auditorium as in the front; the rear and corners of a classroom should provide hearing conditions comparable to the front. The sound should also be equally distributed throughout the entire area of the room; there should be no spots where sound intensity is greater than the norm and none where it is less; there should be no dead spots and no excessively live spots. This problem cannot be solved by the application of a simple formula, but must be treated in a general way.

Large auditoriums may require sound amplification in order to provide proper hearing conditions. If public address systems are installed in such places, they should be engineered so the listener in any part of the room hears sound as if it were coming from the original source.

CONTROL OF ACOUSTIC PROBLEMS — The three acoustic problems of background noise, reverberation, and distribution, are solved by sound isolation, sound absorption, and room shaping. There is no direct relationship between any sound problem and a single solution; isolation, absorption, and shaping, all contribute in varying degrees to the solution of any problem.

Isolation is handled in three ways: by segregation, or getting farther away from the source of the sound; by insulation, or placing a barrier in its path; and by absorption, or using materials that dissipate or absorb sound energy. Depending upon the circumstances of construction, these methods will be used in varying degrees.

The placement of the music room or rooms in relation to the rest of the school plant serves two purposes. In the first place, when properly done, it removes the unwanted sounds of music from the regular classrooms, libraries, and offices. In the second place, it eliminates from the music rooms such unwanted sounds as athletic field noises and shop noises.

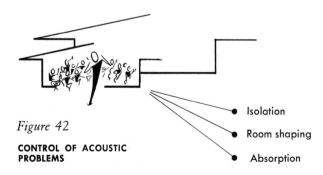

Figure 42

CONTROL OF ACOUSTIC PROBLEMS

Isolation

Room shaping

Absorption

Musicians must not overlook the fact that the sounds of music are noise factors to other classes, libraries, and offices, even though greatly to be desired in music classrooms. Segregation places the environment for each activity so that its sounds will not interfere with those of other activities.

Anything that prevents sounds from travelling from one area to an adjacent or nearby area is an insulation factor or barrier. There are many devices used for insulation in treating acoustic problems. The placement of a storeroom as a sound trap between two music classrooms, for example, is one type of barrier that prevents sounds from carrying between rooms.

Sound absorption is used not only as a method of providing for proper isolation, but also for creating the proper acoustic environment within a room. It does this by using materials that receive the sound energy but reflect only a portion of it. In other words, it *absorbs* part of it and, in effect, destroys it. Some materials are capable of absorbing greater amounts of sound energy than others; some absorb more of the high frequencies than the low, and vice versa. The material used in the solution of any problem depends upon the nature and intensity of the conditions present and the educational functions to be served.

Air volume or mass is another factor to be reasoned with in solving absorption problems. The greater the distance a sound wave has to travel, the weaker it is when it reaches a reflecting surface.

The shape of the room in which sounds must be heard has a great deal to do with reverberation control. Architects and sound engineers have learned much about room shape and its effects upon musical tone. Wisely planned new construction and some remodeling have made excellent use of room design in the control of unwanted reverberation.

The problem of reverberation has been extensively studied and the sound absorption properties of all usual construction materials is known. Formulas have been worked out to determine the amount of such materials needed for rooms containing various properties. The conditions necessary for constructing a room with a specified reverberation time can be achieved with a great deal of accuracy.

The shape of any room governs to a marked degree the manner in which sound is distributed within it. The shape and angle of the walls determine the direction in which reflected sound will travel.

In large rooms, it will be necessary to guard against echoes. Breaking up the rear wall with vertical splays or curves is one device used. Concave surfaces, in auditoriums especially, must be guarded against because they tend to focus sound to certain spots, causing uneven distribution. Also, properly placed reflecting surfaces will help reinforce sound; that is, build up its intensity.

In small rooms, discrete echoes are not a problem since the distances sound may travel are not great. Flutter echoes are a problem that may occur, however, unless steps are taken to avoid them. Flutter echoes are multiple reflections of sound back and forth between hard, parallel surfaces directly opposite each other. They must be eliminated by using nonparallel wall construction, convex curved surfaces, or other such irregularities.

Standing waves may also be a problem at low frequencies in small rooms. These are cured by using sound diffusion methods similar to those mentioned above but in a more irregular way.

Acoustical problems are no longer insurmountable. With all of the advances made in the field of acoustical engineering in recent years, it is inexcusable to permit the construction or remodeling of rooms that are acoustically incompatible to the study of music. Music directors can do themselves, their staffs, their pupils, and their community, a great service by becoming familiar with common problems and modern methods for dealing with them.

Illumination

Music rooms present unusual problems of illumination caused in part by the irregular seating of performing groups. Seating in a band, orchestra, or choir, must be such that all performers can see the conductor with equal ease and still be able to read their scores. With light coming from a single source, all pupils will not be receiving an equal amount of illumination, unless it is provided by supplementing natural light with artificial.

Glare is also a real problem. The stands that hold the music for instrumental players must be tilted at an angle permitting them to see the music easily and at the same time bring the conductor and his signals into the players' range of vision. Unless sufficient light reaches the surface of the stand from a proper angle, glare will result.

Such conditions place urgent demands upon the person planning illumination in music rooms; he must conduct a thorough study of both natural and artificial light and balance the two so that all sections of the room are lighted uniformly.

Most school codes recommend unilateral light. Music rooms, however, demand well-diffused bilateral or even multilateral natural light. It is self-evident that illumination reduces sharply as the distance from the windows increases. A thorough analysis of all factors contained in the problem must be made before reaching a decision as to the most desirable methods of lighting to be used.

East or west exposures are considered to be the best sources of natural light. It must be remembered that such light is affected by weather conditions, architectural design, orientation, window placement, color of walls and ceilings, window shades, positions of trees and other obstructions, and types of building material.

Artificial light is necessary as a supplement to daylight under certain conditions, as a substitute when natural light fails, and for proper illumination at night. Music facilities are always used a great deal at night for extra rehearsals, community music activities, and warming up for concerts. It is extremely important, therefore, to make certain that night lighting is adequate for the best music work.

It is generally considered that indirect artificial lighting is best, but the rapid improvements in fluorescent illumination make it entirely probable that such lighting will become the most important type of artificial lighting for schools. Great care must be exercised to completely eliminate any "hum" from lighting installations. This can become a very persistent unwanted noise that is intolerable in rooms where music is made or studied.

Heating and Ventilation

It is very important to provide proper heating and ventilation for all music rooms. Temperature changes affect the pitch of instruments to a marked degree, but not at the time rate and in the same proportion for all kinds; it is therefore necessary to maintain a uniform temperature if bands and orchestras are to play in tune. Extreme and sudden temperature change is also likely to cause serious damage to certain instruments, especially strings, woodwinds, and those in the percussion group.

A constant temperature ranging from 68 to 70 degrees should be maintained in all music rooms. Where heat is supplied from a central plant, music rooms should be provided with separate thermostatic controls in order to maintain this uniformity.

Singers and players on wind instruments use the oxygen content of air more rapidly than in regular classroom activity. Proper ventilation is essential in order to maintain healthful, invigorating conditions within the room. Mechanical ventilation is the best way to supply these needs, and it has the further advantage of making it possible to seal all windows shut in order to keep the sounds of the rehearsal, practice, and classrooms, from disturbing the remainder of the school.

A word of caution is in order at this point. Whenever air ducts are used in a heating and ventilating system, there is great danger of sounds being carried through the ducts to other areas of the building. This must be prevented at all costs. All ducts supplying, and returning from, music rooms must be lined with fireproof, sound absorbing material and contain frequent baffles and bends to prevent sound transmission.

Serious consideration should be given to complete air conditioning of all space devoted to music activity and storage. Excessive humidity, as well as excessive dryness, is very detrimental to musical instruments, especially the strings. Air conditioning would permit the maintenance of relative humidity within the desirable range of from 30 to 60 per cent.

Equipment

Those physical properties that make the space devoted to the music department serviceable constitute the equipment to be discussed in this section. They are more or less permanently a part of the music rooms, although they may be portable. In themselves they do not produce music but help make the best music possible. A good rule to follow in the purchase of such equipment is to buy the best you can afford and then take good care of it.

CHAIRS — Correct sitting posture is imperative for the best vocal and instrumental performances. The completely satisfactory chair for such purposes has not yet been designed. However, chair manufacturers are now aware of the unique needs of the music department and are seeking to provide products that will satisfy their requirements. The common folding chair is not satisfactory for music because it induces posture not suitable for playing and singing. There are now some folding chairs designed especially for music rooms, and these appear to be quite satisfactory. The preferred chair is still of the straight, non-folding type, sturdily constructed, and permitting comfortably erect posture.

String bass players need stools about thirty inches high, depending upon the height of the player and the size of the instrument he uses. Cellists need a chair slightly higher than the average and one that permits the player to sit on the forward edge with comfort. Chairs with tablet desk arms are needed in the general music room, but are not satisfactory for good vocal work and are entirely unserviceable for instrumental performances.

Chairs must be of a sound, rugged construction in order to give the best service. Considerable movement is expected when instrumentalists and singers perform, and this tends to cause a poorly constructed chair to wear out quickly.

RISERS — The best choral and instrumental work demands that the various rows of performers be at different heights. The rooms used regularly for rehearsals should have built-in risers. For concert purposes, portable ones should be provided for the auditoriums and other places where performing groups are likely to appear.

There are several commercial houses that make a specialty of constructing risers to the specifications of any school and its organizations. It is also possible to have them made in the school shops. Generally speaking, the commercially made collapsible risers are more portable, store more easily, and are more convenient in the long run.

MUSIC STANDS — Music stands constructed entirely of metal and fully adjustable as to height and desk angle are recommended. Light weight folding stands are usually a poor investment. They do not last long enough under the hard usage they receive, necessitating early and frequent replacement. The folding stand does not have a large enough desk to accommodate properly the large folios most bands and orchestras use.

Each school should procure enough stands to supply the largest instrumental organization that will be using them. If two groups rehearse at the same time, it will be necessary to equip each fully and independently. There should be enough stands available so that constant moving from one room to another is unnecessary. Occasional moving to the auditorium for concerts, assemblies, and programs, is expected and proper. The music stands used in the auditorium orchestra pit for operettas and shows should be independently lighted.

When estimating the number of stands needed for any school, a ratio of $1:1\frac{1}{2}$ is a safe guide to follow; this means that one stand should be purchased for each one and one half players to be accommodated at any one time; for example, a band of ninety players would require sixty stands.

CONDUCTOR'S STAND AND PODIUM — All conductors should use a podium. Not only does it make for better conducting, but the players can see the director with greater ease. The podium should be at least three feet square on top and covered with a rubber mat. The height will depend upon the height of the conductor and the size and nature of the performing group. The average height will be approximately eight inches.

The conductor's stand should be similar to that supplied the orchestra and band, but heavier and with the desk tipped almost flat at approximately waist height. A shelf below the desk surface is a great convenience, providing a place for scores not being used at the moment. If this stand is used in the orchestra pit for shows and operettas, it should be independently lighted.

STORAGE EQUIPMENT — The following discusses basic requirements for storing equipment. In a sense, these requirements are ideal, because they provide the most convenient methods possible; yet they are practical, too, because they are basic enough to be adapted to most schools. Some of the storage systems mentioned here are illustrated by photographs in Appendix F.

SHELVES, LOCKERS, AND CABINETS Storage space for musical instruments and equipment can be provided in a separate room, or it may be placed around the sides of the rehearsal room, leaving the front free for a chalkboard, bulletin board, and projection screen. Lockers and cabinets are better for instrument storage than open shelves. They not only afford this valuable equipment better protection, but they can also be kept cleaner and locked. When lockers and cabinets are planned prior to construction, they should be recessed into the walls. Such a plan gives a neater appearance to the room, and it is easier to keep instruments clean and free from harm.

Lockers generally begin at the mop board and run to a height of five or six feet. Certain instruments, such as the tympani, xylophone, and harp, should be provided with closets or lockers that begin at the floor level so they may be moved in and out easily.

Lockers and cabinets should be of various sizes in order to accommodate the many kinds of instruments. Each space should be numbered and assigned to a particular person and instrument.

The larger instruments present a difficult problem. They require a large amount of space, and entrance to that space must be as free as possible to avoid damage when the instrument is being taken from, and being placed in, storage. The exact size and type of space needed for each instrument should be determined before construction begins. There are certain types of roll-away racks for these large instruments that may be procured from their manufacturers. They furnish an ideal type of storage but are quite expensive.

PERCUSSION CABINET The great number and variety of percussion instruments and equipment make it necessary to provide them with special facilities for their protection and accessibility. A large cabinet, mounted on rubber wheels and closed by double doors, which can be locked, should be supplied. It should contain from two to four drawers for small equipment such as wood blocks, bird whistles, drum sticks, brushes, and triangles. The remainder of the space should be given over to a series of shelves for the tambourine, cymbals, tom toms, and other similar equipment.

MUSIC FOLDER CABINET   A cabinet for systematically storing the music folders for each organization when not in use is a great convenience and timesaver; it is economical, too, because it protects folders and music in the best possible manner. Cabinets of this sort can be made in the school shops. They should be large enough to hold all folders without crowding; folders for each organization should be kept in a separate cabinet. One compartment larger than the rest should be provided for the conductor's scores, since full scores require more space than the separate instrumental or vocal parts. The music folder cabinet should be equipped with a lock and mounted on rubber-tired wheels.

MUSIC SORTING RACK   Each music department should have at least one music sorting rack for efficiently placing new music in rehearsal folders and reassembling material after it has been used, before returning it to its proper place in the music library. Such a rack should be of ample size to accommodate the largest organization in the school. All organizations can use the same rack if it is located conveniently to all rehearsal rooms.

The music sorting rack is a series of slanted shelves of proper dimensions for accommodating the largest size of music to be used. It can be made in the school shops at little cost other than the expense of materials. It may be built along the wall of the music library if space is available, or it may be mounted on rubber wheels and easily moved to a convenient place for use.

MUSIC AND RECORD FILING CABINETS   Standard steel, four-drawer letter-and legal-sized files are most adequate and serviceable for the purpose of storing music and phonograph records. All choral and most orchestral and band material may be stored in the letter-size files, while oversized arrangements and records will demand the legal size. Great care must be taken to hold material in a vertical position, especially records, to prevent bending and warping. The files may be made into a unit with shelves built above to the ceiling for additional storage space.

In recent years business equipment firms have developed systems of vertical filing which permit more storage in less floor space. Since the drawers have been eliminated the aisles between rows of such files may be narrower. Also, they are typically from 18 to 24 inches higher than drawer files, and therefore make more efficient use of the storage space provided. Some of these products are engineered to be quite flexible in use, and can be adjusted to the varying sizes of music to be stored.

Several standard 5 × 8, 4 × 6, and 3 × 5 card file drawers should be built into the storage unit in order to provide space for catalog and equipment inventory cards. Even though this space is provided in the storeroom, it may be more convenient for one set of catalog cards and the equipment inventory cards to be placed in the office of the director of music.

New Construction Versus Remodeling

All facilities discussed in this chapter are more easily obtained when they are a part of a new construction program; however, many of them can be worked into an extensive remodeling program. It is not unusual to find that remodeling existing space to meet the particular demands of musical activities is more expensive and less satisfactory than new construction. Older buildings were built before much was known about handling sound problems. Since such materials as insulation must be incorporated in the basic framework of the building itself, it is difficult and expensive to obtain completely satisfactory results from a remodeling program. When remodeling is considered, it is wise to obtain expert advice to determine if it may not be more economical, in the long run, to build a new wing than to remodel an existing structure.

Summary

Providing proper facilities for the performance of music, suitable conditions for hearing it, and storing its distinctive equipment, is an important concern of the music director. Architects and sound engineers have learned a great deal about handling these unique problems of the music department, and wisdom dictates that a thorough study be made of all such conditions before construction of new, or the remodeling of old, facilities is begun. This chapter has singled out many of the factors to be considered in such planning.

The various types of music rooms and their proper location have been discussed. Special acoustical, lighting, heating, and ventilation problems have been considered, and desirable non-musical equipment has been described. A general, non-technical approach has been taken throughout the entire discussion with the recommendation made that the advice of recognized authorities and experts should be sought when detailed technical information is necessary. In this way, the special problems of a particular school may be more adequately solved, and the prudent expenditure of public funds assured.

Suggested Activities

1. Interview a music teacher you know and ask him to point out the most desirable features of the facilities in which he works. Also ask him to identify those features which cause him the most problems. Be sure to consider all aspects of his facilities. Use the major headings of this chapter as an outline for your inquiry.

2. Obtain a set of plans for a music building or facility about to be built and examine them critically from the points of view discussed in this chapter.

3. Examine the rehearsal, instructional, and storage facilities of the music department in which you are now a student. Evaluate them critically, using the suggestions of this chapter as criteria.

4. From your experience as a music student in high school and college sketch out the facilities needed for a high school with an active music department. Be sure to show the most useful and practical arrangements for all instructional and storage facilities. Before you begin to plot facilities, determine and state the music program to be offered by your hypothetical school.

5. Attend concerts in several college, high school, and public auditoriums in your community. Evaluate each acoustically for their suitability and efficiency as concert halls for bands, orchestras, choirs, solos, and small ensembles, both choral and instrumental.

6. Evaluate, acoustically, the classrooms in which music classes of all types are held in your school. What are the acoustical problems? How have they been met? Is the acoustical environment suitable for the types of classes held? How would you rate the hearing conditions?

For Further Reading

Andrews, Frances M., and Cockerille, Clara E. *Your School Music Program.* Englewood Cliffs, N.J., Prentice-Hall, Inc., 1958. Pages 190–217 and 233–236.

Carter, Elwyn. "Planning High School Music Areas." *American School Board Journal*, 136:38–40, March, 1958.

Knudsen, Vern O. "Architectural Acoustics." *Scientific American,* 209, No. 5:78–92, November, 1963.

Leeder, Joseph A., and Haynie, William S. *Music Education in the High School.* Englewood Cliffs, N.J., Prentice-Hall, Inc., 1958. Pages 238–248.

Lewis, Russell LeRoy. "Storage Facilities in the High School Music Department." *American School Board Journal,* 130:60–61, February, 1955.

Masterson, C. T., and Allen, C. J. "Lighting and Color in the Music Room." *Music Journal,* 12:20–22, July, 1954.

Music Educators National Conference. *Music Curriculum in Secondary Schools.* Washington, D.C., The Conference, 1959. Pages 38–39.

Nickerson, James F. "Planning for the Acoustics of Music Rooms." *Kansas Music Review,* February, 1953. Pages 11–15.

_____. "Planning for the Acoustics of Music Rooms. Part II: Excluding Unwanted Sound." *Kansas Music Review,* March, 1953. Pages 21–26.

_____. "Planning for the Acoustics of Music Rooms. Part III: Controlling the Wanted Sounds." *Kansas Music Review,* May, 1953. Pages 19–25.

_____. "Schoolroom Acoustics." *University of Kansas Bulletin of Education,* 7, No. 1:17–21, November, 1952.

_____. "Schoolroom Acoustics. Part II: The Control of Unwanted Sound." *University of Kansas Bulletin of Education,* 7, No. 2:44–48, February, 1953.

_____. "Schoolroom Acoustics. Part III: Control of Wanted Sound." *University of Kansas Bulletin of Education,* 7, No. 3:83–90, May, 1953.

Peterson, W. J. "Sound Control and the Rehearsal Room." *Educational Music Magazine,* 34:12*ff.,* November, 1954.

Sabine, Hale J. "Acoustical Plights of the Instrumental Director." *Educational Music Magazine,* 32:18–20*ff.,* March-April, 1953.

Sur, William R., and Schuller, Charles F. *Music Education for Teen-Agers.* New York, Harper and Brothers, Publishers, 1958. Chapter XV.

Williams, Lloyd J. "How To Design a School for Good Hearing." *American School Board Journal,* 67:103–109, May, 1961.

A Summary

and Challenge

CHAPTER 10

Forward Look

THE BASIC CONCEPT upon which this book is based is that the music educator is expected to be a leader in his school and community. This leadership is exercised in many ways and in many areas, the chief of which have been delineated and patterns of action suggested.

Before this leadership can be effective, no matter how skilled it may be, the music educator must find his place in the total organization of the school and identify himself with the philosophies or purposes which give it its direction. Let us examine these two facets of the music educator's job, beginning with the second.

The American culture is the only form of society in the world that has placed such strong emphasis and hope in universal free education. The purpose behind the school structure that provides this education is to make it possible for all children of all people within our borders to have equal opportunity for improving themselves by means of the experiences there provided. In this manner, the entire social order itself will be made better. All children, no matter what their racial inheritance, religious creed, or economic status, shall be able to receive those benefits of learning that society believes inherent in education. This is the broad, general purpose undergirding the organization of which the music educator finds himself a part.

It is important, also, that the music educator recognize his position as a part of a large organization; he is not alone, he works with other people. The use of the term organization implies that there is system and order in the work effort leading to the attainment of the goals and purposes of the schools. This system or order further implies that each person has an area of particular concern assigned to him for which he accepts responsibility. It is recognized that the system of education has become so large, so vast, so complex, that no single person could possibly carry out its purposes unassisted. For this reason, the work, the areas of responsibility, have been divided, and persons with particular interests and particular abilities have been engaged to carry on the activities unique to each field, but always in cooperation with all other areas and with eyes fixed upon the common goal underlying the activity of the entire organization.

The Educational and Administrative Team

The music educator is a member of a team. The use of the word team implies a unity of purpose in working toward a common goal, or as Webster's New International Dictionary defines the term, "A group of workmen each completing one of a set of operations." Team membership demands those attributes in an individual that make team work successful. He must be loyal to the group with whom and for whom he works; he must also be loyal to the cause or purpose for which the team was organized and set to work. He must be cooperative in his attitudes and activities. He must recognize that the joint effort is important and that the individual effort is important and worthy as it serves the cooperative effort. He must be willing to give assistance to others of the team and also graciously accept their assistance when it is needed. Membership on a team also involves sacrifice; the sacrifice of personal wants and desires on behalf of the team effort; the sacrifice of certain freedoms, personal and social, that might hinder the effectiveness of the organization. All of the attributes of team membership must be employed if the music educator's efforts are to be crowned with success and the school's purposes achieved.

The music educator is also a member of a smaller, inner, or sub-team. This is the administrative group. This smaller group is charged with the responsibility for establishing and maintaining the conditions that make possible the successful functioning of the school as a whole. This area, the administrative, is one of the special spheres of activity and responsibility referred to in the above paragraphs. Again, all of the attributes of successful team work must be employed in the music director's relationships with the administrative group if it is to be successful in achieving the purposes for which it was organized, reaching the goals established for it, and carrying out the responsibilities assigned to it.

The educational team and the administrative team, in their functioning, may be likened to a football squad. All of those players who are a part of the football activity are assembled and become the squad. All members of the squad are trained and ready to play at the proper time and in the proper situation, but only a certain few will be playing on the field at any one particular time. All members of the squad are important and vital members of the team, nevertheless. On the field, each player has his special duties; some are even prescribed by the rules of the game. Only certain ones may advance the ball, others prepare the way for the ball carriers. Certain ones may receive forward passes, others are defined as ineligible. However, all work together to advance the ball for a score and to defend against the other team's advances.

To say that the backs are the heart of the team would be false; to say that the administrative team is the heart of the school organization would be equally false. The administrative staff has its particular duties and responsibilities; the instructional staff has its special part to play; likewise, the clerical and the custodial groups; and so it is throughout the entire team; and yet all are important to the proper functioning and welfare of the school organization as a whole.

The music educator will find that his particular role or the definition of his duties and responsibilities will change as the organizational framework within which he operates changes. In some situations, he will have much responsibility for selecting staff members, in others little or none. Some plans of organization will expect him to accept heavy responsibilities for budgetary planning, others a moderate amount. Whatever his role and its particular duties may be, he must be prepared to cope with them and carry his share of the joint effort in achieving the purposes of the organization as a whole.

It is also possible, and highly probable, that a single music educator will play several roles in the course of a year, or even a day. He will be expected to be teacher, a supervisor, a consultant, a critic, a counsellor, or any one of a host of possibilities. He must recognize, however, that each role will have a certain amount of administrative content. This fact is often overlooked by the music educator

It must be recognized that although the particular role of an individual music educator may change from time to time, and from school to school, the goal of his endeavor does not. He, and all other members of his team, are working for changed lives of individuals and an improved society.

The leadership that the music educator is expected to display will find activity in two areas; the broad field of education, on the one hand, and the special sphere of art, which includes music, on the other. The two areas are again a unity. Education is the goal-seeking activity of the school as a whole, and art is the special area that contributes its share to the attainment of these goals in cooperation with physical education, social studies, reading skills, and all the other special fields of educational concern.

As administration becomes a part of the music educator's activity, the six administrative functions of defining purpose, planning, organizing, directing, evaluating, and improving, discussed in Chapter 1 of this book, are brought into play. Each is continuous in its operation, until the eventual completion of the activity. In a never-ending process such as education, all functions will be present to a certain degree most of the time. The music educator must be able to keep all six phases functioning at peak efficiency all of the time, focusing his attention and that of his staff on first one and then the other phase as each becomes important in the course of educational activity.

Administration is leadership in human relations. The music educator's principal effort will be in working with people. In truth, human relations — dealing with people — is the core of all educational activity. All of the physical accouterments and paraphernalia necessary for carrying on a modern program of education must not blind us to the fact that they are but tools or gadgets useful in achieveing the true purposes of education—changed lives of people and improved society. These ends are reached only by interaction between people and the music educator must play his part in assisting this process to complete fruition.

The music educator has four major areas in which he must practice human relations and show educational and artistic leadership. The first is in his direct, face-to-face contacts with people, pupils, parents, taxpayers, colleagues of the professional and non-professional staffs, and other administrators. The second is in the process of providing those learning experiences that will make possible maximum individual growth for each pupil of the school; in other words, curriculum development. In his work with all members of the staff leading toward improvement of the teaching-learning situation, he will be practicing human relations in the third area. Finally, in the area of public relations, in communicating to, and drawing from, the community the information necessary for making the educational environment productive and wholesome, the music educator is also dealing with human relations.

Administration is also exercising leadership in providing facilities for the best growth and development of children. The music educator is expected to provide this leadership as the musical portions of the school's activities and contributions are affected. Although these administrative activities may be chiefly operational in character, the human element is still tightly interwoven with them. In this area of leadership, the chief focus is, however, the provision of a setting in which music can be most influential in the lives of children. These activities center around schedule making; acquiring and caring for equipment, materials, and supplies; securing, budgeting, and spending, funds in support of the music program; and providing adequate and efficient space and housing for all of its activities.

There is no doubt that the music educator's job is a complex one. He must be a peculiar and particular mixture of musician, educator, humanitarian, diplomat, executive, and administrator. At times, each of these phases will be dominant in his work and activity, while others are more or less dormant. All must be in active reserve so they may be called upon quickly when needed in the business of managing his department and the work assigned to him.

This book has been written in an effort to help the music educator do better those things that are expected of him. It has sought to do this by helping him develop a better understanding of the many ramifications of his job, with particular reference to its administrative duties and responsibilities. Extreme care has been taken to avoid the establishment of rigid rules or patterns of operation because it must be recognized that individuals, purposes, communities, demands, and conditions, are mixed together in such varied proportions that no two situations are alike. Only by understanding basic, underlying principles and exercising creative, constructive thought in their application to a particular place and a definite problem can effective leadership be displayed by a music educator.

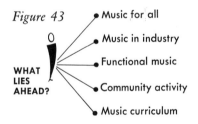

Figure 43

It is the writer's belief and conviction that as insights improve and are applied, educational practice will become better; and as practices improve, results will be more desirable and the objectives of education, the improvement of individuals and society, will be advanced.

The music educator must actively come to grips with this concept and seek to improve his own understandings so that the entire process of education and music may be improved. With this in mind, learning from the past and keeping in mind the experiences of the present, the music educator can turn his eyes toward the future.

Emerging Trends

It is certain that no one possesses all of the powers and information necessary for accurately predicting future events and trends in his personal affairs, world events, or education. It is undoubtedly a good thing that this is so, because such a condition would rob the future of much of its challenge and mystery. It would take away all zest for living and might possibly cause one to face the future with fear and dread. Denied these clairvoyant powers, one can face the future with humility and hope.

The following question will undoubtedly arise in the minds of many, concerning the wisdom of attempting to foresee the direction of educational activity. Should music educators attempt to determine the types of activity and the directions of advances that will characterize the years that lie ahead?

Not to make such an attempt would be to launch out upon an uncharted course and drift aimlessly on the sea of the future, buffeted and tossed about by all of the various currents and tides. An educator in such a position would be much like an object tossed upon the water of mid-ocean, hoping to reach eventually some useful destination.

Progress toward educational goals cannot be made in this way. Society would not move forward, and the dangers of retrogression would be great. The intelligent way to face the future is to envision reasonable, feasible goals and bring all possible resources to bear upon activities leading to the realization of these goals.

We are not, therefore, attempting to predict the future, but rather attempting to make reasonably sound guesses about its direction, based upon the best collected evidence and the best educational thinking. It is our purpose now to identify some of the emerging trends in music education and to anticipate their probable courses. After this is done, various implications for music administrators will be pointed out.

1. GENERAL ACTIVITY — The music education of the foreseeable future will become more and more a general field of activity and less and less a special one. There was a time when the music curriculum in the public schools of America was intended for the specially talented, those who possessed specific interests and abilities; this was particularly true at the secondary level. The bands, the orchestras, and the choruses, were intended for those who could excel in these special activities. Little or no attention was given to those who could not, or did not, care to perform.

Elementary music curriculums claimed to reach all children, but only one type of musical experience—singing—was used. The fact is that although nearly all could be coerced to conform to the vocal music tradition, many never really experienced the full thrill and joy of music. This situation is changing, however, and promises to improve even more in the years that lie ahead.

For a long, long time music has been placed in a category by itself and isolated from other areas of the curriculum. Happily, this is also changing.

> Developments point toward a greater realization that music cannot or at least should not stand alone and apart from the other areas of learning in the school curriculum. While those in charge of the music education program have specific outcomes which they expect to attain at each level, much of what the children do grows out of demands from various sources. The music teacher must in such a program evaluate the demands made upon the music program in terms of their inherent worth, their value for pupil growth, and the time available.[1]

With the new and proper emphasis upon general education at all levels of learning, music is coming into its own. Music as an art, as an expression of man's noblest hopes and aspirations, as an expression of beauty, is a vital part of the common core of the culture of our society. It finds expression not only in song but in the symphonies, the dance music, the church music, in all possible musical forms. Its outlets are as varied as the art itself, and its activities in the curriculum must be just as varied.

2. ACADEMIC RESPECTABILITY — Great strides are being made in moving music out of the "fad and frill" areas of educational thinking. Music is more and more being recognized as a subject of substance on its own merits, on a par with the so-called "solids." This is being brought about, at least in part, by a growing concern on the part of music educators that student performers learn the theoretical, analytical, historical, and esthetic content of music as well as mastery of performance skills.

3. WIDER AUDIENCES — Music is spreading from the drawing rooms and concert halls into the stores, offices, factories, and homes, of our land. It is permeating all phases of human activity more completely than in the past. This does not mean that the concert and recital halls will be left vacant and silent, but through the magic of television, radio, and recordings, plus wider participation in schools and communities, music is reaching areas and activities it has been unable to attain before.

[1] American Association of School Administrators, *American School Curriculum,* Thirty-first Yearbook, Washington, D.C., The Association, 1953, p. 179. Used by permission.

With fewer hours spent at their jobs, the American people are finding more time for the development of artistic and cultural pursuits. There has developed in this country a vast number of musical amateurs as a direct result of the program of public music education in the past years, limited though it may have been. Music has become an avocational interest, a hobby, for many people; the signs indicate that this group will increase in numbers and musical insights in the years ahead.

There is increasing public concern for the development of a typically American culture and its expression in all art forms, music included. Our people are breaking the shackles of foreign influences upon our culture and developing their own culture. This is very apparent in music as our own sons and daughters become the concert artists, the singers, the instrumentalists, and the composers, removing from dominance in these areas musicians trained in foreign lands.

Music will continue to be a very special form of art, but as it continues its march into the lives of our people rather than the select few, it will make tremendous contributions to the social and emotional development of individuals and groups. No expressive medium has the power to draw groups of people together in common cause as does music. No form of art speaks so intimately and strongly to the souls of men, and no better expressive outlet for the emotions of mankind can be found than that of music.

4. COMMUNITY ACTIVITIES — Public education, and with it public music education, is being extended beyond the traditional twelfth year into the thirteenth and fourteenth. The development of community colleges as an extension of the high school and as a setting for adult education is becoming quite widespread. This provides opportunities for music education not only in the years immediately following high school but later adult years.

Community music programs and activities have become widespread and will increase. Amateur orchestras, bands, and choruses, are becoming commonplace in many parts of the country. Community concert associations, music study groups and clubs, and a host of other activities, are becoming an important part of our way of living. The music educator will identify himself with these activities and foster their continued development.

Many communities are extending the school year to provide activities and experiences during those periods in which school facilities have been idle in the past. Summer recreational programs often include music instruction and regularly scheduled concerts by performing groups. These are often truly community groups, encouraging adults and school children to make music together. This is a desirable form for musical activity to take, and its further development is to be encouraged.

5. INDUSTRIAL USE — Music is finding an important place in many businesses and industries. It is performed during lunch periods and even during working hours. Industry-sponsored musical organizations are becoming increasingly common. As workers' lives are made happier, as fatigues and tensions are assuaged, and as men's souls are lifted beyond the commonplaces of life, desirable productivity is increased.

6. FUNCTIONAL USE — Functional music is coming into greater prominence and service. Music is being used to assist in the restoration of sick minds and bodies. It is being used to relieve the tedium of routine tasks and operations. It is being used to stimulate, to motivate, to challenge, to ennoble.

The Challenge for the Music Administrator

What then are the implications for the music administrator as he seeks to provide the leadership for meeting these challenges? First of all, he will extend the horizons of his own thinking to include the expanded functions music will serve. This he must do before he can lead others to see beyond the immediate to the future.

He will seek to widen, deepen, and extend, the music curriculum of his school and community to include meaningful experiences for all people, young and old, and not for merely a selected few. His new curriculum will be flexible and one that can be freely altered and adapted to meet the needs of all children, the community as a whole, and the constantly changing American culture.

He will seek to release music from its ivory tower and enshrine it where it belongs—in the lives of men.

He will recognize and exploit the special abilities of all of his staff, the specialists, the classroom teachers, the administrators, and the non-professional workers, for the good of all children in his community.

He will also seek ways to use lay people in enriching the curriculum of his school. He will in every way seek to create situations in which everyone can contribute his maximum talents in the development of better people and a better society through the medium of music.

He will seek to permit and encourage the contribution music can make to the esthetic development of each person's personality.

Above all, he will recognize that he cannot anchor himself in the present and seek to perpetuate it, nor yearn for the past and attempt to restore it, but rather he must project himself into the future and seek to mold it. Only in this way, can the music administrator provide the leadership expected of him.

For Further Reading

Brameld, Theodore. "What Is the Central Purpose of American Education?" *Phi Delta Kappan,* 43, No. 1:9–14, October, 1961.

Britton, Allen P. "Music Education in the Nineteen-Sixties." *Music Educators Journal,* 50, No. 6:23–26, June-July, 1961.

Cady, Henry L. "The Sociology of Music: A Perspective." *Music Educators Journal,* 50, No. 2:25–27, November-December, 1963.

Carlsen, James. "Toward Academic Excellence in Music." *Music Educators Journal,* 50, No. 4:117–122, February-March, 1964.

Engleman, Finis. "The Arts and American Education." *Music Educators Journal,* 50, No. 4:30–32ff., February-March, 1964.

Fawcett, Novice G. "An Educator Looks at Music and the Arts in a Day of Science." *Music Educators Journal,* 44, No. 5:22, April-May, 1958.

Fowler, Charles B. "Music: A Sound Approach to Living." *Music Educators Journal,* 50, No. 4:51–52ff., February-March, 1964.

Hanson, Howard. "A Plea for the Arts." *Music Journal,* 21, No. 8: 25ff., November, 1963.

———. "Music Education Faces the Scientific Age." *Music Educators Journal,* 45, No. 6:17–19, June-July, 1959.

Hartshorn, William C. "The Study of Music as an Academic Discipline." *Music Educators Journal,* 49, No. 3:25–28, January, 1963.

Lang, William C. "An Expanding Role for Music in a Science-Centered Age." *Music Educators Journal,* 50, No. 4: 123–126, February-March, 1964.

Lerner, Max. "New Dimensions." *Music Educators Journal,* 50, No. 6: 29–33, June-July, 1964.

Lowry, W. McNeil. "The Arts in Today's Society." *Music Educators Journal,* 50, No. 6: 28, June-July, 1964.

Mesthene, Emmanuel G. "Music as a Means of Communication in a Scientific Age." *Music Educators Journal,* 48, No. 1:42–44, September-October, 1961.

Nitz, Donald. "Music Education in a Cultural Epoch." *Music Journal,* 21, No. 7:40ff., October, 1963.

Novak, Benjamin, J., and Barnett, Gladys R. "Are Music and Science Compatible?" *Music Educators Journal,* 46, No. 6:44–48, June-July, 1960.

Smith, Carleton Sprague. "The Study of Music as an Academic Subject." *Music Educators Journal,* 49, No. 1:31–43, September-October, 1962.

Van Bodegraven, Paul. "New Horizons in Music Education." *International Musician,* 60:14ff., February, 1962.

Appendixes

APPENDIX A

Music Educator's Bookshelf

At VARIOUS PLACES in this book, reference has been made to the professional library all music educators should acquire and use. The following books and periodicals are suggested as a nucleus for this personal library. Some other writer might very well come up with a different set of titles, but these have been helpful to the present writer and are recommended to the reader. In keeping with the central theme of the preceding pages, these books have been selected from wide areas in the field of education. An effort has been made to list each title in the area to which it makes its greatest contribution. It must be remembered, however, that each book may well contain implications for other fields and should be read in this light.

Lest one be frightened away from so worthwhile a project as the development of a personal, professional library, the writer would like to suggest that the retention of all books used as texts in one's college career makes a good start toward this objective. With this beginning, a planned program of purchasing and reading a few new books each year will soon result in a practical, useful professional library.

Educational Foundations

Broudy, Harry S. *Building a Philosophy of Education.* Englewood Cliffs, N.J., Prentice-Hall, Inc., 1954. 480 pp.

Brubaker, John S. *Modern Philosophies of Education.* 2nd ed. New York, McGraw-Hill Book Co., 1950. 349 pp.

Butts, R. Freeman. *A Cultural History of Western Education.* 2nd ed. New York, McGraw-Hill Book Co., 1955. 645 pp.

Counts, George S. *Education and American Civilization.* New York, Bureau of Publications, Teachers College, Columbia University, 1952. 491 pp.

Havighurst, Robert J., and Neugarten, Bernice L. *Society and Education.* Boston, Allyn and Bacon, Inc., 1957. 465 pp.

Johnson, Earl A., and Michael, R. Eldon. *Principles of Teaching.* Boston, Allyn and Bacon, Inc., 1958. 501 pp.

Kilpatrick, William H. *Philosophy of Education.* New York, Macmillan Co., 1951, 465 pp.

McGrath, Earl J., and others. *Toward General Education.* New York, Macmillan Co., 1948. 224 pp.

O'Connor, David John. *An Introduction to the Philosophy of Education.* New York, Philosophical Library, 1957. 148 pp.

Scheffler, Israel. *Philosophy and Education.* Boston, Allyn and Bacon, Inc., 1958. 312 pp.

Administration

American Association of School Administrators. *The American School Superintendency.* Thirtieth Yearbook. Washington, D.C., The Association, 1952. 661 pp.

Bartky, A. John. *Administration as Educational Leadership.* Stanford, Calif., Stanford University Press, 1956, 256 pp.

Campbell, Roald F., Ramseyer, John A., and Corbally, John E. Jr. *Introduction to Educational Administration.* Boston, Allyn and Bacon, Inc., 1958. 480 pp.

Elsbree, Willard S., and McNally, Harold J. *Elementary School Administration and Supervision.* New York, American Book Co., 1951. 457 pp.

French, Will, Hull, J. Dan, and Dodds, B. L. *American High School Administration.* rev. ed. New York, Rinehart & Co., Inc., 1957. 604 pp.

Hagman, Harlan L. *The Administration of American Public Schools.* New York, McGraw-Hill Book Co., 1951. 428 pp.

Horn, Gunnar. *Public School Publicity.* New York, Inor Publishing Co., 1948. 226 pp.

Mort, Paul R. *Principles of School Administration.* New York, McGraw-Hill Book Co., 1946. 388 pp.

Mort, Paul R., and Reusser, Walter C. *Public School Finance.* 2nd ed. New York, McGraw-Hill Book Co., 1951. 639 pp.

Sears, Jesse B. *The Nature of the Administrative Process.* New York, McGraw-Hill Book Co., 1950. 623 pp.

Supervision

Association for Supervision and Curriculum Development. *Group Processes in Supervision.* Washington, D.C., The Association, 1948. 130 pp.

Bartky, John A. *Supervision as Human Relations.* Boston, D.C. Heath & Co., 1953. 308 pp.

Beckhard, Richard. *How to Plan and Conduct Workshops and Conferences.* New York, Association Press, 1956. 64 pp.

Burton, William H. *The Guidance of Learning Activities.* 2nd ed. New York, Appleton-Century-Crofts, Inc., 1952. 737 pp.

Keltner, John W. *Group Discussion Processes.* New York, Longmans, Green & Co., 1957, 373 pp.

Wiles, Kimball. *Supervision for Better Schools.* New York, Prentice-Hall, Inc., 1950. 330 pp.

Curriculum Development

American Association of School Administrators. *American School Curriculum.* Thirty-first Yearbook. Washington, D.C., The Association, 1953. 551 pp.

Anderson, Vernon Ellsworth. *Principles and Procedures of Curriculum Improvement.* New York, Ronald Press Co., 1956. 468 pp.

Association for Supervision and Curriculum Development. *Research for Curriculum Improvement.* Washington, D.C., The Association, 1957. 350 pp.

Beauchamp, George A. *Planning the Elementary School Curriculum.* Boston, Allyn and Bacon, Inc., 1956. 295 pp.

Corey, Stephen Maxwell. *Action Research to Improve School Practices.* New York, Bureau of Publications, Teachers College, Columbia University, 1953. 161 pp.

Miel, Alice. *Changing the Curriculum.* New York, Appleton-Century-Crofts, Inc., 1946. 242 pp.

Smith, B. Othanel, Stanley, William A., and Shores, J. Harlan. *Fundamentals of Curriculum Development.* Yonkers-on-Hudson, N.Y., World Book Co., 1950. 780 pp.

Spears, Harold. *Curriculum Planning through In-Service Programs.* Englewood Cliffs, N.J., Prentice-Hall, Inc., 1957. 350 pp.

Stratemeyer, Florence B., Forkner, Hamden L., and McKim, Margaret T. *Developing a Curriculum for Modern Living.* New York, Bureau of Publications, Teachers College, Columbia University, 1947. 558 pp.

Psychology

Almy, Millie Corinne. *Child Development.* New York, Henry Holt & Co., 1955. 490 pp.

Crow, Lester Donald, and Crow, Alice. *Human Development and Learning.* New York, American Book Co., 1956. 578 pp.

Jersild, Arthur T. *Child Psychology.* 3rd ed. Englewood Cliffs, N.J., Prentice-Hall, Inc., 1947. 623 pp.

Kuhlen, Raymond G. *The Psychology of Adolescent Development*. New York, Harper & Brothers, 1952. 675 pp.

Mursell, James L. *Psychology for Modern Education*. New York, W.W. Norton & Co., 1952. 610 pp.

Sawrey, James M., and Telford, Charles W. *Educational Psychology*. Boston, Allyn and Bacon, Inc., 1958. 512 pp.

Musical Foundations

Apel, Willi. *Harvard Dictionary of Music*. Cambridge, Mass., Harvard University Press, 1947. 824 pp.

Bartholomew, Wilmer T. *Acoustics of Music*. Englewood Cliffs, N.J., Prentice-Hall, Inc., 1942. 242 pp.

Boyden, David D. *An Introduction to Music*. New York, Alfred A. Knopf, 1956. 449 pp.

Demuth, Norman. *Musical Trends in the Twentieth Century*. London, Rockcliff, 1952. 359 pp.

Edwards, Arthur C. *The Art of Melody*. New York, Philosophical Library, 1956. 266 pp.

Grove, Sir George. *Dictionary of Music and Musicians*. Eric Blom, ed. 5th ed. London, Macmillan Co., 1954. 9 volumes.

Hansen, Peter S. *An Introduction to Twentieth Century Music*. Boston, Allyn and Bacon, Inc., 1961. 376 pp.

Lang, Paul Henry. *Music in Western Civilization*. New York, W.W. Norton & Co., 1941. 1107 pp.

McKinney, Howard D., and Anderson, W. R. *Discovering Music*. 3rd ed. New York, American Book Co., 1952. 576 pp.

Olson, Harry Ferdinand. *Musical Engineering*. New York, McGraw-Hill Book Co., 1952. 369 pp.

Music Education

Andrews, Francis M., and Cockerille, Clara E. *Your School Program*. Englewood Cliffs, N.J., Prentice-Hall, Inc., 1958. 289 pp.

Andrews, Frances M., and Leeder, Joseph A. *Guiding Junior High School Pupils in Music Experiences*. Englewood Cliffs, N.J., Prentice-Hall, Inc., 1953. 372 pp.

Andrews, Gladys. *Creative Rhythmic Movement for Children*. Englewood Cliffs, N.J., Prentice-Hall, Inc., 1954. 198 pp.

Birge, Edward Bailey. *History of Public School Music in the United States*. Bryn Mawr, Pa., Oliver Ditson Co., 1937. 523 pp.

Brand, Erick D. *Band Instrument Repairing Manual.* 4th ed. Auburn, Ind., Auburn Printing Co., 1947. 198 pp.

Cooper, Irvin, and Kuersteiner, Karl O. *Teaching Junior High School Music: General Music and the Vocal Program.* Boston, Allyn and Bacon, Inc., 1965. 448 pp.

Dykema, Peter W., and Cundiff, Hannah M. *School Music Handbook.* Evanston, Ill., C.C. Birchard & Co., 1955. 696 pp.

Farnsworth, Paul R. *The Social Psychology of Music.* New York, Dryden Press, 1958. 304 pp.

Flagg, Marion Elizabeth. *Musical Learning.* Evanston, Ill., C.C. Birchard & Co., 1949. 195 pp.

Garretson, Robert L. *Conducting Choral Music.* Boston, Allyn and Bacon, Inc., 1961. 246 pp.

Glenn, Neal E. *Teaching Music in Our Schools.* 2d ed. Dubuque, Iowa, William C. Brown Co., 1954. 139 pp.

Goldman, Richard Franko. *The Wind Band: Its Literature and Technique.* Boston, Allyn and Bacon, Inc., 1962. 312 pp.

Graham, Floyd Freeman. *Public Relations in Music Education.* New York, Exposition Press, Inc., 1954. 241 pp.

Hovey, Nilo W. *The Administration of School Instrumental Music.* Rockville Center, N.Y., Belwin, Inc., 1952. 62 pp.

Krone, Beatrice Perham. *Music in the New School.* rev. ed. Chicago, Neil A. Kjos Music Co., 1950. 148 pp.

Krone, Beatrice, and Krone, Max. *Music Participation in the Elementary School,* Park Ridge, Ill., Neil A. Kjos Co., 1952, 88 pp.

———. *Music Participation in the Secondary School.* Park Ridge, Ill., Neil A. Kjos Music Co., 1952. 88 pp.

Kuhn, Wolfgang E. *Instrumental Music: Principles and Methods of Instruction.* Boston, Allyn and Bacon, Inc., 1962. 232 pp.

Landeck, Beatrice. *Children and Music.* New York, Sloane, 1952. 279 pp.

Leeder, Joseph A., and Haynie, William S. *Music Education in the High School.* Englewood Cliffs, N.J., Prentice-Hall, Inc., 1958. 366 pp.

Lundin, Robert W. *An Objective Psychology of Music.* New York, Ronald Press Co., 1953. 303 pp.

Mathews, Paul R. *You Can Teach Music.* New York, E.P. Dutton & Co., Inc., 1953. 178 pp.

Meyer, Leonard B. *Emotion and Meaning in Music.* Chicago, The University of Chicago Press, 1957. 307 pp.

Morgan, Russell Van Dyke, and Morgan, Hazel Nohavec. *Music Education in Action.* Park Ridge, Ill., Neil A. Kjos Music Co., 1954. 186 pp.

Mursell, James L. *Education for Musical Growth.* Boston, Ginn & Co., 1948. 343 pp.

———. *Music and the Classroom Teacher.* Morristown, N.J., Silver Burdett Co., 1951. 304 pp.

————. *Music Education, Principles and Programs.* Morristown, N.J., Silver Burdett Co., 1956. 386 pp.

————. *Music in American Schools.* rev. ed. Morristown, N.J., Silver Burdett Co., 1953. 312 pp.

Music Educators National Conference. *Bibliography of Research Studies in Music Education.* Washington, D.C., The Conference, 1957. 225 pp.

————. *Music Buildings, Rooms, and Equipment.* Washington, D.C., The Conference, 1955. 96 pp.

————. *Music in American Education.* Music Education Source Book No. 2. Washington, D.C., The Conference, 1955. 365 pp.

————. *The Music Teacher and Public Relations.* Washington, D.C., The Conference, 1958. 48 pp.

Music Industry Council. *Business Handbook of Music Education.* Washington, D.C., 1962. 31 pp.

Myers, Louise Kifer. *Music Fundamentals through Song.* Englewood Cliffs, N.J., Prentice-Hall, Inc., 1954. 90 pp.

————. *Teaching Children Music in the Elementary School.* 2nd ed. Englewood Cliffs, N.J., Prentice-Hall, Inc., 1956. 327 pp.

National Society for the Study of Education. *Basic Concepts in Music Education.* Fifty-seventh Yearbook, Part I. Chicago, The Society, 1958. 362 pp.

Nordholm, Harriet, and Thompson, Carl. *Keys to Teaching Elementary School Music.* Minneapolis, Schmitt Publications, Inc., 1949. 271 pp.

Normann, Theodore F. *Instrumental Music in the Public Schools.* Bryn Mawr, Pa., Oliver Ditson Co., 1941. 349 pp.

Pitts, Lilla Belle. *The Music Curriculum in a Changing World.* Morristown, N.J., Silver Burdett Co., 1944. 165 pp.

————. *Music Integration in the Junior High School.* Evanston, Ill., C.C. Birchard & Co., 1935. 206 pp.

Prescott, Gerald R., and Chidester, Lawrence W. *Getting Results with School Bands.* New York, Carl Fischer, Inc.; Minneapolis, Paul A. Schmitt Music Co., 1938. 273 pp.

Righter, Charles B. *Success in Teaching School Orchestras and Bands.* Minneapolis, Paul A. Schmitt Music Co., 1945. 211 pp.

Roggensack, Delinda. *Eyes and Ears for Music.* St. Louis, Educational Publications, 1954. 115 pp.

Rorke, Genevieve A. *Choral Teaching at the Junior High School Level.* Minneapolis, Hall & McCreery Co., 1947. 114 pp.

Sheehy, Emma Dickson. *There's Music in Children.* New York, Henry Holt & Co., 1952. 152 pp.

Singleton, Ira C. *Music in Secondary Schools.* Boston, Allyn and Bacon, Inc., 1963. 404 pp.

Squire, Russel H. *Introduction to Music Education.* New York, Ronald Press Co., 1952. 185 pp.

Sur, William R., and Schuller, Charles F. *Music Education for Teen-Agers.* New York, Harper & Bros., 1958. 478 pp.

Timm, Everett. *The Woodwinds: Performance and Instructional Techniques.* Boston, Allyn and Bacon, Inc., 1964. 212 pp.

Timmerman, Maurine. *Let's Teach Music.* Evanston, Ill., Summy-Birchard Publishing Co., 1958. 216 pp.

Tooze, Ruth, and Krone, Beatrice. *Literature and Music as Resources for Social Studies.* Englewood Cliffs, N.J., Prentice-Hall, Inc., 1955. 478 pp.

Van Bodegraven, Paul, and Wilson, Harry R. *The School Music Conductor.* Minneapolis, Hall & McCreery Co., 1942. 168 pp.

Winter, James H. *The Brass Instruments: Performance and Instructional Techniques.* Boston, Allyn and Bacon, Inc., 1964. 136 pp.

Periodicals

The Instrumentalist. 1418 Lake Street, Evanston, Ill.

Journal of Research in Music Education. Music Educators National Conference, 1201 Sixteenth Street, Northwest, Washington, D.C.

Music Educators Journal. Music Educators National Conference, 1201 Sixteenth Street, Northwest, Washington, D.C.

The Music Journal. 1270 Sixth Avenue, New York 20, N.Y.

Musical America. 113 West Fifty-seventh Street, New York 19, N.Y.

Judging Piano Quality

Tone is the basic material with which the musician works. The cabinet-maker works with wood, the tinsmith with metal, the artist with paints, and the musician with tone.

The musician is dependent upon the inherent tonal quality of his instrument for the tones he must produce. If they are not there, he cannot put them there. The instrument he uses must be capable of producing beautiful, responsive, controllable tones.

These tones must be related and compatible. They must be consistent in quality from low bass to the highest treble.

Properties of Tone

Tones have three basic properties: pitch, dynamics, and quality or timbre. Pitch has to do with highness and lowness. High pitches have a fast rate of vibration, and low pitches, a slow rate. The length, density, and tension, of the strings govern vibration rate. Since the bass strings produce low sounds, these strings must be long and thick. Treble strings must vibrate faster in order to give off higher pitches; hence, they must be short, less thick, and under greater tension. The strings of a piano must be carefully graded as to length and density so that as the pitch rises, the strings gradually become shorter and less thick. The manner in which this is done affects the quality of sound from a piano.

Dynamics has to do with the degree of loudness and softness of a tone. A piano must be capable of producing the loudest sounds demanded by the music without distortion, as well as the softest whispers of tone without losing vitality or character.

Quality, or timbre, has to do with the essential "goodness," beauty, or color of the sound. This is dependent upon the manner in which the instrument produces, amplifies, and distributes the natural partials (overtones) of the various pitches. Here the performer is absolutely dependent upon the maker of the instrument, for he cannot control or alter to any great extent the quality of sound the piano is built to produce.

Tone Production

Strings produce the sound coming from any piano. The quality of the string is largely responsible for the quality of sound coming from an instrument. The sound any piano string is capable of producing would be weak, thin, and not useful, if it were not amplified and reinforced by the sounding board, the frame, and the rim. These are all critical factors in determining the quality and manageability of the tone coming from an instrument.

ACTION — The pianist can produce sounds upon his instrument only by exerting force upon the piano key, which activates a series of levers conducting this force to the hammer, which strikes the string and at the same time releases a felt damper to permit the string to sound. This is an extremely complicated yet delicate mechanism. At any point in the mechanism where painstaking care is not exerted in its manufacture, impairment of the tone the performer is capable of producing will inevitably result. There are eighty-eight such mechanisms on each piano, each containing innumerable parts. The action must be "light" enough that extremely soft, rapid performance is possible, yet contain enough resistance to the touch so that the action and, by it, the tone can be controlled. The action must be sturdy enough that full fortissimo or loud tones can be played without danger of breaking under the force applied to the keys. In short, the action must be responsive to the pianist's touch so that all gradations of tone, from loud to soft, from fast to slow, may be produced with equal ease.

HAMMERS — Hammers are the means by which the force the performer exerts upon the key is applied to the string to cause it to vibrate and thereby produce sound. The hammers must be sturdy enough to withstand this abuse and yet delicate enough to provide the performer with full dynamic range possible.

PEDALS — The three pedals upon the grand piano have sometimes been referred to as the "soul of the instrument." Certainly they have an extremely important bearing upon what the piano is capable of producing. The *una corda* pedal must shift the entire mechanism in such a manner that the hammers strike only two of the three strings tuned to any single pitch. This is a shift of less than an eighth of an inch. If it shifts too far, it causes two pitches to sound although only one key is being played. If it does not shift far enough, it does not reduce the string sound by one third as it is supposed to do. The *sostenuto* pedal must be able to select and sustain any tone or group of tones the performer calls for throughout the entire range of the instrument. There is also no room for error here. The *damper* pedal must remove all dampers from the strings when the performer demands and yet stop the vibrations instantly when the pedal is released.

Piano Maintenance

Only expertly trained and skilled craftsmen can tune a piano properly. It is a highly skilled art, and the pianist is dependent, utterly, upon him for keeping his instrument in tune. School pianos in classrooms and auditoriums must be tuned at least three or four times a year to maintain them in the best condition. A quality instrument will give good service for this long a time, if temperature and humidity are carefully controlled. An important factor in a piano keeping its tune is the pinblock, or wrestplank, and its construction. The texture of the wood, as well as the laminations used in the construction of the pinblock, and the manner in which the tuning pins are seated in the block, determine the ability of the instrument to hold its tune. An inferior instrument will get out of tune more quickly and therefore be more costly to maintain.

VOICING — Voicing deals with adjusting the hardness or density of the felt of the hammer so that the tones produced are of the proper loudness when related to one another (from bass to treble). This also controls the brilliance of the tone in relation to its environment, the concert hall, the classroom, the rehearsal hall, the practice room, or the living room. The quality of the felt is of paramount importance in this process, and the manner in which the felt is affixed to the hammer head is also important. An inferior instrument demands more frequent voicing and is therefore more costly to maintain.

ACTION REGULATIONS — The importance of the proper relationship of all parts of the action to each other was mentioned before. Here we consider the regulation of the action. This is also a task for a skilled and highly trained piano mechanic. A quality instrument is engineered in a way that the action can be regulated and will hold its regulation over longer periods of time. This reduces maintenance costs.

CASE — The case, or exterior, of the piano to be used in a school must be hard and wear-resistant. Every protection possible is taken to protect all pianos from damage. The quality piano keeps its finish longer and is less frequently in the shop for overhaul to its exterior. Inferior pianos have a soft finish, never look as well, and must be repaired at more frequent intervals, again adding to maintenance costs.

APPENDIX C

Sources of Equipment and Supplies

There are many business firms that supply the music education profession. A complete listing of such firms would be difficult, if not impossible, to obtain. Since all music educators on occasion need to consult some list of this sort, the author has asked the officers of the Music Industry Council for permission to include their membership roster as a representative list of such firms. Membership in the Council signifies a special interest in the music education profession, since the Music Industry Council is an affiliate of the Music Educators National Conference.

The music educator seeking business houses to supply his needs is urged to consult this list of firms and contact those that can supply the types of goods and services he seeks. He is also urged to locate and deal with his local music merchants, since they may be better equipped to serve his special needs.

Audio-Visual Aids and Equipment

The Audio Recording & Manufacturing Company, Inc., Box 56, Franklin Square, N.Y.
The Stanley Bowmar Co., Valhalla, N.Y.
Bowmar Records, 4921 Santa Monica Boulevard, Los Angeles 29, Cal.
Capitol Record Distributing Co., 1750 Vine Street, Hollywood 28, Cal.
Century Record, Box 308, Saugus, Cal.
Children's Music Center, 2858 W. Pico Boulevard, Los Angeles 6, Cal.
Columbia Records, Inc., 799 Seventh Avenue, New York, N.Y.
Crest Records, 220 Broadway, Huntington Station, N.Y.
Custom Fidelity Co., 136 Annendale Road, Pasadena, Cal.
Delta Records, 4304 West Fullerton, Chicago 39, Ill.
Deutsche Grammophon Records, MGM Records, 1540 Broadway, New York, N.Y.
Educational Record Sales, 157 Chambers Street, New York 7, N.Y.

Encyclopaedia Britannica, 425 North Michigan Avenue, Chicago 11, Ill.
Fleetwood Records, 152 Commercial Street, Lynn, Mass.
Folkways Records, 121 W. 47th Street, New York 36, N.Y.
Full Fidelity Recordings, 9745 Lockland Road, Cincinnati 15, Ohio.
The Jam Handy Organization, 2821 East Grand Boulevard, Detroit 11, Mich.
Kaybank Recording Co., 2541 Nicollet Avenue, Minneapolis 4, Minn.
Ken-Del Productions, Inc., 515 Shipley Street, Wilmington, Del.
Location Recording Service, 2201 West Burbank Boulevard, Burbank, Cal.
The Magnavox Co., Bueter Road, Fort Wayne, Ind.
Minnesota Audio-Visual Co., 1012 Marquette Avenue, Minneapolis 3, Minn.
Music Education Record Corp., Box 445, Englewood, N.J.
Philadelphia Record Co., Div. Stitzinger Service Co., 8612 Germantown
    Avenue, Philadelphia, Pa.
RCA Victor Records, 155 E. 24th Street, New York 10, N.Y.
Radio-Matic of America, 760 Ramsey Avenue, Hillside, N.J.
Scholastic Stereo, 312 Oxford Valley Road, Fairless Hills, Pa.
Society for Visual Education, 1345 Diversey Parkway, Chicago 14, Ill.
Technifax Corporation, 195 Appleton Street, Holyoke, Mass.
Teeter Corporation, Felton, Cal.
Vogt Quality Recordings, Box 302, Needham 92, Mass.

Band and Orchestra Instrument Manufacturers

W. T. Armstrong Co., Inc., 200 East Sycamore, Elkhart, Ind.
The Cundy-Bettoney Co., Inc., 96 Bradlee Street, Hyde Park 36, Boston,
    Mass.
Fox Products Corp., South Whitley, Ind.
K. G. Geimeinhardt Co., Inc., P.O. Box 19, Route 19, South, Elkhart, Ind.
The Getzen Company, Inc., 431 E. Genevya Street, Elkhorn, Wisc.
Frederick Gretsch Mfg. Co., 60 Broadway, Brooklyn 11, N.Y.
Harmolin, Inc., P.O. Box 244, La Jolla, Cal.
William S. Haynes Co., 10 Piedmont Street, Boston, Mass.
M. Hohner, Inc., Andrews Rd., Hicksville, N.Y.
Frank Holton & Co., Elkhorn, Wisc.
G. C. Jenkins Co., Box 149, Decatur, Ill.
Kay Musical Instrument Co., 2201 W. Arthur Ave., Elk Grove, Ill.
G. LeBlanc Co., 2210 60th Street, Kenosha, Wisc.
Leedy Drum Company, 6633 North Milwaukee Ave., Niles 48, Ill.
Lesher Woodwind Co., 1306 West Bristol Street, Elkhart, Ind.
William Lewis & Son, 30 E. Adams Street, Chicago 3, Ill.
Linton Manufacturing Co., Inc., 919 N. Nappanee Street, Elkhart, Ind.
Ludwig Drum Co., 1728 N. Damen Avenue, Chicago 47, Ill.

Mirafone Corporation, 950 South Broadway Avenue, Los Angeles 15, Cal.

Musser Marimbas, Inc., 8947 Fairview Avenue, Brookfield, Ill.

F. E. Olds & Son, 7373 North Cicero Avenue, Chicago 46, Ill.

Peripole Products, Inc., 51-17 Rockaway Beach Blvd., Far Rockaway 91, N.Y.

Polisi Bassoon, 117 West 48th Street, New York 36, N.Y.

B. Portnoy Clarinet Accessories, 205 West 89th Street, New York 24, N.Y.

Premier Drums Co., 315 Decatur Street, New Orleans, La.

C. Pruefer Manufacturing Co., Inc., 185 Union Avenue, Providence 9, R.I.

The Recorder Shop, 432 South Hill Street, Los Angeles 13, Cal.

Rhythm Band Incorporated, 407-409 Throckmorton Street, Fort Worth 2, Texas.

Richards Musical Instruments, Inc., 431 Baldwin Street, Elkhart, Ind.

Rogers Drums, Inc., 744 Bolivar Road, Cleveland 15, Ohio.

Scherl & Roth Inc., 1729 Superior Avenue, Cleveland, Ohio

Oscar Schmide-International, Inc., 87 Ferry Street, Jersey City 7, N.J.

Schulmerich Carillons, Inc., Sellersville, Pa.

H. & A. Selmer, Inc., Selmer Building, Elkhart, Ind.

Slingerland Drum Co., 6633 N. Milwaukee Ave., Niles 48, Ill.

H. N. White Co., 5225 Superior Avenue, Cleveland 3, Ohio.

Avedis Zildjian Co., 39 Fayette Street, North Quincy 71, Mass.

Band Uniforms and Choir Gown Manufacturers

Bentley & Simon Inc., 7 W. 36th Street, New York 18, N.Y.

Collegiate Cap & Gown Co., 1000 N. Market Street, Champaign, Ill.

The Craddock Company, Box 1039, Kansas City 41, Mo.

Eastwood Apparel, Ltd., Eastwood Bldg., Box 351, St. George 1, N.Y.

Fechheimer Bros. Co., Corner Fourth & Pike Streets, Cincinnati, Ohio

Sol Frank Uniforms, Inc., P.O. Box 1846, San Antonio 6, Texas.

Ireland Needlecraft, 3661 San Fernando Road, Glendale 4, Cal.

Manhattan Costume Co., Inc., 614 West 51st Street, New York 19, N.Y.

E. R. Moore Co., 932 Dakin Street, Chicago 13, Ill.

De Moulin Brothers & Co., Greenville, Ill.

Robert Rollins Blazers, Inc., 242 Park Avenue South, New York 3, N.Y.

Saxony Clothes, 230 Canal Street, New York 13, N.Y.

Uniforms by Ostwald, Inc., 73 Henry Street, Staten Island 1, N.Y.

Musical Equipment Manufacturers

American Rawhide Manufacturing Co., 1103 N. North Branch Street, Chicago, Ill.

Brilhart Musical Instrument Co., 505 Oak Avenue, Carlsbad, Cal.
Clarin Manufacturing Co., 4640 W. Harrison Street, Chicago 44, Ill.
Handy-Folio Music Co., Box 3185, Milwaukee 18, Wisc.
Krauth & Benninghofen, Hamilton, Ohio
Manhasset Specialty Company, Route 6, Box 373, Yakima, Wash.
Midwest Folding Products, Roselle, Ill.
Mitchell Manufacturing Co., 2740 S. 34th Street, Milwaukee 46, Wisc.
The Norwood Co., Inc., 8040 N. Austin Avenue, Morton Grove, Ill.
Rico Products, 819 N. Highland Ave., Hollywood 38, Cal.
School Specialties, 48 West Northfield Road, Livingston, N.J.
E. H. Sheldon Equipment Co., Muskegon, Mich.
Stagecraft Manufacturing Corp., 25 Belden Avenue, Norwalk, Conn.
Wenger Music Equipment Co., Owatonna, Minn.

Music Magazines

Down Beat Magazine, 205 West Monroe Street, Chicago 6, Ill.
High Fidelity Magazine, Great Barrington, Mass.
The Instrumentalist, 1418 Lake Street, Evanston, Ill.
Keyboard Jr., 1346 Chapel Street, New Haven 11, Conn.
Musical America, 111 West 57th Street, New York 19, N.Y.
The Music Journal, Inc., 1776 Broadway, New York 19, N.Y.
The School Musician, 4 E. Clinton Street, Joliet, Ill.

Music Textbook Publishers

Allyn and Bacon, Inc., 150 Tremont Street, Boston 11, Mass.
American Book Co., 55 Fifth Avenue, New York 3, N.Y.
Wm. C. Brown Co., 135 South Locust, Dubuque, Iowa.
Follett Publishing Co., 1010 West Washington Blvd., Chicago 7, Ill.
Ginn & Co., Statler Building, Boston 17, Mass.
Holt, Rinehart & Winston, Inc., 383 Madison Avenue, New York 17, N.Y.
Lerner Publications Co., 133 First Avenue North, Minneapolis 1, Minn.
Prentice-Hall, Inc., Englewood Cliffs, N.J.
Charles Scribner's Sons, 597 Fifth Avenue, New York, N.Y.
Silver Burdett Co., Morristown, N.J.
Sing Out, Inc., 121 West 47th Street, New York 36, N.Y.
Summy-Birchard Co., 1834 Ridge Avenue, Evanston, Ill.
Wadsworth Publishing Co., Inc., 10 Davis Drive, Belmont, Cal.

Piano and Organ Manufacturers

Aeolian American Corp., East Rochester, N.Y.
The Baldwin Piano and Organ Co., 1801 Gilbert Avenue, Cincinnati 2, Ohio.
Conn Organ Corp., 1101 Beardsley, Elkhart, Ind.
Hammond Organ Co., 4200 W. Diversey Avenue, Chicago 39, Ill.
Lowrey Organ Co., 7171 North Cicero, Lincolnwood, Chicago 46, Ill.
Steinway & Sons, Steinway Place, Long Island City 5, N.Y.
Story and Clark Piano Co., 28 E. Jackson Boulevard, Chicago, Ill.
The Wurlitzer Co., De Kalb, Ill.

Sheet Music and Instrument Dealers and Distributors

Bregman, Cocco, and Conn, Inc., 1619 Broadway Avenue, New York 19, N.Y.
Brodt Music Co., Box 1207, Charlotte 1, N.C.
Bronen's Music Co., 406 East 189th Street, Bronx 58, N.Y.
C. Bruno and Son, Inc., 1110 Broadway, San Antonio, Texas.
Byron Hoyt Sheet Music Service, 531 S. W. Park Avenue, Portland 5, Ore.
Chesterfield Music Shops, Inc., 12 Warren Street, New York 7, N.Y.
City Music Center, 82 Springfield Avenue, Newark 3, N.J.
Coast Wholesale Music Co. of Los Angeles, 1201 S. Olive Street, Los Angeles, Cal.
Cross Music Centre, 1819 Capitol Avenue, Cheyenne, Wyo.
Dorn & Kirschner Band Instruments Co., 77 Springfield Avenue, Newark, N.J.
Educational Music Bureau, Inc., 434 South Wabash, Chicago 5, Ill.
The Empire Music Co., Ltd., 934 Twelfth Street, Box 270, New Westminister, B.C., Canada.
Carl Fischer Musical Instrument Co., 105 East 16th Street, New York 3, N.Y.
Fuhrman Music Co., 29 N. California Street, Stockton, Cal.
The Getzen Company, Inc., 431 East Geneva Street, Elkhorn, Wisc.
David Gornston, 117 West 48th Street, New York 19, N.Y.
William R. Gratz Co., Inc., 14 Bixley Heath, Lynnbrook, L.I., N.Y.
Grossman Music Corp., 740 Bolivar Road, Cleveland 15, Ohio.
Hargail Music Press, 157 West 57th Street, New York 19, N.Y.
L. D. Heater Music Co., 1930 N.W. Irving Street, Portland 9, Ore.
Hershman Musical Instrument Co., 53 West 23rd Street, New York 10, N.Y.
Hunleth Music Company, 415 North Broadway Avenue, St. Louis, Mo.
Informal Music Service, Deleware, Ohio

Jenkins Music Co., 1217 Walnut Street, Kansas City, Mo.
Johnson West Music Co., 500 Denny Way, Seattle 9, Wash.
Georgia Kelischek Workshop, 2725 Knox Street, N.E., Atlanta 17, Ga.
Kendor Music Co., East Aurora, N.Y.
Keynote Music Service, 837 South Olive Street, Los Angeles 14, Cal.
B. F. Kitching & Co., Inc., 8947 Fairview Avenue, Brookfield, Ill.
Lockie Music Exchange, 950 South Broadway, Los Angeles 15, Cal.
Lyon & Healy, Inc., Wabash & Jackson Boulevards, Chicago 4, Ill.
Lyons Band Instrument Co., Inc., 223 W. Lake Street, Chicago 6, Ill.
Magna Music Distributors, Inc., Sharon, Conn.
C. Meisel Music Co., 2332 Morris Avenue, Union, N.J.
Merson Musical Products Co., 6 W. 20th Street, New York, N.Y.
Meyer's Music Co., 3448 Grand River, Detroit 8, Mich.
Music Products, Inc., 223 West Lake Street, Chicago 6, Ill.
New Jersey Educational Music Co., 99 Springfield Avenue, Summit, N.J.
Pacific Music Supply Co., 1143 Santee Street, Los Angeles 15, Cal.
J. W. Pepper & Son, Inc., 321 N. 3rd Street, Philadelphia 6, Pa.
Philadelphia Music Co., Limerick, Pa.
Plymouth Music, Inc., 1841 Broadway, Suite 611, New York 23, N.Y.
Morse M. Preeman, Inc., 733 S. Hill Street, Los Angeles 55, Cal.
Remo, Inc., 12804 Raymer Street, North Hollywood, Cal.
St. Louis Music Supply, 3711 W. Pine, St. Louis 8, Mo.
Southern Music Co., 1100 Broadway, San Antonio 6, Texas.
Stanbury & Company, 120 West Brooks Street, Brookfield, Mo.
Targ & Dinner, Inc., 2451 N. Sacramento, Chicago, Ill.
Robert S. Taylor, 8710 Garfield Street, Bethesda 14, Md.
Van Horn & Son, Inc., 232 North Eleventh Street, Philadelphia 7, Pa.
Vibra-Art, 5 Guilford Lane, Trenton, N.J.
Waterloo Music Co., Ltd., 3 Regina Street North, Waterloo, Ont., Canada
David Wexler & Co., 838 S. Wabash, Chicago 5, Ill.
Wingert-Jones Music Co., 1211 Walnut Street, Kansas City 6, Mo.

Sheet Music Publishers

Associated Music Publishers, Inc., 1 West 47th Street, New York 36, N.Y.
Augsburg Publishing House, 426 S. Fifth Street, Minneapolis 15, Minn.
Belwin, Inc., 250 Maple Avenue, Rockville Center, N.Y.
The Big 3 Music Corp., 1540 Broadway, New York 36, N.Y.
Boosey & Hawkes, Inc., Oceanside, N.Y.
Boston Music Co., 116 Boylston Street, Boston 16, Mass.
Bourne, Inc., 136 W. 52nd Street, New York 19, N.Y.

Canyon Press, Inc., 17 Kearney Street, East Orange, N.J.

Chappell & Co., Inc., 609 Fifth Avenue, New York 17, N.Y.

Cole Corporation, 421 Melrose Avenue, Chicago, Ill.

Concordia Publishing House, 3558 S. Jefferson Avenue, St. Louis 18, Mo.

Consolidated Music Publishers, Inc., 240 W. 55th Street, New York 19, N.Y.

Educators Music Supply Co., 114 N. Broadway Avenue, Sylacauga, Ala.

Henri Elkan Music Publisher, 1316 Walnut, Philadelphia 7, Pa.

Elkan-Vogel Company, Inc., 1716 Sansom Street, Philadelphia 3, Pa.

Fearon Publishers, 828 Valencia Street, San Francisco 10, Cal.

Carl Fischer, Inc., 56 Cooper Square, New York 3, N.Y.

J. Fischer & Bro., Glen Rock, N.J.

H. T. Fitzsimons Co., 615 N. La Salle Street, Chicago 10, Ill.

Harold Flammer, Inc., 251 W. 19th Street, New York 11, N.Y.

Charles Foley, 67 West 44th Street, New York, N.Y.

Sam Fox Publishing Co., 11 W. 60th Street, New York 23, N.Y.

Frank Music Corp., 119 W. 57th Street, New York 19, N.Y.

Samuel French, Inc., 25 West 45th Street, New York 36, N.Y.

Galaxy Music Corp., 2121 Broadway, New York 23, N.Y.

The H. W. Gray Company, Inc., 159 E. 48th Street, New York 17, N.Y.

Highland Music Co., 1311 North Highland Avenue, Hollywood 28, Cal.

Bruce Humphries Publishers, 48 Melrose Street, Boston, Mass.

Neil A. Kjos Music Co., 525 Busse, Park Ridge, Ill.

Lawson-Gould Music Publishing Co., 609 Fifth Avenue, New York 17, N.Y.

Leeds Music Corp., 322 W. 48th Street, New York 36, N.Y.

Hal Leonard Music, Inc., 64 E. Second Street, Winona, Minn.

Wm. D. Lockwood, Inc., 39 Tremont Avenue, Binghamton, N.Y.

Ludwig Music Publishing Co., 557 E. 140th Street, Cleveland 10, Ohio.

Edward B. Marks Music Corp., 136 W. 52nd Street, New York 19, N.Y.

Merson Musical Products Corporation, 6 West 20th Street, New York 11, N.Y.

Mills Music, Inc., 1619 Broadway, New York 19, N.Y.

Edwin H. Morris & Co., Inc., 31 W. 54th Street, New York 19, N.Y.

Music Publishers Association, 609 Fifth Avenue, New York, N.Y.

Music Publishers Holding Corp., 488 Madison Avenue, New York 22, N.Y.

New Sounds in Modern Music, 315 West 53rd Street, New York 19, N.Y.

Oxford University Press, 417 Fifth Avenue, New York 16, N.Y.

C. F. Peters Corporation, 373 Fourth Avenue, New York 16, N.Y.

Pointer System, Inc., 64 East 2nd Street, Winona, Minn.

Theodore Presser Company, Bryn Mawr, Pa.

Pro Art Publications, 469 Union, Westbury, Long Island, N.Y.

Rubank, Inc., Music Publishers, 5544 W. Armstrong Avenue, Chicago 30, Ill.

G. Schirmer, Inc., 609 Fifth Avenue, New York 17, N.Y.

Schmitt, Hall, McCreery Co., Park Avenue at Sixth Street, Minneapolis 25, Minn.

Schroeder & Gunther, Associated Music Publishers, Inc., 1 W. 47th Street, New York, N.Y.

Shapiro, Bernstein & Co., Inc., 666 Fifth Avenue, New York 19, N.Y.

Shawnee Press, Inc., Delaware Water Gap, Pa.

Southern Music Publishing Co., 1619 Broadway, New York 19, N.Y.

Jack Spratt Woodwind Shop, 77 W. Brand Street, Stanford, Conn.

Staff Music Publishing Co., 374 Great Neck Rd., Great Neck, N.Y.

Summy-Birchard Co., 1834 Ridge, Evanston, Ill.

Tams-Witmark Music Library, Inc., 757 Third Avenue., New York 17, N.Y.

Gordon V. Thompson, Ltd., 32 Alcorn Avenue, Toronto 7, Ont., Canada.

Volkwein Bros., Inc., 632-634 Liberty Avenue, Pittsburgh 22, Pa.

Walton Music Corporation, 12069 Ventura Place, North Hollywood, Cal.

Willis Music Co., 124 E. Fourth Street, Cincinnati 2, Ohio.

B. F. Wood Music Co., 1619 Broadway, New York 19, N.Y.

Miscellaneous

American Society of Composers, Authors and Publishers, 575 Madison Avenue, New York 22, N.Y.

Americana Corporation, 575 Lexington Avenue., New York 22, N.Y.

Andante-Belmont Publications, 1232 Jackson Street, Denver 26, Colo.

Association Conventions Exhibits, 342 Madison Avenue, New York 17, N.Y.

Baton Music Company, 6503 Delmar Boulevard, St. Louis 30, Mo.

Broadcast Music Inc., 589 Fifth Avenue, New York 17, N.Y.

Buegeleisen & Jacobson, Inc., 5 Union Square, New York 3, N.Y.

Al Cass, 12 Short Street, Milford, Mass.

Childhood Interests, 180 West Westfield Avenue, Roselle Park, N.J.

Franco Colombo, Inc., 16 West 61st Street, New York 23, N.Y.

Electro-Voice, Cecil & Carroll Streets, Buchanan, Mich.

Evans Products, Inc., Box 58, 201 First Avenue, Dodge City, Kans.

Farham Stationery & School Supply, 301 South Fifth Street, Minneapolis 15, Minn.

Fechheimer Bros. Co., Corner 4th & Pike Street, Cincinnati, Ohio.

Interlochen Press, National Music Camp, Interlochen, Mich.

J. & J. Tool & Machine Co., 9505 South Prairie Avenue, Chicago 28, Ill.

Lutton Music Personnel Service, 64 E. Jackson Boulevard, Chicago, Ill.

Match-a-Tach, Inc., 4950 North Ardmore Avenue, Milwaukee 17, Wisc.

Mitchell Lurie Enterprises, 116 South La Brea Avenue, Los Angeles 36, Cal.

Modern Music Masters Society, Inc., Box 347, Park Ridge, Ill.

Music Mend Plastic Covers, 223 North Moore Street, Monterey Park, Cal.

National Manufactures Association of America, 333 North Michigan Avenue, Chicago 3, Ill.

Nelson Knitting Mills Co., 2105 West Superior Street, Duluth 6, Minn.

Pacific Music Paper, 1305 North Highland Avenue, Hollywood 28, Cal.

Panama-Beaver, Inc., 2633 Touhy Avenue, Chicago 45, Ill.

Piano Technicians Guild, Inc., 1121 Drew Avenue, Houston 6, Texas.

Playground as Music Teacher, 1 Sherbrooke Road, Scarsdale, N.Y.

School of Music, University of Denver, Denver 3, Colo.

Walter E. Sear, 111 West 48th Street, New York 36, N.Y.

Sesac, Inc., 10 Columbus Circle, New York, N.Y.

Standard Oil Co. of California, Standard Oil Building, Room 2173, San Francisco 20, Cal.

Sun Valley Music Camp, Inc., Box 491, Boise, Idaho.

West Shore Mfg. Co., Inc., Kewaunee, Wisc.

APPENDIX D

Copyright Law

All music educators should be well informed about the copyright law, its intent, coverage, and penalties. In an effort to assist in informing the profession of this law as it affects the profession's use of copyrighted material, this statement from the Music Industry Council is presented.

Provisions of the Copyright Law are frequently violated as a result of ignorance of the law. This does not in any way lessen the offense, nor does it abrogate the publisher's right to protect his property. It is important, therefore, that all users of music understand the copyright law and its applications.

The moral basis of the Copyright Law may be expressed by paraphrasing a celebrated quotation by Abraham Lincoln: "No fruits of man's labor are more peculiarly his own than the fruits obtained from the labor of his mind."

Among the virtues on which Americans pride themselves are respect for the property of others, a sense of fair play, and respect for the law of the land.

Quite apart from the reasons outlined above, the law expressly provides civil and criminal liability incurred by persons making any unauthorized use of copyright material.

The following uses, among others, without the express permission of the copyright owner or his authorized representative, of all or any part of a copyrighted work are ILLEGAL acts which must be avoided and guarded against with the greatest of care, regardless of purpose or intent, and whether for religious, educational, theatrical use or use in any other fields:

1. Printing, reprinting, copying or publishing by any means and methods whatsoever, including by hand or machine; on paper or blackboard; by photostating, multigraphing or mimeographing.

2. Translating, arranging, adapting, including the making of orchestrations, arrangements and parodies upon lyrics.
3. Performing publicly for profit (without proper license or compliance with established requirements) anywhere including radio stations, restaurants, cabarets, theatres, or any place where an audience fee is charged.
4. Recording or producing by mechanical methods such as piano rolls, phonograph records, electrical transcriptions and motion pictures. This includes recording broadcasts on home recording machines; it includes making your own LP records from older, 78 r.p.m. records or recording of any sort.
5. Making of contact, slide or roll film reproduction to be shown on screens or other surfaces by the use of projection.
6. Making, reproducing, selling, distribution, dealing or in any way trafficking with any of the infringing matter referred to above.

The Copyright Law of the United States provides penalties which may be imposed on anyone committing illegal acts. The penalties include damages of not less than $250.00 for each infringement. Additional penalties may be imposed in the case of willful infringement for profit.

We hope that you will help us eliminate these illegal appropriations from the "fruits of a man's mind which are most peculiarly his own." [1]

[1] Music Industry Council, "The Business Handbook of Music Education," 7th ed., Washington, D.C., The Council, 1956, p. 10. Used by permission.

Typical Budgets

SEVERAL BUDGETS taken from actual schools are presented in the following pages. They are illustrative of several types of budgets, budget forms, and budget practices. In each instance, the actual dollar amounts budgeted are not important for our purposes, but the form and the clarity of presentation are.

Budget Estimate Form

Many school districts develop their own budgetary system and use estimate forms and code numbers that are meaningful only to them. This is rather common practice, and the music educator should become familiar with the form and code used by his system early in his first year on the job. In the three examples given on following pages, notice that the classification number and budget identification code change as music (band arrangements, folios, solo and ensemble material), repairs, and new instruments, are listed.

Budget Estimate Form, No. 1

Note: This form should be made in *duplicate*. Original sent to the Assistant Superintendent-Business Services and duplicate kept in your files for future references.

2
_____
Classification

BUDGET ESTIMATES, 19___–___

School or department *Instrumental Music* Budget identification *2c3m*
(Supplies, equipment, etc.)

Quantity	Item description and source (*be specific and detailed*)	Unit	Total
Example: 6	Yard benches—metal with hardwood top—12′	$30.00	$180.00
	DISTRICT ORCHESTRA		
17 folios	"All Popular" (replacement-addition)	.85	14.45
7 folios	"Famous Favorites" (replacement-addition)	.85	5.95
55 folios	"Our Director" (new)	.85	46.75
5	Orchestrations for festival and concert	12.00	60.00
	SOLO AND ENSEMBLE MATERIAL		
15	Festival solos for students	.70	10.50
8	Dance band arrangements	3.00	24.00
15 folios	String ensemble	.75	11.15
	MISCELLANEOUS		
2 boxes	Music ditto paper	10.00	20.00
30 sheets	Onionskin music copying paper	.06	1.80
25	Shoulder pads for violin and viola	3.00	75.00
	ACCESSORIES		
	Strings (replacements); drum sticks; drum slings; drum beaters; rosin; pitch pipes; oboe, bassoon, sax, and clarinet reeds; trumpet and trombone oil; drum heads; string adjusters; nine gallons of zepherine chloride for tonette sterilizing; pre-festival concert fee.		500.00

BUDGET ESTIMATE FORM, NO. 2

Note: This form should be made in *duplicate.* Original sent to the Assistant Superintendent-Business Services and duplicate kept in your files for future references.

$$\frac{5}{\text{Classification}}$$

BUDGET ESTIMATES, 19___-___

School or department *Instrumental Music* Budget identification *5b3*

(Supplies, equipment, etc.)

Quantity	Item description and source (*be specific and detailed*)	Unit	Total
Example: 6	Yard benches—metal with hardwood top—12'	$30.00	$180.00
	REPAIRS *Strings* Repair cracks, set sound posts, fit bridges, replace worn cases.		
	Woodwinds Overhaul as needed (pads, springs, etc.), replace cases.		
	Brass Overhaul as needed, relacquer mouthpieces, replace work cases.		
	Percussion Replace worn or broken heads and torn canvas bags.		$800.00

Budget Estimate Form, No. 3

Note: This form should be made in *duplicate*. Original sent to the Assistant Superintendent-Business Services and duplicate kept in your files for future references.

10
————————
Classification

BUDGET ESTIMATES, 19___-___

School or department *Instrumental Music* Budget identification *10d2*

(Supplies, equipment, etc.)

Quantity	Item description and source (*be specific and detailed*)	Unit	Total
Example: 6	Yard benches—metal with hardwood top—12′	$30.00	$180.00
1	Bundy bass clarinet		294.00
1	Schreibers Perc-Rite percussion cabinet		175.00
30	Hamilton Model 400N music stands	3.25	97.50
1	Bassoon		400.00
1	E♭ recording tuba		390.00
1 pr.	18″ medium thin orchestra cymbals		75.00
1	Bass viol		200.00
1	Bass drum, 16x32		100.00
1	Oboe		300.00
2	B♭ French horns	165.00	330.00
1	Vibra graver		10.00
1	Bass viol bow		15.00
4	Viola bows	7.50	30.00
3	Cello bows	10.00	30.00
1	Electric A-B♭ tuner		25.00
	State sales tax @ 4%		98.86
			$2570.36

Financing Outside the Total School Budget

The following excerpts of a letter from the band director at Springdale, Arkansas, illustrate how one community started its band program and maintained it. It is published by permission.

I am quite happy to be able to tell you of the budget and finance here in S.H.S. with relationship to the instrumental dept.

In the past bands have been rather in and out of the school. If you are acquainted with the bandmaster who spent one night a week in four or five towns, that is what I mean. So when I organized . . . we had exactly one empty room, no music, and no equipment of any description.

Our first attempt at "money" was through the "Band Builders" club, which started several projects, and we purchased music racks, a brass horn, and several other necessary instruments.

We used all the devices and means to make a few dollars now known to man and some he has forgotten. Uniforms were purchased by the several service clubs in Springdale. Some people purchased 1 uniform, some $\frac{1}{2}$, some $\frac{1}{4}$, and others donated whatever money they felt like giving. Anyway, in a week's time we had sixty uniforms all paid.

Our most immediate need was for money to maintain a band. The parents and superintendent decided to charge a fee of $2 per month of all students enrolled in band. This seems wrong to many educators, but they should try to maintain an organization sometime without school aid. The schools at that time in Arkansas were rather poor, and fees were the only way that several departments were able to exist. And if you look at it this way—"Them that gets, pays"—maybe it isn't so wrong. Anyway, we charged them and still do. We have enough to keep us on a cash-and-carry basis, which is sometimes unusual with school bands.

Once a year our club made a one-day drive which we called Band Day. This would net a considerable amount ($900 to $1,500), but as so many money drives were organized, the community decided to put them all in one drive and give each a proportionate share. Consequently, the band came in for a $1,200 share which has since been raised to $1,300. This is used to replace uniforms, instruments, pay insurance, and repair bills. We do not have a bank account to point to, but we are able to meet all bills with cash and to keep away from the public with our hands in a begging position.

The band appears in all parades and some events in neighboring cities, all football games at home, and those games away from home that are reasonably close. All concerts are free to the public.

We, the superintendent, public, and myself, are quite happy with our system.

Fees Collected: 125 students @ $2 per month will average for the year $2,200; One Community Fund Drive, $1,300. This is a total of $3,500. All money is spent by the director with checks signed or paid by the office of the superintendent. While this is not a large sum, we find that it is adequate for our purposes.

An Example of a Flexible Budget

The following is an excerpt from a letter to the author from the band director, Mr. J. Raymond Brandon, of the North Little Rock Senior High School, North Little Rock, Arkansas. It is used by permission.

Our school uses a flexible budget; we set up a tentative budget but do not make an attempt to follow it to the letter. As the year progresses, we make changes as the need arises.

A sample of our plan is as follows:

19___-19___	
Travel, including two football trips	$ 850.00
Music (other than solo and ensemble material)	800.00
Ensembles and instruction books	50.00
Instruments repaired	500.00
Uniform repair and accessories	275.00
New instruments	1400.00
Supplies, teaching aids, films, etc.	300.00
TOTAL	$4175.00

The Instrumental Music Department handles the football program, advertising and sales, and operates the concessions stands for all games in the stadium. The Band Parents Club takes care of the operation under the supervision of the stadium manager, who takes care of all purchases, sets up the stands and co-ordinates the operation.

The Board of Education purchases all uniforms and helps financially in "emergency" cases.

Budgeting in a Large System

The following budgets are from a State Teachers College and supplied for inclusion in this book by the head of the music department. He has asked that both he and his school remain anonymous. They are offered as examples of an exceedingly complicated budgetary system. This is not unusual in state college systems and large city school systems.

Our budget is a complicated affair, for we receive our money from several sources. We operate on a state purchasing plan, all purchases made from submitted bids . . . . . . For example: I submit a budget, divided into categories of equipment and supplies; I specifically list each item with its description, title, etc. This is done TWO years in advance! . . . . . Needless to say, this presents many problems when current needs develop. [In] April I will receive notification that a certain amount for supplies and another amount for equipment has been awarded my department for 19___-19___. At that time I re-juggle the budget I submitted last April, and order specific items to match the amount awarded me—usually cut appreciably. As an illustration, I submitted a budget request for the instrumental and music education needs two years ago totaling some $3088.00. My final order for this past year's program totaled $1235.04; $885.44 for equipment and $349.60 for supplies. (This state has a listing categorizing equipment as distinguished from supplies. Music is listed under *supplies*; all musical instruments are listed under *equipment*.)

My request for the current year totaled $2582.50; $2097.00 for equipment and the balance for supplies. My actual award was $1000.00 for equipment, and $116.35 for supplies.

In short, we have complete control of what we request; it is submitted along with the total college budget to the State Department of Education, then it is pared down and returned. I find that I am able to obtain some of the equipment which the state turns down through some of the other sources of revenue.

Much of our current operating expense and equipment which must be ordered comes from our Student Congress:

BUDGET ESTIMATE

ESTIMATED BUDGET 19___-19___.
(Submitted in May two years prior.)

Instruments	*Estimated Discount Price*
2 Blessing standard (student line) trumpets and cases Vendor:	$150.00
1 Olds Ambassador tenor trombone and case Vendor:	120.00
1 Conn Director sousaphone and case, model No. 14K Vendor:	385.00

1 Pair Ludwig and Ludwig tympani, pedal tuned	475.00
Fibre covers for heads	25.00
Mallets for tympani	10.00
Vendor:	
1 Harold Freeman bassoon and case	340.00
This instrument imported from France	
Vendor:	
1 Bundy flute	95.00
Vendor:	
1 Orchestra size snare drum (approximately 5½x14″)	60.00
Slingerland, or Ludwig, or comparable	
Vendor:	
1 Dressell double horn (German import) and case	350.00
Vendor:	
1 Viola (Juzek made) with bow and case, #610 Strad	
model	160.00
1 Set orchestra bells, Deagan 2½ octaves, #871	40.00
Vendor:	
1 Harold Freeman oboe (French import) and case	250.00
TOTAL	$2635.00

Music

Assorted band, orchestra music, and conductors' scores—	
Various publishers	$ 300.00
TOTAL	$ 300.00

Equipment

11 Manhasset music stands @ $8.50	$ 93.50
Vendor:	
50 Stiff cover manuscript size music folders for band,	
#4 Concert Fale brand	$ 69.50
TOTAL	$ 163.00
GRAND TOTAL	
(Instruments, music, equipment)	$3088.00

ACTUAL ORDER TWO YEARS LATER

Equipment	*Estimated Discount Price*
One (1) set W. F. pedal tuned tympani (two), #885	$ 367.50
Manufacturer:	
Vendor:	

Two (2) sets tympani mallets (total of four mallets),
  #711 Slingerland or comparable mallets by
  W. F. Ludwig.   7.50
    Vendor:
Two (2) fibre covers for above tympani   12.00
    Manufacturer:
    Vendor:
Eight (8) Manhasset music stands (fully adjustable),
  @ $8.50   68.00
    Vendor:
One (1) Harold Freeman brand bassoon and case,
  (French import)   300.00
    Vendor:
One (1) set of Deagan orchestra bells, $2\frac{1}{2}$ octaves, #871   40.00
    Vendor:
Eighteen (18) music stand lamps, #104, bronze finish   45.00
    Vendor:
One (1) sousaphone stand   18.00
    Vendor:
One (1) Pep mouthpiece puller, #MP-11   5.49
    Vendor:
One (1) twelve bar autoharp, #P 12 A   21.95
                                           TOTAL $ 885.44

Supplies

Fifty (50) concert sized music folders, #4, Fale brand $ 60.00
    Vendor:
Fifty (50) Goddard loose-leaf folios (march size #2919   50.00
    Vendor:
One (1) "Tru Dot Note Placer," #H 2905 C   3.00
    Vendor:
Two hundred (200) B and O filing envelopes: as follows
  100 No. 11 (march size)   2.70
  100 No. 13 (concert size)   6.50
    Vendor:
Four hundred (400) four-way reference music library cards   3.00
  100 each of four different colors
    Vendor:
Three (3) reels Scotch magnetic recording tape,
  No. 190A-18-100G, ($\frac{1}{4}$"x1800'; 190 extra play)   20.00

Music

From four (4) specified publishers 26 specific titles
  were ordered amounting to   139.35

Recordings
>   Listed by title, composer, and recording number.

Sixteen (16) titles were ordered amounting to	$ 65.05
TOTAL	$ 349.60
GRAND TOTAL	
(equipment, supplies)	$1235.04

PROPOSED BUDGET, STUDENT CONGRESS FUNDS

PROPOSED BUDGET 19___-19___.

A. Proposed Income (Student Congress only)

B. Proposed Expenditures (following not furnished by state funds):

	Discount Price
One bass clarinet (new)	$ 400.00
One baritone saxophone stand	15.00
One bass clarinet stand	10.00
Seventeen folders for dance band music @ $1.00	17.00
Seventeen lights for Porta desk music stands (dance band)	35.00
One set of mutes for brass (dance band) as follows:	69.65
Trumpets, 5 each plungers, straight, and cup	
Trombones, 4 each plungers, straight, and cup	
Band awards for 50 members @ $1.50	65.00
Music manuscript and arrangements for dance band	50.00
Majorette awards, 5 @ $2.00	10.00
Majorette hats (they furnish boots), 5 @ $15.00	75.00
One used tuba	350.00
Expenses for proposed recruiting trip to _____	
and _____	450.00

45 people (including Madrigals who will share cost)		
Travel 400 miles, bus	$270.00	
Meals for two days	275.00	
Hotel for two nights	360.00	
TOTAL	$905.00	
TOTAL AMOUNT REQUESTED		$1546.65

Band and Orchestra Parents Association Budget

Frequently, the music director will be called upon to assist his PTA, Band Boosters, or some other organization of parents that supports the music program, with their budgetary problems. The following budgets illustrate this type of financial planning.

*Baldwin Park (California) Elementary Band and
Orchestra Parents Association*

PROPOSED BUDGET: SEPTEMBER, 19___ TO SEPTEMBER, 19___

Balance on Hand, September, 19___ $ 160.12

I

Estimated income

Candy bar sale (net)	550.00
Scholarship Dinner (net)	350.00
Two (2) parades	50.00
TOTAL ESTIMATED INCOME	$ 950.00

II

Estimated expenditures

Two skating parties for district band and orchestra	$ 85.00
Two "Newsette" issues	50.00
Material for stripes	10.00
Refreshments for Beginners Concert	35.00
Pictures of band and orchestra and certificates	15.00
Accompanists for Festival soloists	20.00
Spring Concert—trophies, certificates, and decorations	65.00
Annual Picnic—punch and prizes	30.00
Pre-Festival Clinic Concert by Los Angeles City Band	25.00
Arrowbear awards	300.00
Film and film developing	50.00
Courtesy—flowers and gifts	35.00
Incidentals (upkeep, etc.)	20.00
TOTAL ESTIMATED EXPENDITURES	$ 740.00
UNBUDGETED BALANCED	$ 370.12

*Baldwin Park Elementary Band and
Orchestra Parents Association*

SUMMARY OF BUDGET FOR OPERATING EXPENSES: 19___–19___

Two skating parties	$ 80.50
Two "Newsettes"	22.32
Beginners Concerts	24.93
Wide angles lens for camera	98.17
Film and film developing	44.57
Spring Concert, awards and trophies	54.73
Pictures—certificate and framing	11.83
Annual Picnic—punch and prizes	32.13

Courtesy—flowers and gifts	25.63
Knives for dinner (108)	37.07
Oboe lessons	20.00
Courtesy breakfast—music directors	30.45
Courtesy director	25.00
Patterns for Pom Pom girls	2.22
Soloist accompanist	20.00
Arrowbear awards	325.00

TOTAL OPERATING EXPENSE $ 854.55

The following expenditures, although run through our account, were self-supported with few exceptions and did not result in a cost to be Association.

19___–19___

	Received	Paid Out
Band and orchestra pictures	$ 56.00	$ 56.00
Candy expenses	1431.20	946.14
Reeds for reed machine	38.80	44.11
Instrument insurance	84.60	84.60
Scholarship Dinner	596.73	239.47
Spring Concert program	73.75	81.40
Spring Concert recordings	255.00	276.00
Three parades	75.00	
	$2584.08	$1727.72

Seeking Bids

The following letter asking for bids on musical instruments illustrates the detail in order to assure the type, make, and quality, of merchandise desired. This is an exact copy of a bid request sent by a junior high school in California to five music stores in the school community. The school's identity is stricken from the letter at the school's own request.

The . . . bid was sent to five local music stores. This gave us the lowest price on each instrument and gave each music store an equal opportunity to do business with the school. We do this on the purchase of all student body instruments.

_____ JUNIOR HIGH SCHOOL

_____, CALIFORNIA

OCTOBER 5, 19___

_____ Musical Instrument Co.

_____ Boulevard

_____, California

Gentlemen:

We are interested in buying some musical instruments. If you would like to bid on these items, we should be happy to have you do so. Following is a list of the instruments that we are in the market for, together with specifications that must be met:

	Bid Price	*Delivery Date*
1 BASS CLARINET, Horst Moennig. Must have low E♭ Key. Complete with plush-lined case and swab.		
1 LOCKIE BARITONE STAND WITH ROLLERS No. 922	_____	_____
1 CONCERT, KAY BASS VIOL S8 (or equal German bass). Must have spruce top, maple back and sides, hard maple neck. Genuine ebony fingerboard and tailpiece, hand inlaid purfling on top and back edges. Regulation 3/4 size, with cloth case.	_____	_____
1 GERMAN STYLE BASS BOW. Must be of select lemonwood. Full lined ebony finish composition frog. Leather grip.	_____	_____
1 J. G. PFRETZCHNER CELLO (or equal). Full size. Must have good quality ebony trimmings. Complete with cloth case.	_____	_____
1 E♭ BARITONE SAXOPHONE, BUE-SCHER, No. 129. Complete with fabrikoid covered plush-lined case. Clear lacquer finish.	_____	_____

SPECIFICATIONS TO APPLY TO ALL NEW MUSICAL INSTRUMENTS THAT
MAY BE PURCHASED

   a. All instruments *must be new.*

   b. All instruments and equipment shall be subjected to inspection
      before purchase. The instruments shall be inspected for intona-
      tion, free action of keys and movable parts.

   c. Please quote lowest price and *earliest* delivery date in the spaces
      provided on this sheet. Bids must be sealed and filed with _____
      _____, Associate Financial Manager, Junior High
      School Body, _____ Street, _____
      _____, California, *not later than* October 15, 19—.

   d. Manufacturer shall guarantee instrument against imperfections of
material and/or workmanship for a period of one year.

    Thank you for your early response as we are interested in obtaining
these instruments as soon as possible.

                                            Yours very truly,

Facilities for Housing and Storage

On the following pages are illustrations of several types of facilities for music. It must be borne in mind that facilities are ideal or adequate only as they serve the needs of a particular program in a particular school and community. The drawings submitted here are judged by the author to have desirable features for the programs in the schools where they are located. No one should make use of these same ideas unless they serve the curriculum of the school and community in which he works.

Standard music facilities for Senior High Schools in the Los Angeles, California, City School District. Courtesy of William C. Hartshorn, Supervisor of Music Education.

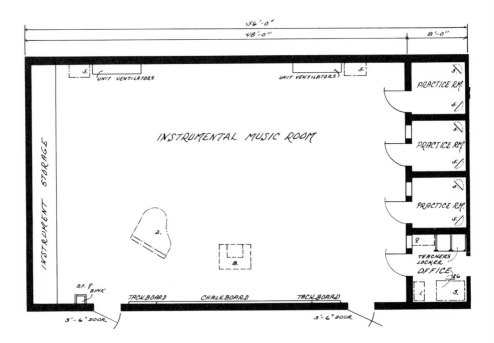

1. FILING CABINET	2	6. RECORD STORAGE CAB	5
2. GRAND PIANO	2	7. CHAIRS, TEACHERS	2
3. DESK, TEACHERS	2	8. PODIUM	1
4. CHAIRS, TABLE ARM	62	9. FILE, ORCH. MUSIC	1
5. CHAIRS	90		

LEGEND

GRAPHIC SCALE
0 1 2 3 4 5 6 7 8 9

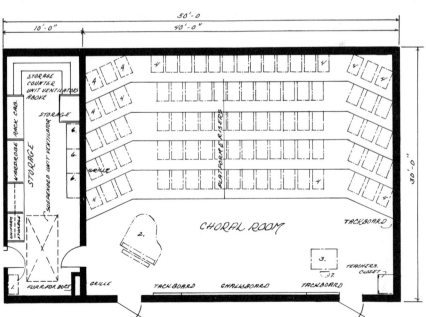

CHORAL ROOM

Standard instrumental, choral, and general music facilities for Junior High Schools in Los Angeles, California, City School District. Courtesy of William C. Hartshorn, Supervisor of Music Education.

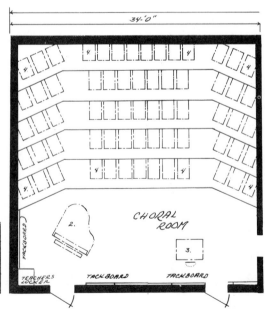

LEGEND

1. FILE CABINET	2
2. GRAND PIANO	2
3. TEACHERS DESK	2
4. TABLE ARM CHAIRS	150
5. RECORD STORAGE CABINET	1
6. CHAIRS	1
7. TAPE RECORDER	1
8. PHONOGRAPH	2

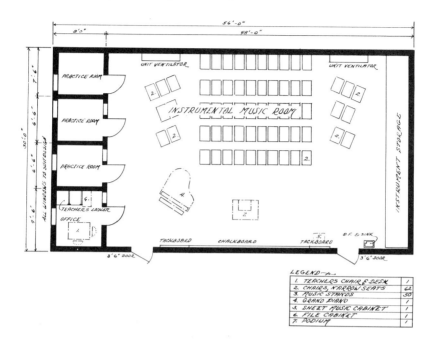

LEGEND

1. TEACHERS CHAIR & DESK	1
2. CHAIRS, NARROW SEATS	62
3. MUSIC STANDS	50
4. GRAND PIANO	1
5. SHEET MUSIC CABINET	1
6. FILE CABINET	1
7. PODIUM	1

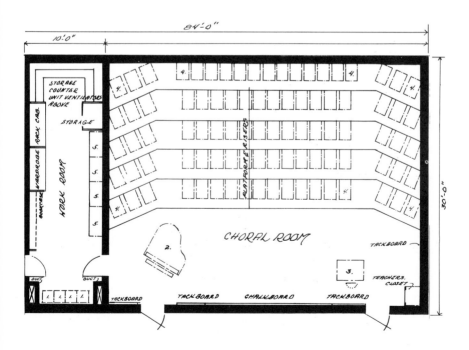

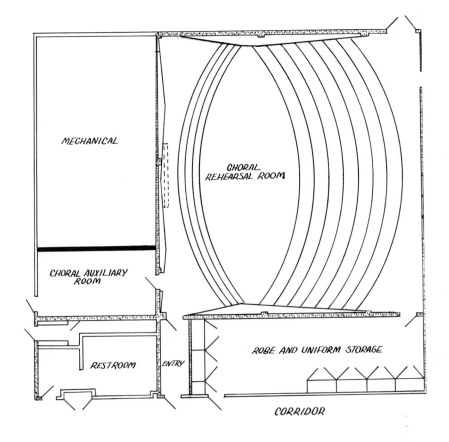

Choral rehearsal room and combination band and orchestra rehearsal room at California State College at Los Angeles. Each area is surrounded by its auxiliary service areas. The control room and announcer's booth serve both areas. The following three pages contain photographs illustrating some of these service areas and rehearsal rooms at California State College at Los Angeles.

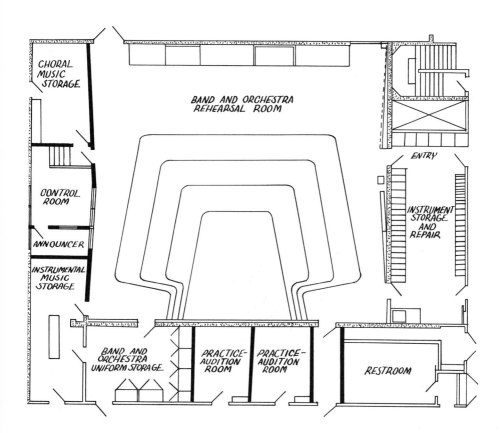

ABOVE: *The instrumental storage room.* Each intrument is identified by a number stenciled on the case. A record is kept in a card file. BELOW: *A storage wall in the instrumental rehearsal room.* This storage area is located on the top level of the built-in risers. From this location, the instruments may be moved across the width of the riser into playing position.

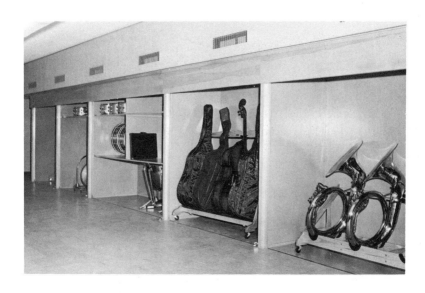

ABOVE: *The band uniform room adjacent to the instrumental rehearsal hall.* The room also serves for committee meetings and conferences. BELOW: *A music sorting rack.* A librarian is using it for placing music in rehearsal folders. The rack is mounted on wheels for ease in moving from one location to another.

ABOVE: *The choral rehearsal room.* The windows at the back indicate the location of the recording control room. The door at the rear of the room leads to the robe storage area, which is acoustically treated and large enough so that sectional rehearsals may be held in it. BELOW:*The instrumental rehearsal hall.* The door at the left gives access to the uniform storage area, and the one in the center to the instrumental music library. The door at the extreme right leads to the recording control room, which is situated between the instrumental and choral rehearsal rooms and serves both areas. The chalkboards behind the conductor slide aside to expose a large tackboard and mirror.

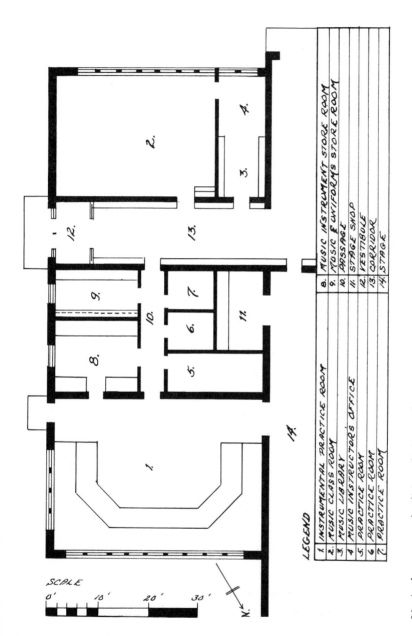

LEGEND

1. INSTRUMENTAL PRACTICE ROOM	8. MUSIC INSTRUMENT STORE ROOM
2. MUSIC CLASS ROOM	9. MUSIC & UNIFORMS STORE ROOM
3. MUSIC LIBRARY	10. PASSAGE
4. MUSIC INSTRUCTOR'S OFFICE	11. STAGE SHOP
5. PRACTICE ROOM	12. VESTIBULE
6. PRACTICE ROOM	13. CORRIDOR
7. PRACTICE ROOM	14. STAGE

SCALE
0'   10'   20'   30'

N.

Music department facilities adjoining the stage of a new junior-senior high school in Nanuet, New York. Mr. Wellington A. Brewster, Principal; Ralph Evans Hacker, Architect.

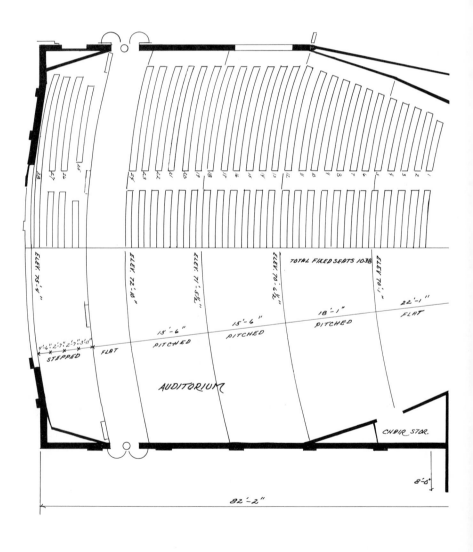

Music department facilities added to the existing stage of the senior high school auditorium. Courtesy of Donald R. Sullivan, Music Teacher, Junior High School West, Arlington, Massachusetts.

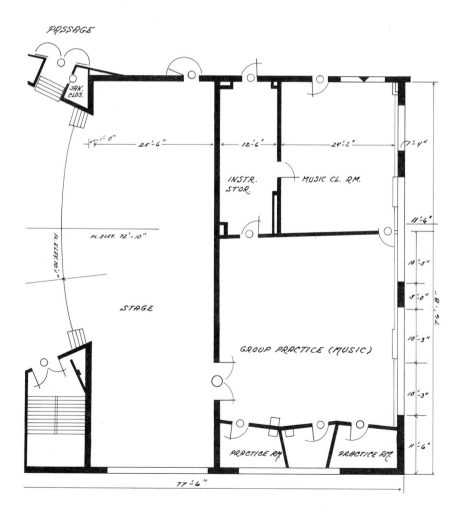

APPENDIX G

Bibliography

Books

Andrews, Frances M., and Cockerille, Clara E. *Your School Music Program.* Englewood Cliffs, N.J., Prentice-Hall, Inc., 1958. 289 pp.

Andrews, Frances M., and Leeder, Joseph A. *Guiding Junior High School Pupils in Music Experiences.* Englewood Cliffs, N.J., Prentice-Hall, Inc., 1953. 372 pp.

Andrews, Gladys. *Creative Rhythmic Movement for Children.* Englewood Cliffs, N.J., Prentice-Hall, Inc., 1954. 198 pp.

Bartholomew, Wilmer T. *Acoustics of Music.* Englewood Cliffs, N.J., Prentice-Hall, Inc., 1942. 242 pp.

Bartky, A. John. *Administration as Educational Leadership.* Stanford, Calif., Stanford University Press, 1956. 256 pp.

————. *Supervision as Human Relations.* Boston, D.C. Heath & Co., 1953. 308 pp.

Boardman, Charles W., Douglass, Harl R., and Bent, Rudyard K. *Democratic Supervision in Secondary Schools.* Boston, Houghton Mifflin Co., 1953. 557 pp.

Brand, Erick D. *Band Instrument Repairing Manual.* 4th ed. Auburn, Ind., Auburn Printing Co., 1947. 198 pp.

Broudy, Harry S. *Building a Philosophy of Education.* Englewood Cliffs, N.J., Prentice-Hall, Inc., 1954. 480 pp.

Brown, Edwin John. *Managing the Classroom.* New York, Ronald Press Co., 1952. 424 pp.

Burton, William H. *The Guidance of Learning Activities.* 2nd ed. New York, Appleton-Century-Crofts, 1952. 737 pp.

Carnegie, Dale. *How To Win Friends and Influence People.* New York, Simon and Schuster, 1936, 246 pp.

Chamberlain, Leo M., and Kindred, Leslie W. *The Teacher and School Organization.* 2nd ed. Englewood Cliffs, N.J., Prentice-Hall, Inc., 1949. 681 pp.

Corey, Stephen Maxwell. *Action Research to Improve School Practices.* New York, Bureau of Publications, Teachers College, Columbia University, 1953. 161 pp.

Crosby, Muriel Estelle. *Supervision as Co-operative Action.* New York, Appleton-Century-Crofts, 1957. 334 pp.

Davis, Ennis. *More Than a Pitch-pipe.* Evanston, Ill., C.C. Birchard & Company, 1941. 177 pp.

Dykema, Peter W., and Cundiff, Hannah M. *School Music Handbook.* Evanston, Ill., C.C. Birchard & Co., 1955. 669 pp.

Dykema, Peter W., and Gehrkens, Karl W. *The Teaching and Administration of High School Music,* Evanston, Ill., C.C. Birchard & Co., 1941. 614 pp.

Farnsworth, Paul R. *The Social Psychology of Music.* New York, Dryden Press, 1958. 304 pp.

Flagg, Marion Elizabeth. *Musical Learning.* Evanston, Ill., C.C. Birchard, 1949. 195 pp.

Frandsen, Arden N. *How Children Learn: An Educational Psychology.* New York, McGraw-Hill Book Co., Inc., 1957. 546 pp.

French, Will, and associates. *Behavioral Goals of General Education in High School.* New York, Russell Sage Foundation, 1957. 247 pp.

French, Will, Hull, J. Dan, and Dodds, B. L. *American High School Administration.* rev. ed. New York, Rinehart & Co., 1957. 604 pp.

Glenn, Neal E. *Teaching Music in Our Schools.* 2nd ed. Dubuque, Iowa, William C. Brown Co., 1954. 139 pp.

Graham, Floyd Freeman. *Public Relations in Music Education.* New York, Exposition Press, Inc., 1954. 241 pp.

Hagman, Harlan L., and Schwartz, Alfred H. *Administration in Profile for School Executives.* New York, Harper & Brothers, 1955. 315 pp.

Havighurst, Robert J., and Neugarten, Bernice L. *Society and Education.* Boston, Allyn and Bacon, Inc., 1957. 465 pp.

Hovey, Nilo W. *The Administration of School Instrumental Music.* Rockville Center, N.Y., Belwin Inc., 1952. 62 pp.

Jones, L. Bruce. *Building the Instrumental Music Department.* New York, Carl Fischer, Inc., 1949. 143 pp.

Kelter, John W. *Group Discussion Processes.* New York, Longmans, Green & Co., 1957. 373 pp.

Krone, Beatrice Perhan. *Music in the New School.* rev. ed. Park Ridge, Ill., Neil A. Kjos Music Co., 1950. 148 pp.

Krone, Beatrice, and Krone, Max. *Music Participation in the Elementary School.* Park Ridge, Ill., Neil A. Kjos Music Co., 1952. 88 pp.

———. *Music Participation in the Secondary School.* Park Ridge, Ill., Neil A. Kjos Music Co., 1952. 88 pp.

Landeck, Beatrice. *Children and Music.* New York, Sloane, 1952. 279 pp.

Lang, Paul Henry. *One Hundred Years of Music in America.* New York, G. Schirmer, Inc., 1961. 322 pp.

Leeder, Joseph A., and Haynie, William S. *Music Education in the High School.* Englewood Cliffs, N.J., Prentice-Hall Co., Inc., 1958. 366 pp.

Lundin, Robert W. *An Objective Psychology of Music.* New York, Ronald Press Co., 1953. 303 pp.

McGrath, Earl J., and others. *Toward General Education.* New York, Macmillan Co., 1948. 224 pp.

Mackenzie, Gordon N., Corey, Stephen M., and associates. *Instructional Leadership.* New York, Bureau of Publications, Teachers College, Columbia University, 1954. 209 pp.

Mathews, Paul R. *You Can Teach Music.* New York, E. P. Dutton & Co., Inc., 1953. 178 pp.

Meyers, Louise Kifer. *Music Fundamentals through Song.* Englewood Cliffs, N.J., Prentice-Hall., Inc., 1954. 90 pp.

———. *Teaching Children Music in the Elementary School.* 2nd ed. Englewood Cliffs, N.J., Prentice-Hall Co., 1956. 327 pp.

Moehlman, Arthur B. *School Administration: Its Development, Principles, and Function in the United States.* Boston, Houghton Mifflin Co., 1951. 514 pp.

Morgan, Russell Van Dyke, and Morgan, Hazel N. *Music Education in Action.* Park Ridge, Ill., Neil A. Kjos Music Co., 1954. 186 pp.

Morphet, Edgar L., Johns, Roe L., and Reller, Theodore L. *Educational Administration: Concepts, Practices and Issues.* Englewood Cliffs, N.J., Prentice-Hall, Inc., 1959. 556 pp.

Morse, Arthur D. *Schools of Tomorrow—Today!* New York, Doubleday & Co. Inc., 1960. 191 pp.

Mort, Paul R., and Reusser, Walter C. *Public School Finance.* 2nd ed. New York, McGraw-Hill Book Co., Inc., 1951. 639 pp.

Mursell, James L. *Education for Musical Growth.* Boston, Ginn & Company, 1948. 343 pp.

————. *Music and the Classroom Teacher.* Morristown, N.J., Silver Burdett Co., 1951. 304 pp.

————. *Music Education, Principles, and Programs.* Morristown, N.J., Silver Burdett Co., 1956. 386 pp.

————. *Music in American Schools.* rev. ed. Morristown, N.J., Silver Burdett Co., 1953. 312 pp.

————. *Principles of Democratic Education.* New York, W. W. Norton & Co., 1955. 461 pp.

————. *Psychology for Modern Education.* 1st ed. New York, W. W. Norton & Co., 1952. 610 pp.

————. *Psychology of Music.* New York, W. W. Norton & Co., 1937. 389 pp.

Nordholm, Harriett, and Thompson, Carl O. *Keys to Teaching Elementary School Music.* Minneapolis, Paul A. Schmitt Music Co., 1949. 271 pp.

Normann, Theodore F. *Instrumental Music in the Public Schools.* Bryn Mawr, Pa., Oliver Ditson Co., 1941. 349 pp.

Nye, Robert E., and Bergethon, Bjornar. *Basic Music for Classroom Teachers.* Englewood Cliffs, N.J., Prentice-Hall, Inc., 1954. 134 pp.

O'Connor, David John. *An Introduction to the Philosophy of Education.* New York, Philosophical Library, 1957. 148 pp.

Olson, Harry Ferdinand. *Musical Engineering.* New York, McGraw-Hill Book Co., 1952. 369 pp.

Pitts, Lilla Belle. *The Music Curriculum in a Changing World.* Morristown. N.J., Silver Burdett Co., 1944. 165 pp.

Prescott, Gerald R., and Chidester, Lawrence W. *Getting Results with School Bands.* New York, Carl Fischer; Minneapolis, Paul A. Schmitt Music Co., 1938. 273 pp.

Righter, Charles B. *Success in Teaching School Orchestras and Bands.* Minneapolis, Paul A. Schmitt Music Co., 1945. 211 pp.

Roggensack, Delinda. *Eyes and Ears for Music.* St. Louis, Educational Publishers, 1954. 115 pp.

Rorke, Genevieve A. *Choral Teaching at the Junior High School Level.* Minneapolis, Hall & McCreery Co., 1947, 114 pp.

Sawrey, James M., and Telford, Charles W. *Educational Psychology.* 2nd ed. Boston, Allyn and Bacon, Inc., 1964. 600 pp.

Scheffler, Israel. *Philosophy and Education.* Boston, Allyn and Bacon, Inc. 1958. 312 pp.

Sears, Jesse B. *The Nature of the Administrative Process.* New York, Mc-Graw-Hill Book Co., 1950. 623 pp.

————. *Public School Administration.* New York, Ronald Press Co., 1947. 433 pp.

Sharp, George M. *Curriculum Development as Re-education of the Teacher.* New York, Bureau of Publications, Teachers College, Columbia University, 1951. 132 pp.

Sheehy, Emma Dickson. *There's Music in Children.* New York, Henry Holt & Co., Inc., 1952. 152 pp.

Spears, Harold. *Curriculum Planning through In-Service Programs.* Englewood Cliffs, N.J., Prentice-Hall, Inc., 1957. 350 pp.

Squire, Russel H. *Introduction to Music Education.* New York, Ronald Press Co., 1952. 185 pp.

Sur, William R., and Schuller, Charles F. *Music Education for Teen-Agers.* New York, Harper & Brothers, 1958. 478 pp.

Tead, Ordway. *The Art of Administration.* New York, McGraw-Hill Book Co., 1951. 223 pp.

————. *The Art of Leadership.* New York, McGraw-Hill Book Co., 1935. 308 pp.

————. *Democratic Administration.* New York, Avon Press, 1945. 78 pp.

Timmerman, Maurine. *Let's Teach Music.* Evanston, Ill., Summy-Birchard Publishing Co., 1958. 216 pp.

Tooze, Ruth, and Krone, Beatrice. *Literature and Music as Resources for Social Studies.* Englewood Cliffs, N.J., Prentice-Hall, Inc., 1952. 478 pp.

Trump, J. Lloyd, and Braynham, Dorsey. *Focus on Change—Guide to Better Schools.* Chicago, Rand McNally Company, 1961. 147 pp.

Wiles, Kimball. *Supervision for Better Schools.* Englewood Cliffs, N.J., Prentice-Hall, Inc., 1950. 330 pp.

Publications of Learned Societies and Other Organizations

American Association of School Administrators. *American School Buildings.* Twenty-seventh Yearbook. Washington, D.C., The Association, 1949. 525 pp.

————. *American School Curriculum.* Thirty-first Yearbook. Washington, D.C., The Association, 1953. 551 pp.

————. *The American School Superintendency.* Thirtieth Yearbook. Washington, D.C., The Association, 1952. 661 pp.

————. *Public Relations for American Schools.* Twenty-eighth Yearbook. Washington, D.C., The Association, 1950. 497 pp.

————. *Staff Relations in School Administration.* Thirty-third Yearbook. Washington, D.C., The Association, 1955. 470 pp.

————. *The Superintendent as Instructional Leader.* Thirty-fifth Yearbook. Washington, D.C., The Association, 1957. 484 pp.

Association for Supervision and Curriculum Development. *Group Planning in Education.* Washington, D.C., The Association, 1945. 153 pp.

————. *Group Processes in Supervision.* Washington, D.C., The Association, 1948. 130 pp.

————. *Leadership for Improving Instruction.* 1960 Yearbook. Washington, D.C., The Association, 1960. 198 pp.

————. *Research for Curriculum Improvement.* 1957 Yearbook. Washington, D.C., The Association, 1957. 350 pp.

Best, Clarence J. *Music Rooms and Equipment.* Music Education Research Bulletin No. 17. Washington, D.C., Music Educators National Conference, 1949. 111 pp.

Hartsell, O. M. *Teaching Music in the Elementary School: Opinion and Comment.* Washington, D.C., Association for Supervision and Curriculum Development, 1963. 53 pp.

Johns, R. L., and Morphet, E. L., editors. *Problems and Issues in Public School Finance.* New York, National Conference of Professors of Educational Administration, 1952. 492 pp.

Junior High School Principals Association and Junior High School Association of Illinois. *Block of Time Scheduling Practices in Junior High Schools.* Danville, Illinois, The Associations, 1960. Pamphlet. 35 pp.

Music Education Research Council. *Music Supervision and Administration in the Schools.* Bulletin No. 18. Washington, D.C., Music Educators National Conference, 1949. 30 pp.

————. *Self Survey for School Music Systems.* Bulletin No. 15. Washington, D.C., Music Educators National Conference, 1934. 14 pp.

Music Educators National Conference. *Bibliography of Research Studies in Music Education.* Washington, D.C., The Music Educators National Conference, 1957. 225 pp.

————. *Music in American Education.* Music Education Source Book No. 2. Washington, D. C., The Conference, 1955. 365 pp.

————. *Music Buildings, Rooms, and Equipment.* Washington, D.C., The Conference, 1955. 96 pp.

————. *Music Curriculum in Secondary Schools.* Washington, D.C., The Conference, 1959. 115 pp.

————. *The Music Teacher and Public Relations.* Washington, D.C., The Conference, 1958. 48 pp.

National Association of Secondary School Principals. *Focus on Change.* Chicago, Rand McNally & Co., 1961. 147 pp.

————. *The Function of Music in the Secondary School Curriculum.* Bulletin of the Association. Washington, D.C., The Association, 1952. Vol. 36, November, 1952. 126 pp.

————. *Public Relations in Secondary Schools.* Bulletin No. 152. Washington, D.C., The Association, 1948. 342 pp.

National Education Association. *Music and Art in the Public Schools.* Washington, D.C., The Association. Research Monograph 1963-M3.

————. *NEA Handbook.* Washington, D.C., The Association, 1957–58. 328 pp.

National School Public Relations Association. *It Starts in the Classroom.* Washington, D.C., The Association, 1951. 64 pp.

————. *Teaming Up for Public Relations.* Washington, D.C., The Association, 1952. 48 pp.

National Society for the Study of Education. *Basic Concepts in Music Education.* Fifty-seventh Yearbook, Part I, Nelson B. Henry, ed. Chicago, The Society, 1958. 362 pp.

Taba, Hilda. *Leadership Training in Intergroup Action.* Washington. D.C., American Council on Education, 1953. 243 pp.

Periodicals

Ashby, Lloyd W. "What Supervisory Practices Promote Teacher Growth and Cooperation?" *National Association of Secondary School Principals Bulletin.* 36:26–32, April, 1952.

Avery, Frank D. "A Building and Departmental Budget System." American School Board Journal. 135:47–48, September, 1957.

Bakkegard, B. M. "Public School Music as a Public Relations Agent." *Music Educators Journal,* 39:61–63, September-October, 1952.

Barr, Arvil S. "Characteristics of Successful Teachers." *Phi Delta Kappan.* 39, No. 6:282–284, March, 1958.

————. "Measurement of Teacher Characteristics and Prediction of Teaching Efficiency." *Review of Educational Research.* 22:169–74. June, 1952.

Benne, Kenneth D. "Theory of Cooperative Planning in Education." *Teachers College Record.* 53:429–35, May, 1952.

Best, Clarence J. "Building Facilities for Music Education." *School Executive,* 65, No. 7:57–72, March, 1946.

Blumberg, Arthur, and Amidon, Edmund. "Teacher Reactions to School Faculty Meetings." *The Journal of Educational Research.* 56, No. 9:466–470, May-June, 1963.

Brameld, Theodore. "What Is the Central Purpose of American Education?" *Phi Delta Kappan.* 43, No. 1:9–14, October, 1961.

Britton, Allen P. "Music Education in the Nineteen-Sixties." *Music Educators Journal.* 47, No. 6:23–26, June-July, 1961.

Brownell, John A. "The Infirmities of Administrators." *Phi Delta Kappan.* 41, No. 2:53–56, November, 1959.

Burrows, Raymond. "Piano Classes Are Fun." *National Elementary Principal,* 30:34–36, February, 1951.

Bush, Robert N., and Allen, Dwight W. "Flexible Scheduling for What?" *Journal of Secondary Education.* 36:346–353, October, 1961.

———. "Flexible Scheduling." *National Association of Secondary School Principals Bulletin.* 47, No. 283:73–98, May, 1963.

Butler, Kenneth B. "How to Win Administrators and Influence School Boards." *Educational Music Magazine,* 30:8–9, September-October, 1950.

Buttleman, Clifford V. "Hunt, Richman, Petrillo Sign the Code." *Music Educators Journal,* 34, No. 1:23–25, September-October, 1947.

Cady, Henry L. "The Sociology of Music: A Perspective." *Music Educators Journal,* 50, No. 2:25–27 *ff.,* November-December, 1963.

Carlsen, James. "Toward Academic Excellence in Music." *Music Educators Journal,* 50, No. 4:117–122, February-March, 1964.

Carruth, Irby B. "Human Relations Inside the School." *School Executive,* 71:73–75, June, 1952.

Carter, Elwyn. "Planning High School Music Areas." *American School Board Journal,* 136:38–40, March, 1958.

———. "School Building Planning for Music and Drama." *Music Educators Journal,* 45, No. 6:37–41, June-July, 1959.

Chase, Francis S. "Factors for Satisfaction in Teaching." *Phi Delta Kappan,* 33:127–32, November, 1951.

Chenault, Robert N. "The Principal's Responsibility for School-Community Relations." *National Elementary Principal,* 32:19–21, October, 1952.

Choate, Robert A. "Music Instruction in the Self-Contained Classroom." *National Elementary Principal,* 30:9–11, February, 1951.

_____. "The Shaping Forces of Music in the Changing Curriculum." *Music Educators Journal*, 47, No. 5:29–32, April-May, 1961.

Clarvoe, Frank A. "Sound Techniques in Public - Relations." *California Journal of Elementary Education*, 20:115–19, November, 1951.

Claye, Clifton M. "Lola Gets What Lola Wants from Supervision." *Journal of Educational Research*, 56, No. 7:358–361, March, 1963.

Coutant, Madeleine Frink. "Public Relations and the School Music Program." *Music Educators Journal*, 40, No. 4:68–70, February-March, 1954.

Cremin, Lawrence A. "The Curriculum Maker and His Critics: A Persistent American Problem." *Teachers College Record*, 54:234–45, February, 1953.

Cremin, Lawrence A., and Weiss, Robert M. "Yesterday's School Critic." *Teachers College Record*, 54:77–82, November, 1952.

Eggert, C. Lee. "Make Budget Planning a Faculty Affair." *School Executive*, 73:42–43, September, 1953.

Ellis, U. Berkley, and Dick, Stanley B. "Scheduling the Practical and the Fine Arts in the Large Junior High School." *National Association of Secondary School Principals Bulletin*, 46, No. 273:36–41, April, 1962.

Empey, Donald W. "Student Self Direction, Flexible Scheduling, and Team Teaching." *National Association of Secondary School Principals Bulletin*, 47, No. 280:118–124, February, 1963.

Engleman, Finis. "The Arts and American Education." *Music Educators Journal*, 50, No. 4:30–32 ff., February-March, 1964.

Ernst, Karl. "What Can Be Expected from the Classroom Teacher?" *National Elementary Principal*, 30:28–32, February, 1951.

Fawcett, Novice G. "An Educator Looks at Music and the Arts in a Day of Science." *Music Educators Journal*, 44, No. 5:22, April-May, 1958.

Finkelstein, Herman. "Copyright, the Author's Property." *Music Educator's Journal*, 44, No. 4:42, February-March, 1958.

Fitzpatrick, Edward A. "Public Education Is Public Business." American School Board Journal, 126, No. 4:54–55, April, 1953.

Flagg, Marion. "Elementary School Principal and His Music Program. *National Elementary Principal*, 30:12–16, February, 1951.

Flora, Frank E. "Successful Administrative Relationships Make Successful Music Programs." *Music Educators Journal*, 47, No. 5:66–67, April-May, 1961.

Flower, George E., Sargent, Cyril G., and Belisle, Eugene L. "Relationships with People Is the Key." *American School Board Journal*, 124:25–27, June, 1952.

Foshay, Arthur W. "Curriculum Improvement Through Action Research." *National Education Association Journal*, 46, No. 4:265–266, April, 1957.

Fowler, Charles B. "Music: A Sound Approach to Living." *Music Educators Journal*, 50, No. 4:51–2 *ff.*, February-March, 1964.

Franseth, J. "Improving the Curriculum and Teaching Through Action Research." *School Life*, 42, No. 4:8–10, December, 1959.

Fraser, Dorothy McClure, and Pullen, Thomas G., Jr., "What to Teach? Curriculum Planning." *National Education Association Journal*, 51, No. 7:34–36, October, 1962.

Frazen, Carl G. F. "What Supervisory Practices Promote Teacher Growth and Cooperation?" *National Association of Secondary School Principals Bulletin*, 31:17–26, April, 1952.

French, Elizabeth. "Administrator as the Director of Community-School Relations." *California Journal of Elementary Education*, 20:171–75, February, 1952.

Gehrkens, Karl Wilson. "An Old Man's Opinion." *Music Educators Journal*, 46, No. 6:48, June-July, 1960.

Glenn, Neal E. "Human Relations and the Music Supervisor." *Education*, 74, No. 1:27, September, 1953.

Hansen, Sigurd, and Harris, Ben M. "Systematic and Democratic Budget Planning." *American School Board Journal*, 135:45, December, 1957.

Hanson, Howard. "Music Education Faces the Scientific Age." *Music Educators Journal*, 45, No. 6:17–19, June-July, 1959.

————. "A Plea for the Arts." *Music Journal*, 21, No. 8:25 *ff.*, November, 1963.

Hartsell, O. M. "How Super Is Your Supervision?" *Music Educators Journal*, 44, No. 5:40, April-May, 1958.

————. "Quality in Elementary School Music." *National Education Association Journal*, 49, No. 3:27–29, March, 1960.

Hartshorn, William C. "The Study of Music as an Academic Discipline." *Music Educators Journal*, 49, No. 3:25–28, January, 1963.

Heffernan, Helen. "Education Through Music." *Education*, 74, No. 1:11–16, September, 1953.

Heller, Dorothy M. "The Psychology of Preadolescence in Teacher-Pupil Planning." *Music Educators Journal*, 50, No. 3:92–96, January, 1964.

Hills, Arthur C. "A New Schedule for a New School." *Music Educators Journal*, 48, No. 5:50–52, April-May, 1962.

Humphreys, Alfred W. "Orienting the Classroom Teacher in Music." *Music Educators Journal*, 39:28–30, September, 1952.

Jaffe, Alexander. "Public Relations Program." *California Teachers Association Journal*, 48:11–12, October, 1952.

James, H. Thomas. "The Nature of Professional Authority." *Phi Delta Kappan*, 41, No. 2:45–48, November, 1959.

Johnson, Beverly E. "Adjustable Ceiling for Band Room Acoustical Control." *Music Educators Journal*, 44, No. 3:54, January, 1958.

Johnson, Burt P. "Music a Must in General Education." *Music Educators Journal*, 37:14–15, June, 1951.

Kennelly, E. F. "Human Relations in Personnel Administration for Education." *Education*, 75, No. 4:214–217, December, 1954.

Kliewer, Vernon L. "The Musician and Aesthetics." *Music Journal*, 21, No. 7:58 *ff.*, October, 1963.

Knudsen, Vern O. "Architectural Acoustics." *Scientific American*, 209, No. 5:78–92, November, 1963.

Knuth, William E. "General Music for the General High School Student." *California Journal of Secondary Education*, 30, No. 4:223–226, April, 1955.

Krebs, Robert M. "Citizens Need to Be Aware of Public Education." *Illinois Education*, 41:58–59, October, 1952.

Lang, William C. "An Expanding Role for Music in a Science-Centered Age." *Music Educators Journal*, 50, No. 4:123–126, February-March, 1964.

Leonhard, Charles. "Place of Music in Our Elementary and Secondary Schools." *National Education Association Journal*, 52, No. 4:40–42, April, 1963.

Lerner, Max. "New Dimensions." *Music Educators Journal*, 50, No. 6:29–33, June-July, 1964.

Lewis, Russel LeRoy. "Storage Facilities in the High School Music Department." *American School Board Journal*, 130:60–61, February, 1955.

Lickey, Harold L. "Scheduling the Music Program in a Small or Middle-sized High School." *Music Educators Journal*, 41, No. 4:42, February-March, 1955.

Lloyd, Elizabeth C. "Building Better Staff Relationships." *National Elementary Principal*, 32:147–50, September, 1952.

Lowry, W. McNeil. "The Arts in Today's Society." *Music Educators Journal*, 50, No. 6:28, June-July, 1964.

Ludeman, W. W. "Teacher's Public Relations." *Education*, 78, No. 6:337–338, February, 1958.

Masterson, C. T., and Allen C. J. "Lighting and Color in the Music Room." *Music Journal*, 12:20–22, July, 1954.

Mayer, Frederick. "Education and the Crisis of Our Time." *Phi Delta Kappan,* 43, No. 7:300–302, April, 1962.

Mesthene, Emmanuel G. "Music as a Means of Communication in a Scientific Age." *Music Educators Journal,* 48, No. 1:42–44, September-October, 1961.

Moran, John. "School Publicity—A Reporter's Eye-view." *School Executive,* 72:68–71, November, 1952.

Morrill, Charles L. "Better Public Relations." *School Executive,* 77, No. 1:74–76, September, 1957.

Nickerson, James F. "Planning for the Acoustics of Music Rooms." *Kansas Music Review,* 15:11–15 *ff.,* February, 1953.

————. "Planning for the Acoustics of Music Rooms. Part II: Excluding Unwanted Sound." *Kansas Music Review,* 15:21–26, March, 1953.

————. "Planning for the Acoustics of Music Rooms. Part III: Controlling the Wanted Sounds." *Kansas Music Review,* 15:19–25, May, 1953.

————. "Schoolroom Acoustics." *University of Kansas Bulletin of Education,* 7, No. 1:17–21, November, 1952.

————. "Schoolroom Acoustics. Part II: The Control of Unwanted Sound." *University of Kansas Bulletin of Education,* 7, No. 2:44–48, February, 1953.

————. "Schoolroom Acoustics. Part III: Control of Wanted Sound." *University of Kansas Bulletin of Education,* 7, No. 3:83–90, May, 1953.

Niemi, Allan L. "Acoustics Most Important in Planning the Music Department." *American School Board Journal,* 125:42–44, December, 1952.

————. "Housing School and Community Music Activities." *American School Board Journal,* 125:44–46, August, 1952.

————. "Music Department: Its Location and Equipment." *American School Board Journal,* 125:37–38, October, 1952.

Nitz, Donald. "Music Education in a Cultural Epoch." *Music Journal,* 21, No. 7:40 *ff.,* October, 1963.

Novak, Benjamin, J., and Barnet, Gladys R. "Are Music and Science Compatible?" *Music Educators Journal,* 46, No. 6:44–48, June-July, 1960.

Ojemann, R. H. "Identifying Effective Classroom Teachers." *National Elementary Principal,* 32:130–38, September, 1952.

Pascucci, Vito. "Improving School Bid Specifications." *Music Journal,* 21, No. 5:48 *ff.,* May, 1963.

Passow, A. Harry. "A Conception of Educational Leadership." *Teachers College Record,* 54:324–31, March, 1953.

Peterson, W. J. "Sound Control and the Rehearsal Room." *Educational Music Magazine*, 34:12 *ff.*, November, 1954.

Picerno, Vincent. "What Is a Successful Teacher?" *Music Journal*, 22, No. 1:74 *ff.*, January, 1964.

Prescott, Gerald R. "School Music Values and the Administrator." *Nations Schools*, 50:65–66, November, 1952.

Rafferty, Sadie M., and Michael, Lloyd S. "Scheduling the Music Program in a Large Senior High School." *Music Educators Journal*, 44, No. 4:43–44, February-March, 1955.

Richardson, E. G. "Orchestral Acoustics." *The Scientific Monthly,* 80, No. 4:211–224, April, 1955.

Righter, Charles B. "Equipment Issue and Accounting." *Educational Music Magazine*, 36:8, March, 1957.

Ringkamp, H. C. "All Activities Are Public Relations." *Catholic School Journal*, 52:240–43, October, 1952.

Rose, Gale W. "Performance Evaluation and Growth in Teaching." *Phi Delta Kappan*, 45, No. 1:48–53, October, 1963.

Rounds, Lester E., "Delegating Administrative Authority." *Nations Schools,* 50:57–59, October, 1952.

Sabine, Hale J. "Acoustical Plights of the Instrumental Director." *Educational Music Magazine*, 32:18–20 *ff.*, March-April, 1952.

Schinnerer, Mark C. "Administrator Talks about Music." *Music Educators Journal*, 37:18–19, April, 1951.

Schnoor, Lois Laverne. "The Attributes of an Effective Teacher." *Music Educators Journal*, 39, No. 5:58, April-May, 1953.

Sears, Jesse B. "The Nature of the Administrative Process in Education—A Partial Analysis of the Factors Involved." *Educational Administration and Supervision*, 31:1–21, January, 1945.

Smith, Carleton Sprague. "The Study of Music as an Academic Subject." *Music Educators Journal*, 49, No. 1:31–34, September-October, 1962.

Smith, Mary. "Action Research to Improve Teacher Planning Meetings." *School Review*, 60, No. 3:146–150, March, 1952.

Sommers, Hobart H. "General Education and the Music Teacher." *Music Educators Journal*, 39, No. 6:19–21, June-July, 1953.

————. "Storm Warning." *Educational Music Magazine*, 31:8–10, March, 1952.

Stapleton, E. G. "Good Public Relations Can Put the Taxpayer in Your Corner." *School Executive*, 72:70–73, October, 1952.

Stoops, Emery. "Keys to Leadership." *Phi Delta Kappan*, 45, No. 1:42–43, October, 1963.

Strickland, Virgil E. "Scheduling Music in Junior High School." *Nations Schools*, 48:43–44, September, 1951.

Sunderman, Lloyd Frederick. "Great Issues in Music Education." *Education*, 74, No. 1:27, September, 1953.

Taylor, James L. "Flexibility in School Facilities." *School Life*, 43, No. 2:11–13, October, 1960.

Thomas, Maurice J. "Real Meaning of a School Budget." *School Executive*, 72:65, November, 1952.

Trump, J. Lloyd. "Developing and Evaluating a Class Schedule to Help Each Pupil Learn Better." *Journal of Secondary Education*, 36:338–345, October, 1961.

————. "Flexible Scheduling, Fad or Fundamental?" *Phi Delta Kappan*, 44, No. 8:367–371, May, 1963.

Van Bodegraven, Paul. "New Horizons in Music Education." *International Musician*, 60:14 *ff.*, February, 1962.

Van Camp, Leonard. "Public Relations and the Secondary School Music Educator." *Music Educators Journal*, 48, No. 2:81–89, November-December, 1961.

Weil, LeRoy. "Financing a Program of School Music." *Kentucky School Journal*, 29:26, May, 1951.

Weir, Bill, and Pearce, David W. "Going Back to Face the Music—Teacher." *American School Board Journal*, 146, No. 4:35–37, April, 1963.

Wesler, Warren A. "A Compact, Useful and Economical School Music Suite." *Music Educators Journal*, 45, No. 1:78–79, September-October, 1958.

Williams, Lloyd J. "How to Design a School for Good Hearing." *American School Board Journal*, 67:93–126, May, 1961.

Wilson, Harry R. "What I Have Learned About Administration." *Music Educators Journal*, 50, No. 4:39–41, February-March, 1964.

Wright, Al G. "Housing the School Music Department." *Music Educators Journal*, 37:20, April, 1951.

Pamphlets

Beckhard, Richard, *How to Plan and Conduct Workshops and Conferences.* New York, Association Press, 1956. 64 pp.

Howsam, Robert B. "Who's a Good Teacher?" Burlingame, California, California Teachers Association, 1960. 48 pp.

Martin, Jack, and others. *Budgeting Practices in Central Schools.* New York, Central School Boards Committee for Educational Research, 1952. 22 pp.

Moore, E. C. *How to Write a Woodwind Specification.* Kenosha, Wisconsin, G. Leblanc Corporation. 8 pp.

Ohm, Robert E. "Toward a Rationale for Team Teaching." *Administrator's Notebook*, 9, No. 7: March, 1961.

Index